Cisco Press
Networkers 2006 Folio

Cisco Press

800 East 96th Street
Indianapolis, IN 46240 USA

Cisco Press Networkers 2006 Folio

Published by:
Cisco Press
800 East 96th Street
Indianapolis, IN 46240 USA

Printed in the United States of America 1 2 3 4 5 6 7 8 9 0

ISBN: 1-58705-267-9

Warning and Disclaimer

This book is designed to provide information about the fundamentals of content networking. Every effort has been made to make this book as complete and as accurate as possible, but no warranty or fitness is implied.

The information is provided on an "as-is" basis. The authors, Cisco Press, and Cisco Systems, Inc., shall have neither liability nor responsibility to any person or entity with respect to any loss or damages arising from the information contained in this book or from the use of the discs or programs that may accompany it.

The opinions expressed in this book belong to the author and are not necessarily those of Cisco Systems, Inc.

Trademark Acknowledgments

All terms mentioned in this book that are known to be trademarks or service marks have been appropriately capitalized. Cisco Press or Cisco Systems, Inc., cannot attest to the accuracy of this information. Use of a term in this book should not be regarded as affecting the validity of any trademark or service mark.

RealNetworks images and information in Chapter 13 provided courtesy of RealNetworks, Inc.:

Copyright © 1995–2005 RealNetworks, Inc. All rights reserved. RealNetworks, Helix, Helix Proxy, RealProxy, RealPlayer, and RealMedia are trademarks or registered trademarks of RealNetworks, Inc.

Feedback Information

At Cisco Press, our goal is the creation of in-depth technical books of the highest quality and value. Each book is crafted with care and precision, undergoing rigorous development that involves the unique expertise of members from the professional technical community.

Readers' feedback is a natural continuation of this process. If you have any comments regarding how we could improve the quality of this book, or otherwise alter it to better suit your needs, you can contact us through email at feedback@ciscopress.com. Please be sure to include the book title and ISBN in your message.

We greatly appreciate your assistance.

Corporate and Government Sales

Cisco Press offers excellent discounts on this book when ordered in quantity for bulk purchases or special sales.

For more information please contact: **U.S. Corporate and Government Sales**   1-800-382-3419
corpsales@pearsontechgroup.com

For sales outside the U.S. please contact: **International Sales**   international@pearsoned.com

Corporate Headquarters
Cisco Systems, Inc.
170 West Tasman Drive
San Jose, CA 95134-1706
USA
www.cisco.com
Tel: 408 526-4000
        800 553-NETS (6387)
Fax: 408 526-4100

European Headquarters
Cisco Systems International BV
Haarlerbergpark
Haarlerbergweg 13-19
1101 CH Amsterdam
The Netherlands
www-europe.cisco.com
Tel: 31 0 20 357 1000
Fax: 31 0 20 357 1100

Americas Headquarters
Cisco Systems, Inc.
170 West Tasman Drive
San Jose, CA 95134-1706
USA
www.cisco.com
Tel: 408 526-7660
Fax: 408 527-0883

Asia Pacific Headquarters
Cisco Systems, Inc.
Capital Tower
168 Robinson Road
#22-01 to #29-01
Singapore 068912
www.cisco.com
Tel: +65 6317 7777
Fax: +65 6317 7799

Cisco Systems has more than 200 offices in the following countries and regions. Addresses, phone numbers, and fax numbers are listed on the
Cisco.com Web site at www.cisco.com/go/offices.

Argentina • Australia • Austria • Belgium • Brazil • Bulgaria • Canada • Chile • China PRC • Colombia • Costa Rica • Croatia • Czech Republic
Denmark • Dubai, UAE • Finland • France • Germany • Greece • Hong Kong SAR • Hungary • India • Indonesia • Ireland • Israel • Italy
Japan • Korea • Luxembourg • Malaysia • Mexico • The Netherlands • New Zealand • Norway • Peru • Philippines • Poland • Portugal
Puerto Rico • Romania • Russia • Saudi Arabia • Scotland • Singapore • Slovakia • Slovenia • South Africa • Spain • Sweden
Switzerland • Taiwan • Thailand • Turkey • Ukraine • United Kingdom • United States • Venezuela • Vietnam • Zimbabwe

Contents at a Glance

Contents

Exerpt from *Content Networking Fundamentals*

Exerpt from *Storage Networking Protocol Fundamentals*

Exerpt from *Firewall Fundamentals*

Exerpt from *Building Multiservice Transport Networks*

Chapter 7   Multiservice Provisioning Platform Network Design   215

Exerpt from *Network Virtualization*

Part I: Fundamentals Series

Understand the Purpose, Application, and Management of Technology

The Cisco Press Fundamentals Series provides experienced networking professionals with trusted, **authoritative introductions to networking topics**, covering network topologies, example deployment concepts, protocols, and management techniques. Skip networking primers and master essential networking concepts and solutions with Cisco Press Fundamentals books.

Fundamentals Book Features

- Chapter objectives provide a roadmap to learning
- Notes, tips, and cautions highlight important information
- Chapter summaries reinforce concepts and technologies
- Chapter review questions and answers
- Case studies illustrate important concepts in a real-world setting and provide valuable insight into practical situations

ISBN: 1-58705-239-3

Intrusion Prevention Fundamentals

An introduction to network attack mitigation with IPS

Earl Carter · Jonathan Hogue

CHAPTER 4

Security in Depth

No single security countermeasure can always stop all attacks. Effective security requires multiple layers of countermeasure, so that if one is bypassed, the attack still has to get through the next layer, the layer after that, and so on. This concept is called *defense-in-depth*, and is illustrated by Figure 4-1.

Figure 4-1 *Layered Defenses*

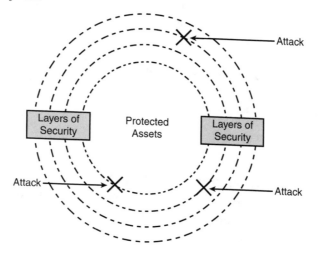

For example, a fence by itself is not enough to secure your home. The fence stops some attackers, but others climb over it. Some people might even knock your fence down. That is why you have doors and windows with locks on them, perhaps an alarm system, and even a safe for your valuables. Each layer makes it more difficult for the attacker to succeed.

Effective computer security should also be based on a defense-in-depth. An Intrusion Prevention System (IPS) is only one of many layers you employ to defend your computing resources. This chapter demonstrates the importance of computer security in depth. It will

■ Give examples of effective defense-in-depth

■ Explain the role of security policy

■ Envision the likely future of IPS and how collaboration between layers greatly enhances defensive capabilities

Defense-in-Depth Examples

Defense-in-depth assumes that every countermeasure can potentially be bypassed by an attacker. However, if you put many countermeasures together, the odds of bypassing all of them without being detected becomes much more unlikely. However, because of operational concerns, the most secure solution cannot always be implemented and is not always practical.

Consider securing houses. The strongest walls are thick concrete walls with no windows. These walls are also more expensive than normal wooden framed walls. Furthermore, people prefer to have natural lighting, so most houses have numerous windows made of glass. The glass lets light in and enables people to view things happening outside their house. Although the glass windows are a weak link (because they are breakable), you can improve on them using the defense-in-depth strategy. By adding a clear plastic laminate to the inside of the window, you can ensure that when the window breaks, the pieces stay together. This laminate then prevents attackers from easily getting through the window even if they break the glass. In conjunction with the laminate, you probably want to add an alarm mechanism that triggers when the window is opened or the glass is broken. Both of these measures make it more difficult for robbers to get into your house through the window without being detected.

This section walks through two examples that show the strength of a defense-in-depth approach:

- External attack against a corporate database
- Internal attack against a management server

External Attack Against a Corporate Database

A prime target on your network is your corporate database. Hopefully, this database is housed on your internal network and protected by various security measures. These security measures should make it difficult for an attacker to launch a successful attack against your corporate database.

Many people might think that an external attack needs to come directly from your network Internet connection. However, external attackers can attack your corporate database in various ways. Some of the attack paths and mechanisms include the following:

- Accessing the database server from Internet
- Accessing the database server from a compromised internal system
- Accessing the database server from compromised DMZ web server
- Accessing the database server from a worm attack

Protecting against these external attacks falls into the following areas or layers:

- Layer 1: The Internet perimeter router

- Layer 2: The Internet perimeter firewall

- Layer 3: The DMZ firewall

- Layer 4: Network IPS

- Layer 5: NetFlow

- Layer 6: Antivirus

- Layer 7: Host IPS

Layer 1: The Internet Perimeter Router

The first layer of protection from an attack is your external router. A router, if properly configured, can prevent traffic from entering your network while spoofing your internal address space. A commonly used and effective method for preventing spoofed traffic is to enable unicast reverse path forwarding (uRPF). uRPF uses the router's routing table to examine incoming traffic on an interface. This means that when traffic arrives on an interface with a source IP address of 10.10.10.1, for example, the router examines its routing table to see which interfaces it would send traffic that had 10.10.10.1 as a destination address. If these two interfaces aren't the same, the spoofed traffic is dropped. Routers can also use access control lists (ACLs). ACLs are rules that permit, deny, or simply identify traffic based on the following parameters:

- Source IP address

- Destination IP address

- Source port

- Destination port

- IP protocol

A weakness of traditional router ACLs is that they must trust information contained within the network traffic. The router does not maintain state information on traffic and instead relies on whether or not bits are set in a packet to determine whether or not the traffic is valid. For example, a crafted attack packet could potentially set the ACK bit to 1, and a router might believe this traffic is response traffic to a session that originated inside the network.

VALID TCP CONNECTION

A valid TCP connection is one that has been initiated with a complete three-way handshake that starts with a SYN packet from the client, followed by a SYN-ACK packet from the server, followed by an ACK from the client. Valid TCP traffic also has sequence and acknowledgment numbers that match the current values for the TCP connection. For more information on the TCP protocol, refer to RFC 793.

For example, suppose ACME's corporate databases run on Microsoft's SQL Server, which defaults to using User Datagram Protocol (UDP) port 1434 for access to the database. Most companies already block this port, but ACME should verify that the ACLs on the router do not allow this port to pass, especially to the SQL Server. Because this traffic is UDP-based, this ACL should block all external traffic to this port. Simply limiting external connections, however, via ACLs is usually not effective because an attacker can spoof UDP traffic fairly easily.

Layer 2: The Internet Perimeter Firewall

Most companies want their default protection to prevent traffic from the Internet to the internal network, although they allow internal systems to easily access the Internet. A perimeter firewall can implement rules to enforce these protections. The firewall, however, also has additional functionality such as the following:

- Application inspection processing

- Stateful connection processing

- Network Address Translation (NAT)

Your perimeter firewall should be configured to prevent an external computer from making connections to your internal database server.

In the example, the perimeter firewall prevents any inbound connections to the internal network. At the same time, this firewall allows internal systems to make outbound connections (allowing return traffic only for connections initiated from the internal network).

The application inspection processing enables your firewall to perform a detailed analysis of network traffic at the application layer. This analysis can automatically alter packet contents (such as performing NAT on IP fields in the application data). It can also open up pinhole connections through the firewall based on application data (such as opening up voice audio streams).

Layer 3: The DMZ Firewall

External users need to access many systems (such as your corporate web server). These systems, therefore, are a prime attack target. By placing these systems in a demilitarized zone (DMZ), you limit the ability of an attacker to impact other areas of your network if they happen to be compromised (see Figure 4-2). If a DMZ server is compromised by an attacker, the only other systems an attacker can attempt to attack from the compromised server are other systems on the same DMZ. Any connectivity to other DMZs or the internal network must be explicitly defined on the firewall.

NOTE   You should also limit the ability of your DMZ servers to initiate connections to other systems on the Internet. This prevents your public servers from attacking other systems on the Internet should they be compromised.

Figure 4-2   *DMZ Zone*

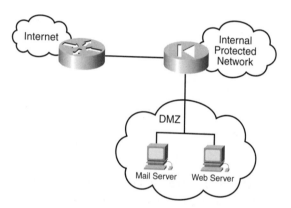

The firewall provides access to your web server and mail server; however, it can also provide some protection against many flooding attacks (such as a SYN flood). For example, the Cisco PIX firewall software version 7.0 and the Adaptive Security Appliance (ASA) provide various measures to protect against SYN flood attacks.

In the example, placing the public servers on a DMZ network prevents them from being used to attack the database server because they have no access to the internal network and the firewall is not configured to allow it. All connections to these public servers are initiated from the internal network.

Layer 4: Network IPS

Your Network IPS is continually analyzing the traffic passing through key points in your network. Using a large database of known attack signatures (a combination of patterns, protocol decodes, anomaly and behavioral analysis) your IPS sensors can prevent many attacks from reaching systems on your network.

If an attacker manages to pass attack traffic through your firewall, your Network IPS should detect it and take action. Actions are usually predefined and can include setting off an alarm or stopping the attack. You can also configure your Network IPS to alarm if it detects unauthorized traffic, such as connections originating from the database server destined to systems on the Internet.

Layer 5: NetFlow

NetFlow enables you to analyze the connections that occur on your network. Looking at the following connection parameters, you can identify patterns and other potentially anomalous activity:

■ Source IP address

■ Destination IP address

■ Source port

■ Destination port

■ IP protocol

■ Amount of data transmitted

In the example, NetFlow is used for anomaly identification. A baseline of connections patterns is established. Then using NetFlow, any connections that deviate from the established baseline are investigated.

In fact, Cisco Security Monitoring, Analysis and Response System (CS-MARS) accepts NetFlow data from routers and Layer 3 switches and then automates the security analysis of the NetFlow information. By learning what normal traffic is on the network, CS-MARS is able to alert on sudden changes in behavior.

Layer 6: Antivirus

Antivirus software protects systems on your network from a wide variety of viruses, Trojans, and worms. Antivirus software runs on the actual system that it protects. Therefore, the protection moves with the system. This is especially beneficial for highly mobile systems, such as laptops. Your business network might have a wide variety of security measures in place, but when your users take their corporate laptops home, those same protections are usually not in place (except for those that run on the laptops themselves).

In the example, antivirus software protects user systems from becoming compromised by known viruses. Protecting user systems prevents the user computers from being used as a launching point for attacks against the network.

Layer 7: Host IPS

Similar to antivirus, Host IPS runs on the actual system being protected. If your Host IPS implements behavioral signatures, it has the ability to protect your systems from day zero attacks.

DAY ZERO ATTACKS

Day zero attacks refer to attacks that were previously unpublished when they are used. Therefore, these attacks are not included in the signature database of many antivirus products.

Another advantage of Host IPS is that it can detect malicious software, such as keyloggers and Trojans, that an attacker might attempt to install on your systems.

A Host IPS system such as Cisco Security Agent (CSA) can be installed on the database systems, as well as all user systems. CSA protects the systems from buffer overflow attacks and from the installation of malicious software. It also alerts the user whenever it appears that software is being installed on the system. These alerts provide a visual indication to the user indicating that software is being installed on the system. This enables users to prevent many malicious applications and spyware from being installed on the system while still allowing them to install other software successfully. CSA can also be configured to protect against many malicious applications automatically (without informing the user).

Internal Attack Against a Management Server

Besides external attacks, you also need to worry about internal people who attempt to access unauthorized resources (either intentionally or accidentally). Because your management systems control the configuration on devices throughout your network, protecting these systems is a vital component of your overall network security strategy. Hopefully, an attacker must compromise several security mechanisms to access your management systems.

Protecting against these internal attacks falls into the following areas or layers:

- Layer 1: The switch

- Layer 2: Network IPS

- Layer 3: Encryption

- Layer 4: Strong authentication

- Layer 5: Host IPS

Layer 1: The Switch

The first layer of protection on your network is the switch ports that connect devices to your internal network. By separating different ports into different VLANs, you force traffic between different VLANs to go through your Layer 3 protection mechanisms, such as ACLs on your routers. When you turn off unused ports or use a port-based authentication system like 802.1x, you decrease the chances that someone can plug into an unused port and gain access to important systems.

802.1X

802.1x is a protocol that requires a device to be authenticated before the port that the device is connected to is allowed to access the protected network. Initially, the port provides the device with access only to the switch itself. Then if the device can authenticate successfully, the switch reconfigures the port and provides the device with greater access to the network.

In this example, the only ports configured for the server VLAN are the three server systems. Furthermore, ACLs limit access to only specific user systems. You can also get benefit by enabling port security on the switch's ports. Port security restricts the number of Ethernet addresses that a specific switch port is allowed to use, along with preventing a device from pretending to be another device's Ethernet address using Address Resolution Protocol (ARP) spoofing (common techniques used by tools such as Ettercap and DSNIFF).

Layer 2: Network IPS

Your Network IPS is constantly monitoring the traffic on your network looking for potential attack traffic. In this example, you can also use your Network IPS to identify anomalous connections to or from your management servers. Sensors running in inline mode can actually prevent connections from or to unauthorized systems. If attackers do compromise one of the servers, they can attempt to establish a connection to an external system on the Internet. This connection can be observed by the Network IPS.

Layer 3: Encryption

Many tools are available to sniff (or capture) the traffic on a network. To prevent successful sniffing, encrypt traffic to your management servers so that you stop an attacker from capturing vital information (such as login credentials). Common encrypted protocols for management include Secure Shell (SSH) and Secure Socket Layer (SSL).

In the example, encrypting the network traffic makes it almost impossible for an internal attacker (who has access to the network) to gain login credentials by using a simple network sniffer unless the attacker is able to successfully initiate a man-in-the-middle attack.

NOTE   Enabling port security, however, can minimize or eliminate the ability of the attacker to initiate a successful man-in-the-middle attack.

Layer 4: Strong Authentication

Strong authentication is important to protect critical assets (such as your management systems). One way to implement strong authentication is to implement one-time passwords. Even if an attacker manages to observe the password during a login attempt, the password could not be used by the attacker to gain access to the management system.

ONE-TIME PASSWORDS

By stealing basic username and passwords, an attacker can log in to vital systems. Using one-time passwords, your accounts are protected even if the password is observed because a new password is generated for each login attempt and is usually valid only for a short period of time. These passwords are generated by a smartcard, token, or computer program.

Layer 5: Host IPS

Finally, Host-based IPS, like CSA, protects the management system from attempts at exploiting vulnerabilities in the operating system or applications running on it. In addition, it can enforce policies that define what applications are allowed to run, which systems they are allowed to communicate with, and which users are allowed to run them. This final line of defense provides a final hurdle for an internal attacker.

The Security Policy

Although some people do not recognize it, your corporate security policy has an important role to play in defense-in-depth. It contains policies, procedures, guidelines, standards, implementation specifications, and requirements that should guide every facet of your security strategy. A typical corporate security policy contains four sections:

- Administrative safeguards

- Physical safeguards

- Technical safeguards

- Organizational framework

Each section defines a layer of security. For example, the administrative safeguards determine who should have access to a protected resource, the physical safeguards determine what physical access controls should protect the resource, and the technical safeguards define the technical countermeasures that should be in place. An IPS would likely be a tool used in the technical safeguards section.

The technical safeguards section also defines implementation guidelines for each layer of technical security. It covers how each layer should be configured, what layers should protect each type of resource, and how the layers are to interact. If you do not already use IPS, be sure to add it to your security policy.

You might find that as you add IPS to your security policy that you have to revise other sections to reflect the IPS' impact on other layers. For example, some IPS can reconfigure other types of devices, like firewalls, in response to an attack. The firewall section of the policy must be updated to define which interface should be reconfigured by the IPS, how the configuration request should be handled, and how the communications channel is to be secured.

The Future of IPS

The desire to become proactive instead of reactive has prompted most of the major improvements in IPS technology over the last few years. For example, movement of IPS devices into the data stream improves their ability to stop attacks before any damage can occur. The transition away from purely signature-based detection methods and into detection methods that can stop new and unknown attacks is another example. Refer to Chapter 1, "Intrusion Prevention Overview," for more information about the historical evolution of IPS.

As time goes on, IPS will likely reach a threshold where it is as proactive as it needs to be. At that time, IPS developers will have to find other ways to improve the technology. This section gives three examples of improvements that might be the future of IPS:

- Intrinsic IPS

- Collaboration between layers

- Automatic configuration and response

Intrinsic IPS

Chapter 7, "Network Intrusion Prevention Overview," covers some of Network IPS' limitations. One of the limitations covered there is that a NIPS device cannot inspect traffic it doesn't see. For a NIPS to be effective, it must bridge or capture the traffic between the attacker and the victim. Host IPS has the same problem in that it cannot protect a device that it is not installed on (see

Chapter 5, "Host Intrusion Prevention Overview"). Therefore, it is likely that in the future, IPS will transition away from a network or host add-on and become an intrinsic part of your network or endpoint.

In the case of Network IPS, this means that it will be built into every device that powers your network. Firewalls, routers, switches, and practically any other device through which network traffic passes will have the capability to inspect and act on that traffic. The only traffic that will escape inspection is that which passes directly from host to host with no intermediary.

On the host side, HIPS will run on a wider variety of operating systems and endpoints like IP phones, mobile phones, personal digital assistants (PDAs), and any other device that can connect to the network. It might be that product vendors will ship their products with built-in HIPS. Also, mechanisms that check for the presence of a HIPS before granting network access will become more foolproof and sophisticated.

Eventually, IPS might cease to exist as a standalone technology. If it's built into everything, it might become a standard feature rather than an add-on.

Collaboration Between Layers

Traditionally, each layer of protection operates separately from all of the others. A few exceptions exist, but for the most part, firewalls do not communicate with the NIPS—the NIPS does not talk to the HIPS, the HIPS does not interface with antivirus, and so on. Each layer has weaknesses for which other layers can make up. In the future, the layers will collaborate together, and the whole will be greater than the sum of the parts. This collaboration will result in

- Enhanced accuracy

- Better detection capability

- Automated configuration and response

Enhanced Accuracy

In the near future, accuracy enhancing interfaces between HIPS and NIPS will appear. When NIPS sees a malicious event, HIPS can corroborate it and vice versa. For example, if a HTTP service attack is detected by a NIPS device, it can ask the HIPS running on the target if a web service is running. If a web service is running, the attack is corroborated. If no web service is running, the attack is marked as a false alarm.

Another example would be the case where HIPS sees anomalous network activity on a host. The HIPS will consult with the NIPS to see if the activity is dangerous or benign. The NIPS can report back that the host from which the activity originated was recently identified as an attacker. The HIPS then knows that the anomalous activity is an actual attack and can respond appropriately.

Currently, CS-MARS is a Cisco product that can read syslogs, application logs, and IPS events and correlate them together to help to perform attack research and also mitigate and isolate attacks. You can find out more information on the MARs product at http://www.cisco.com/go/mars. The result of MARs event correlation is less false positive events from security devices and a much better understanding of what the various security event messages mean when looked at as a collective picture of the state of your network.

Better Detection Capability

An attack has a much harder time avoiding detection if all of the layers through which it has to pass share information with each other. Think of a suspicious-looking person passing through a series of manned checkpoints. If the checkpoints do not communicate, the guard at each stop might think the person looks "funny" but not have enough supporting evidence to take action. However, if the guards communicated, they would all agree that the person is suspicious-looking and should be stopped and questioned.

The same concept will be applied to computer security. In the future, each countermeasure will share information with all of the others. For example, a firewall, a NIPS, and a HIPS all detect suspicious, but potentially not dangerous, reconnaissance activity originating from a single host. They all report their findings to a single collection and correlation device. The device sees three similar reports and sends a message to all three devices indicating that a reconnaissance effort is underway and that the attacking host should be shunned.

The same function might take the form of a "tag" applied to network traffic as it passes through defensive layers. If a firewall detects traffic that is anomalous it adds a "potentially dangerous" flag to the traffic. An IPS sees the flag and knows that the firewall thinks the traffic is strange. If the IPS also determines that the traffic is suspicious, it drops the traffic based on its suspicion and the firewall's tag.

Automated Configuration and Response

In the future, security countermeasures will be able to take collaborative, rather than individual, action during an incident. As it stands, when an IPS detects an attack it takes action according to its configuration settings. Moving forward, when the IPS detects an attack originating from an internal host, it can take its usual action and also configure the network to contain the attack. Routers, switches, and firewalls will be reconfigured by the IPS to make sure the attack cannot propagate throughout the network.

HIPS and NIPS can also work together to configure each other. For example, if a HIPS sees an attack against a protected host, it can notify the NIPS. The NIPS can take that notification and reconfigure itself to take more stringent action against traffic from the attacker. Furthermore, if IPS functionality is integrated into many different devices on the network (such as firewalls and routers), all of these devices can participate collaboratively to maintain a strong security posture on your network.

Summary

No single security countermeasure can always stop all attacks. Effective security requires multiple layers of countermeasure, so that if one is bypassed, the attack still has to get through the next layer, the layer after that, and so on. The concept of utilizing multiple layers of defense is called *defense-in-depth.*

A prime target on your network is your corporate database. Hopefully, this database is housed on your internal network and protected by various security measures. However, an external attacker can attack your corporate database in various ways. Some of the attack paths and mechanisms include the following:

- Accessing the database server from Internet

- Accessing the database server from a compromised internal system

- Accessing the database server from compromised DMZ web server

- Accessing the database server from a worm attack

Protecting against these external attacks falls into the following areas or layers:

- Layer 1: The Internet perimeter router

- Layer 2: The Internet perimeter firewall

- Layer 3: The DMZ firewall

- Layer 4: Network IPS

- Layer 5: NetFlow

- Layer 6: Antivirus

- Layer 7: Host IPS

Besides external attacks, you also need to worry about internal people who attempt to access unauthorized resources (either intentionally or accidentally). Protecting against these internal attacks falls into the following areas or layers:

- Layer 1: The switch

- Layer 2: Network IPS

- Layer 3: Encryption

- Layer 4: Strong authentication

- Layer 5: Host IPS

Your corporate security policy has an important role to play in defense-in-depth. It contains policies, procedures, guidelines, standards, implementation specifications, and requirements that should guide every facet of your security strategy. A typical corporate security policy contains four sections:

- Administrative safeguards

- Physical safeguards

- Technical safeguards

- Organizational framework

ISBN: 1-58705-222-9

Campus Network Design Fundamentals

The all-in-one guide to modern routed and switched campus network design

ciscopress.com

Diane Teare · Catherine Paquet

This chapter discusses switching network design and includes the following sections:

- Making the Business Case

- Switching Types

- Spanning Tree Protocol

- Virtual LANs

- Multilayer Switching and Cisco Express Forwarding

- Switching Security

- Switching Design Considerations

CHAPTER 2

Switching Design

This first chapter in Part II, "Technologies: What You Need to Know and Why You Need to Know It," discusses switching network design. After introducing why switches are an important part of a network, we examine the different types of switching and then discuss the Spanning Tree Protocol (STP), which is key in Layer 2 switched environments to ensure that redundancy does not cause the network performance to deteriorate. Virtual local-area networks (VLANs) are then described. Two types of Layer 3 switching, multilayer switching (MLS) and Cisco Express Forwarding (CEF), are then introduced. Security in a switched environment is examined next. The chapter concludes with considerations and examples of switched designs.

> **NOTE** Appendix B, "Network Fundamentals," includes material that we assume you understand before reading the rest of the book. Thus, you are encouraged to review any of the material in Appendix B that you are not familiar with before reading the rest of this chapter.

Making the Business Case

Switches can enhance the performance, flexibility, and functionality of your network.

The first networks were LANs; they enabled multiple users in a relatively small geographical area to exchange files and messages, and to access shared resources such as printers and disk storage. A hub—an Open Systems Interconnection (OSI) Layer 1 device—interconnected PCs, servers, and so forth as the number of devices on the network grew. However, because all devices connected to a hub are in the same bandwidth (or collision) domain—they all share the same bandwidth—using hubs in anything but a small network is not efficient.

To improve performance, LANs can be divided into multiple smaller LANs, interconnected by a Layer 2 LAN switch. Because each port of the switch is its own collision domain, multiple simultaneous conversations between devices connected through the switch can occur.

By default, all ports of a switch are in the same broadcast domain. Recall (from Appendix B) that a broadcast domain includes all devices that receive each other's broadcasts (and multicasts). A *broadcast* is data meant for all devices; it uses a special broadcast address to indicate this. A *multicast* is data destined for a specific group; again, a special address indicates this. Note that

Layer 3 broadcast packets are typically encapsulated in Layer 2 broadcast frames, and Layer 3 multicast packets are typically encapsulated in Layer 2 multicast frames (assuming that the packets are going over a data-link technology that supports these types of frames, such as Ethernet).

The implications of this for modern networks are significant—a large switched OSI Layer 2 network is one broadcast domain, so any broadcasts or multicasts traverse the entire network. Examples of broadcast traffic include Internet Protocol (IP) Address Resolution Protocol (ARP) packets, and routing protocol traffic such as Routing Information Protocol (RIP) version 1 (RIPv1). Multicast traffic includes packets from more advanced routing protocols such as Open Shortest Path First (OSPF) and applications such as e-learning and videoconferencing. As network use increases, the amount of traffic—including multicast and broadcast traffic—will also increase.

Today's switches support VLANs so that physically remote devices can appear to be on the same (virtual) LAN. Each VLAN is its own broadcast domain. Traffic within a VLAN can be handled by Layer 2 switches. However, traffic between VLANS, just like traffic between LANs, must be handled by an OSI Layer 3 device. Traditionally, routers have been the Layer 3 device of choice. Today, Layer 3 switches offer the same functionality as routers but at higher speeds and with additional functionality.

The rest of this chapter explains how switches—Layer 2 and Layer 3—and the protocols associated with them work, and how they can be incorporated into network designs.

Switching Types

Switches were initially introduced to provide higher-performance connectivity than hubs, because switches define multiple collision domains.

Switches have always been able to process data at a faster rate than routers, because the switching functionality is implemented in hardware—in Application-Specific Integrated Circuits (ASICs)—rather than in software, which is how routing has traditionally been implemented. However, switching was initially restricted to the examination of Layer 2 frames. With the advent of more powerful ASICs, switches can now process Layer 3 packets, and even the contents of those packets, at high speeds.

The following sections first examine the operation of traditional Layer 2 switching. Layer 3 switching—which is really routing in hardware—is then explored.

Layer 2 Switching

KEY POINT | Layer 2 switches segment a network into multiple collision domains and interconnect devices within a workgroup, such as a group of PCs.

The heart of a Layer 2 switch is its Media Access Control (MAC) address table, also known as its content-addressable memory (CAM). This table contains a list of the MAC addresses that are reachable through each switch port. (Recall that the physical MAC address uniquely identifies a device on a network. When a network interface card is manufactured, the card is assigned an address—called a burned-in address [BIA]—which doesn't change when the network card is installed in a device and is moved from one network to another. Typically, this BIA is copied to interface memory and is used as the MAC address of the interface.) The MAC address table can be statically configured, or the switch can learn the MAC addresses dynamically. When a switch is first powered up, its MAC address table is empty, as shown in the example network of Figure 2-1.

Figure 2-1 *The MAC Address Table Is Initially Empty*

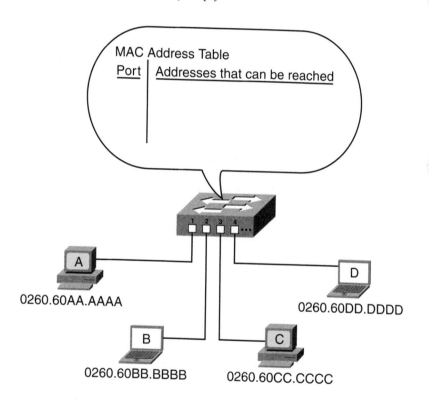

In this example network, consider what happens when device A sends a frame destined for device D. The switch receives the frame on port 1 (from device A). Recall that a frame includes the MAC address of the source device and the MAC address of the destination device. Because the switch does not yet know where device D is, the switch must *flood* the frame out of all the other ports; therefore, the switch sends the frame out of ports 2, 3, and 4. This means that devices B, C, and D all receive the frame. Only device D, however, recognizes its MAC address as the destination address in the frame; it is the only device on which the CPU is interrupted to further process the frame.

In the meantime, the switch now knows that device A can be reached on port 1 (because the switch received a frame from device A on port 1); the switch therefore puts the MAC address of device A in its MAC address table for port 1. This process is called *learning*—the switch is learning all the MAC addresses that it can reach.

At some point, device D is likely to reply to device A. At that time, the switch receives a frame from device D on port 4; the switch records this information in its MAC address table as part of its learning process. This time, the switch knows where the destination, device A, is; the switch therefore forwards the frame only out of port 1. This process is called *filtering*—the switch is sending the frames only out of the port through which they need to go—when the switch knows which port that is—rather than flooding them out of all the ports. This reduces the traffic on the other ports and reduces the interruptions that the other devices experience.

Over time, the switch learns where all the devices are, and the MAC address table is fully populated, as shown in Figure 2-2.

Figure 2-2   *The Switch Learns Where All the Devices Are and Populates Its MAC Address Table*

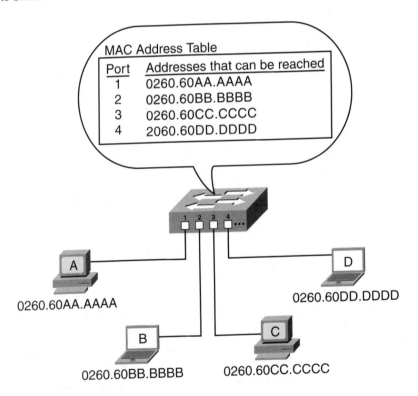

The filtering process also means that multiple simultaneous conversations can occur between different devices. For example, if device A and device B want to communicate, the switch sends their data between ports 1 and 2; no traffic goes on ports 3 or 4. At the same time, devices C and

D can communicate on ports 3 and 4 without interfering with the traffic on ports 1 and 2. Thus, the overall throughput of the network has increased dramatically.

The MAC address table is kept in the switch's memory and has a finite size (depending on the specific switch used). If many devices are attached to the switch, the switch might not have room for an entry for every one, so the table entries will time out after a period of not being used. For example, the Cisco Catalyst 2950 switch defaults to a 300-second timeout. Thus, the most active devices are always in the table.

> **NOTE**   Cisco LAN switches are also known as *Catalyst switches.*

KEY POINT   Broadcast and multicast frames are, by default, flooded to all ports of a Layer 2 switch, other than the incoming port. The same is true for unicast frames that are destined to any device that is not in the MAC address table.

MAC addresses can also be statically configured in the MAC address table, and you can specify a maximum number of addresses allowed per port.

One advantage of static addresses is that less flooding occurs, both when the switch first comes up and because of not aging out the addresses. However, this also means that if a device is moved, the switch configuration must be changed. A related feature available in some switches is the ability to *sticky-learn* addresses—the address is dynamically learned, as described earlier, but is then automatically entered as a static command in the switch configuration. Limiting the number of addresses per port to one and statically configuring those addresses can ensure that only specific devices are permitted access to the network; this feature is particularly useful when addresses are sticky-learned.

Layer 3 Switching

KEY POINT   A Layer 3 switch is really a router with some of the functions implemented in hardware to improve performance. In other words, some of the OSI model network layer routing functions are performed in high-performance ASICs rather than in software.

In Appendix B and Chapter 3, "IPv4 Routing Design," we describe the following various functions and characteristics of routers:

- Learning routes and keeping the best path to each destination in a routing table.

- Determining the best path that each packet should take to get to its destination, by comparing the destination address to the routing table.

- Sending the packet out of the appropriate interface, along the best path. This is also called *switching the packet,* because the packet is encapsulated in a new frame, with the appropriate framing header information, including MAC addresses.

- Communicating with other routers to exchange routing information.

- Allowing devices on different LANs to communicate with each other and with distant devices.

- Blocking broadcasts. By default, a router does not forward broadcasts, thereby helping to control the amount of traffic on the network.

These tasks can be CPU intensive. Offloading the switching of the packet to hardware can result in a significant increase in performance.

A Layer 3 switch performs all the previously mentioned router functions; the differences are in the physical implementation of the device rather than in the functions it performs. Thus, functionally, the terms *router* and *Layer 3 switch* are synonymous.

Layer 4 switching is an extension of Layer 3 switching that includes examination of the contents of the Layer 3 packet. For example, as described in Appendix B, the protocol number in the IP packet header indicates which transport layer protocol (for example, Transmission Control Protocol [TCP] or User Datagram Protocol [UDP]) is being used, and the port number in the TCP or UDP segment indicates the application being used. Switching based on the protocol and port numbers can ensure, for example, that certain types of traffic get higher priority on the network or take a specific path.

Depending on the switch, Layer 3 switching can be implemented in two different ways within Cisco switches—through multilayer switching and Cisco Express Forwarding. These terms are described in the section "Multilayer Switching and Cisco Express Forwarding," later in this chapter (after we discuss VLANs, which you must understand before you read that section).

Spanning Tree Protocol

KEY POINT | STP is a Layer 2 protocol that prevents logical loops in switched networks that have redundant links.

In the following sections, we first examine why such a protocol is needed in Layer 2 networks. We then introduce STP terminology and operation.

NOTE   In the following sections, we are only concerned with Layer 2 switching; as you see in Chapter 3, routed (Layer 3) networks inherently support networks with multiple paths, so a protocol such as STP is not required.

Redundancy in Layer 2 Switched Networks

Redundancy in a network, such as that shown in Figure 2-3, is desirable so that communication can still take place if a link or device fails. For example, if switch X in this figure stopped functioning, devices A and B could still communicate through switch Y. However, in a switched network, redundancy can cause problems.

Figure 2-3   *Redundancy in a Switched Network Can Cause Problems*

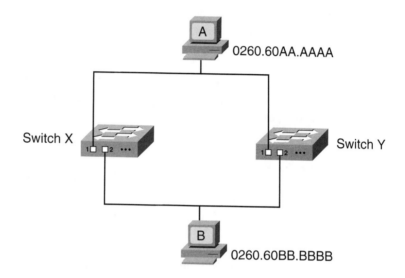

The first type of problem occurs if a broadcast frame is sent on the network. (Recall that a switch floods broadcast frames to all ports other than the one that it came in on.) For example, consider what happens when device A in Figure 2-3 sends an ARP request to find the MAC address of device B. The ARP request is sent as a broadcast. Both switch X and switch Y receive the broadcast; for now, consider just the one received by switch X, on its port 1. Switch X floods the broadcast to all its other connected ports; in this case, it floods it to port 2. Device B can see the broadcast, but so can switch Y, on its port 2; switch Y floods the broadcast to its port 1. This broadcast is received by switch X on its port 1; switch X floods it to its port 2, and so forth. The broadcast continues to loop around the network, consuming bandwidth and processing power. This situation is called a *broadcast storm.*

The second problem that can occur in redundant topologies is that devices can receive multiple copies of the same frame. For example, assume that neither of the switches in Figure 2-3 has learned where device B is located. When device A sends data destined for device B, switch X and switch Y both flood the data to the lower LAN, and device B receives two copies of the same frame. This might be a problem for device B, depending on what it is and how it is programmed to handle such a situation.

The third difficulty that can occur in a redundant situation is within the switch itself—the MAC address table can change rapidly and contain wrong information. Again referring to Figure 2-3, consider what happens when neither switch has learned where device A or B are located, and device A sends data to device B. Each switch learns that device A is on its port 1, and each records this in its MAC address table. Because the switches don't yet know where device B is, they flood the frame, in this case on their port 2. Each switch then receives the frame, from the other switch, on its port 2. This frame has device A's MAC address in the source address field; therefore, both switches now learn that device A is on their port 2. The MAC address table is therefore overwritten. Not only does the MAC address table have incorrect information (device A is actually connected to port 1, not port 2, of both switches), but because the table changes rapidly, it might be considered to be unstable.

To overcome these problems, you need a way to logically disable part of the redundant network for regular traffic while still maintaining the redundancy for the case when an error occurs. The Spanning Tree Protocol does just that.

STP Terminology and Operation

The following sections introduce the Institute of Electrical and Electronics Engineers (IEEE) 802.1d STP terminology and operation.

STP Terminology

STP terminology can best be explained by examining how an example network, such as the one in Figure 2-4, operates.

Figure 2-4 *STP Chooses the Port to Block*

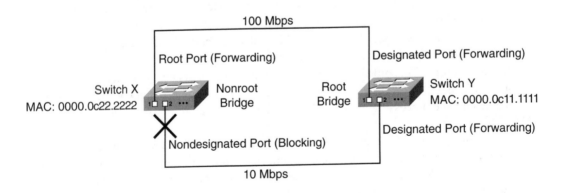

NOTE   Notice that STP terminology refers to the devices as *bridges* rather than *switches*. Recall (from Appendix B) that bridges are previous-generation devices with the same logical functionality as switches; however, switches are significantly faster because they switch in hardware, whereas bridges switch in software. Functionally, the two terms are synonymous.

Within an STP network, one switch is elected as the *root bridge*—it is at the root of the spanning tree. All other switches calculate their best path to the root bridge. Their alternate paths are put in the blocking state. These alternate paths are logically disabled from the perspective of regular traffic, but the switches still communicate with each other on these paths so that the alternate paths can be unblocked in case an error occurs on the best path.

All switches running STP (it is turned on by default in Cisco switches) send out bridge protocol data units (BPDUs). Switches running STP use BPDUs to exchange information with neighboring switches. One of the fields in the BPDU is the bridge identifier (ID); it is comprised of a 2-octet bridge priority and a 6-octet MAC address. STP uses the bridge ID to elect the root bridge—the switch with the lowest bridge ID is the root bridge. If all bridge priorities are left at their default values, the switch with the lowest MAC address therefore becomes the root bridge. In Figure 2-4, switch Y is elected as the root bridge.

NOTE   The way that STP chooses the root bridge can cause an interesting situation if left to the default values. Recall that the MAC address is a 6-octet or 48-bit value, with the upper 24 bits as an Organizational Unique Identifier (OUI) (representing the vendor of the device) and the lower 24 bits as a unique value for that OUI, typically the serial number of the device. A lower MAC address means a lower serial number, which likely means an older switch. Thus, because STP by default chooses a switch with a lower MAC address, the oldest switch is likely to be chosen. This is just one reason why you should explicitly choose the root bridge (by changing the priority), rather than getting the STP default choice.

All the ports on the root bridge are called *designated ports,* and they are all in the *forwarding state*—that is, they can send and receive data. (The STP states are described in the next section of this chapter.)

On all *nonroot bridges,* one port becomes the *root port,* and it is also in the forwarding state. The root port is the one with the lowest cost to the root. The cost of each link is by default inversely proportional to the bandwidth of the link, so the port with the fastest total path from the switch to the root bridge is selected as the root port on that switch. In Figure 2-4, port 1 on switch X is the root port for that switch because it is the fastest way to the root bridge.

NOTE If multiple ports on a switch have the same fastest total path costs to the root bridge, STP considers other BPDU fields. STP looks first at the bridge IDs in the received BPDUs (the bridge IDs of the next switch in the path to the root bridge); the port that received the BPDU with the lowest bridge ID becomes the root port. If these bridge IDs are also equal, the port ID breaks the tie; the port with the lower port ID becomes the root port. The port ID field includes a port priority and a port index, which is the port number. Thus, if the port priorities are the same (for example, if they are left at their default value), the lower port number becomes the root port.

Each LAN segment must have one designated port. It is on the switch that has the lowest cost to the root bridge (or if the costs are equal, the port on the switch with the lowest bridge ID is chosen), and it is in the forwarding state. In Figure 2-4, the root bridge has designated ports on both segments, so no more are required.

NOTE The root bridge sends configuration BPDUs on all its ports periodically, every 2 seconds by default. (These configuration BPDUs include the STP timers, therefore ensuring that all switches in the network use the same timers.) On each LAN segment the switch that has the designated port forwards the configuration BPDUs to the segment; all switches in the network therefore receive these BPDUs, on their root port.

All ports on a LAN segment that are not root ports or designated ports are called *nondesignated ports* and transition to the *blocking state*—they do not send data, so the redundant topology is logically disabled. In Figure 2-4, port 2 on switch X is the nondesignated port, and it is in the blocking state. Blocking ports do, however, listen for BPDUs.

If a failure happens—for example, if a designated port or a root bridge fails—the switches send topology change BPDUs and recalculate the spanning tree. The new spanning tree does not include the failed port or switch, and the ports that were previously blocking might now be in the forwarding state. This is how STP supports the redundancy in a switched network.

STP States

Figure 2-5 illustrates the various STP port states.

Figure 2-5 *A Port Can Transition Among STP States*

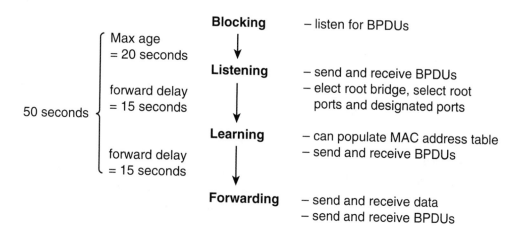

When a port initially comes up, it is put in the blocking state, in which it listens for BPDUs and then transitions to the listening state. A blocking port in an operational network can also transition to the listening state if it does not hear any BPDUs for the *max-age time* (a default of 20 seconds). While in the listening state, the switch can send and receive BPDUs but not data. The root bridge and the various final states of all the ports are determined in this state. If the port is chosen as the root port on a switch or as a designated port on a segment, the port transitions to the learning state after the listening state. In the learning state, the port still cannot send data, but it can start to populate its MAC address table if any data is received. The length of time spent in each of the listening and learning states is dictated by the value of the *forward-delay* parameter, which is 15 seconds by default. After the learning state, the port transitions to the forwarding state, in which it can operate normally. Alternatively, if in the listening state the port is not chosen as a root port or designated port, it becomes a nondesignated port and it transitions back to the blocking state.

KEY POINT

Do not confuse the STP learning state with the learning process that the switch goes through to populate its MAC address table. The STP learning state is a transitory state. While a switch can learn MAC addresses from data frames received on its ports that are in the STP learning state, it does not forward those frames. In a stable network, switch ports are in either the forwarding or blocking state. Ports in the blocking state do not listen to data frames and therefore do not contribute to the switch's MAC address table. Ports in the forwarding state do, of course, listen to (and forward) data frames, and those frames populate the switch's MAC address table.

STP Options

Figure 2-5 illustrates that it could take up to 50 seconds for a blocked port to transition to the forwarding state after a failure has occurred in the forwarding path. This lengthy time is one of the drawbacks of STP.

Several features and enhancements to STP can help to reduce the convergence time, that is, the time it takes for all the switches in a network to agree on the network's topology after that topology has changed. The following are some of these features that are implemented in Cisco switches:

- **PortFast**—This feature should be used for ports that have only end-user stations or servers attached to them, in other words, for ports that are not attached to other switches (so that no BPDUs are received on the port). Because no other switches are attached, the port cannot be part of a loop, so the switch immediately puts the port in the forwarding state. Thus, the port transitions to the forwarding state much faster than it otherwise would.

- **UplinkFast**—This feature is intended to be used on redundant ports on access layer switches.[1] If the root port (pointing to the root bridge) on a switch goes down, the nondesignated port (the redundant blocking port) on the switch is quickly put in the forwarding state, rather than going through all the other states.

- **BackboneFast**—This feature helps to reduce the convergence time when links other than those directly connected to a switch fail. This feature must be deployed on all switches in the network if it is to be used.

Rapid STP (RSTP)

RSTP is defined by IEEE 802.1w. RSTP incorporates many of the Cisco enhancements to STP, resulting in faster convergence. Switches in an RSTP environment converge quickly by communicating with each other and determining which links can be forwarding, rather than just waiting for the timers to transition the ports among the various states. RSTP ports take on different roles than STP ports. The RSTP roles are root, designated, alternate, backup, and disabled. RSTP port states are also different than STP port states. The RSTP states are discarding, learning, and forwarding. RSTP is compatible with STP.

Virtual LANs

As noted earlier, a broadcast domain includes all devices that receive each other's broadcasts (and multicasts). All the devices connected to one router port are in the same broadcast domain. Routers block broadcasts (destined for *all* networks) and multicasts by default; routers only forward *unicast* packets (destined for a specific device) and packets of a special type called *directed broadcasts*. Typically, you think of a broadcast domain as being a physical wire, a LAN. But a broadcast domain can also be a VLAN, a logical construct that can include multiple physical LAN segments.

> **NOTE** IP multicast technology, which enables multicast packets to be sent throughout a network, is described in Chapter 10, "Other Enabling Technologies."

> **NOTE** An IP directed broadcast is a packet destined for all devices on an IP subnet, but which originates from a device on another subnet. A router that is not directly connected to the destination subnet forwards the IP directed broadcast in the same way it would forward unicast IP packets destined to a host on that subnet.
>
> On Cisco routers, the **ip directed-broadcast** interface command controls what the last router in the path, the one connected to the destination subnet, does with the packet. If **ip directed-broadcast** is enabled on the interface, the router changes the directed broadcast to a broadcast and sends the packet, encapsulated in a Layer 2 broadcast frame, onto the subnet. However, if the **no ip directed-broadcast** command is configured on the interface, directed broadcasts destined for the subnet to which that interface is attached are dropped. In Cisco Internet Operating System (IOS) version 12.0, the default for this command was changed to **no ip directed-broadcast**.

KEY POINT | We found the Cisco definition of VLANs to be very clear: "[A] group of devices on one or more LANs that are configured (using management software) so that they can communicate as if they were attached to the same wire, when in fact they are located on a number of different LAN segments. Because VLANs are based on logical instead of physical connections, they are extremely flexible."[2]

Figure 2-6 illustrates the VLAN concept. On the left side of the figure, three individual physical LANs are shown, one each for Engineering, Accounting, and Marketing. (These LANs contain workstations—E1, E2, A1, A2, M1, and M2—and servers—ES, AS, and MS.) Instead of physical LANs, an enterprise can use VLANs, as shown on the right side of the figure. With VLANs, members of each department can be physically located anywhere, yet still be logically connected with their own workgroup. Thus, in the VLAN configuration, all the devices attached to VLAN E (Engineering) share the same broadcast domain, the devices attached to VLAN A (Accounting) share a separate broadcast domain, and the devices attached to VLAN M (Marketing) share a third broadcast domain. Figure 2-6 also illustrates how VLANs can span across multiple switches; the link between the two switches in the figure carries traffic from all three of the VLANs and is called a *trunk*.

Figure 2-6   *A VLAN Is a Logical Implementation of a Physical LAN*

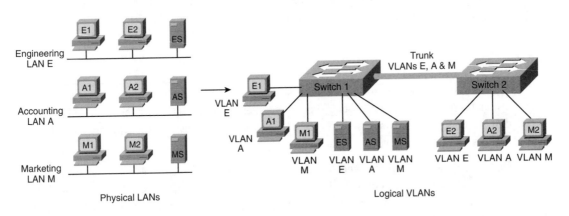

VLAN Membership

A switch port that is not a trunk can belong to only one VLAN at a time. You can configure which VLAN a port belongs to in two ways: statically and dynamically.

Static port membership means that the network administrator configures which VLAN the port belongs to, regardless of the devices attached to it. This means that after you have configured the ports, you must ensure that the devices attaching to the switch are plugged into the correct port, and if they move, you must reconfigure the switch.

Alternatively, you can configure dynamic VLAN membership. Some static configuration is still required, but this time, it is on a separate device called a *VLAN Membership Policy Server (VMPS)*. The VMPS could be a separate server, or it could be a higher-end switch that contains the VMPS information. VMPS information consists of a MAC address-to-VLAN map. Thus, ports are assigned to VLANs based on the MAC address of the device connected to the port. When you move a device from one port to another port (either on the same switch or on another switch in the network), the switch dynamically assigns the new port to the proper VLAN for that device by consulting the VMPS.

Trunks

As mentioned earlier, a port that carries data from multiple VLANs is called a trunk. A trunk port can be on a switch, a router, or a server.

A trunk port can use one of two protocols: Inter-Switch Link (ISL) or IEEE 802.1q.

ISL is a Cisco-proprietary trunking protocol that involves encapsulating the data frame between an ISL header and trailer. The header is 26 bytes long; the trailer is a 4-byte cyclic redundancy check (CRC) that is added after the data frame. A 15-bit VLAN ID field is included in the header to identify the VLAN that the traffic is for. (Only the lower 10 bits of this field are used, thus supporting 1024 VLANs.)

The 802.1q protocol is an IEEE standard protocol in which the trunking information is encoded within a Tag field that is inserted inside the frame header itself. Trunks using the 802.1q protocol define a native VLAN. Traffic for the native VLAN is not tagged; it is carried across the trunk unchanged. Thus, end-user stations that don't understand trunking can communicate with other devices directly over an 802.1q trunk, as long as they are on the native VLAN. The native VLAN must be defined to be the same VLAN on both sides of the trunk. Within the Tag field, the 802.1q VLAN ID field is 12 bits long, allowing up to 4096 VLANs to be defined. The Tag field also includes a 3-bit 802.1p user priority field; these bits are used as class of service (CoS) bits for quality of service (QoS) marking. (Chapter 6, "Quality of Service Design," describes QoS marking.)

The two types of trunks are not compatible with each other, so both ends of a trunk must be defined with the same trunk type.

NOTE   Multiple switch ports can be logically combined so that they appear as one higher-performance port. Cisco does this with its Etherchannel technology, combining multiple Fast Ethernet or Gigabit Ethernet links. Trunks can be implemented on both individual ports and on these Etherchannel ports.

STP and VLANs

Cisco developed per-VLAN spanning tree (PVST) so that switches can have one instance of STP running per VLAN, allowing redundant physical links within the network to be used for different VLANs and thus reducing the load on individual links. PVST is illustrated in Figure 2-7.

Figure 2-7 *PVST Allows Redundant Physical Links to Be Used for Different VLANs*

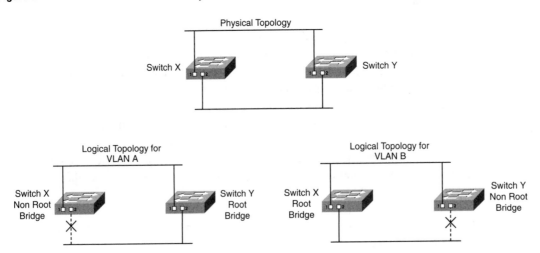

The top diagram in Figure 2-7 shows the physical topology of the network, with switches X and Y redundantly connected. In the lower-left diagram, switch Y has been selected as the root bridge for VLAN A, leaving port 2 on switch X in the blocking state. In contrast, the lower-right diagram shows that switch X has been selected as the root bridge for VLAN B, leaving port 2 on switch Y in the blocking state. With this configuration, traffic is shared across all links, with traffic for VLAN A traveling to the lower LAN on switch Y's port 2, while traffic for VLAN B traveling to the lower LAN goes out switch X's port 2.

PVST only works over ISL trunks. However, Cisco extended this functionality for 802.1q trunks with the PVST+ protocol. Before this became available, 802.1q trunks only supported Common Spanning Tree (CST), with one instance of STP running for all VLANs.

Multiple-Instance STP (MISTP) is an IEEE standard (802.1s) that uses RSTP and allows several VLANs to be grouped into a single spanning-tree instance. Each instance is independent of the other instances so that a link can be forwarding for one group of VLANs while blocking for other VLANs. MISTP therefore allows traffic to be shared across all the links in the network, but it reduces the number of STP instances that would be required if PVST/PVST+ were implemented.

VLAN Trunking Protocol

KEY POINT The VLAN Trunking Protocol (VTP) is a Cisco-proprietary Layer 2 protocol that allows easier configuration of VLANs on multiple switches. When VTP is enabled in your network, you define all the VLANs on one switch, and that switch sends the VLAN definitions to all the other switches. On those other switches, you then have to only assign the ports to the VLANs; you do not have to configure the VLANs themselves. Not only is configuration easier, but it is also less prone to misconfiguration errors.

A switch in a VTP domain (a group of switches communicating with VTP) can be in one of three modes: server (which is the default mode), client, or transparent mode. The VTP server is the one on which you configure the VLANs; it sends VTP advertisements, containing VLAN configuration information, to VTP clients in the same VTP domain, as illustrated in Figure 2-8. Note that VTP advertisements are only sent on trunks.

Figure 2-8 *VTP Eases VLAN Definition Configuration*

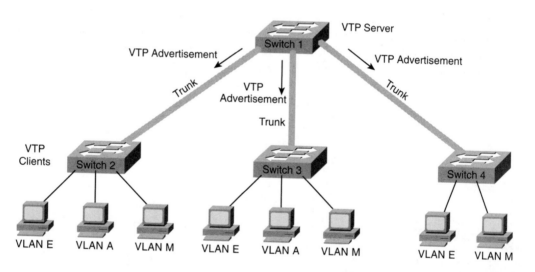

You cannot create, modify, or delete VLANs on a VTP client; rather, a VTP client only accepts VLAN configuration information from a VTP server. A VTP client also forwards the VTP advertisements to other switches.

You can create, modify, or delete VLANs on a switch that is in VTP transparent mode; however, this information is not sent to other switches, and the transparent-mode switch ignores advertisements from VTP servers (but does pass them on to other switches).

VTP pruning is a VTP feature that helps reduce the amount of flooded traffic (including broadcast, multicast, and unicast) that is sent on the network. With VTP pruning enabled, the switches communicate with each other to find out which switches have ports in which VLANs; switches that have no ports in a particular VLAN (and have no downstream switches with ports in that VLAN) do not receive that VLAN's traffic. For example, in Figure 2-8, switch 4 has no need for VLAN A traffic, so VTP pruning would prevent switch 1 from flooding VLAN A traffic to switch 4. VTP pruning is disabled by default.

Inter-VLAN Routing

You have learned how devices on one VLAN can communicate with each other using switches and trunks. But how do networked devices on different VLANs communicate with each other?

KEY POINT | Just like devices on different LANs, those on different VLANs require a Layer 3 mechanism (a router or a Layer 3 switch) to communicate with each other.

A Layer 3 device can be connected to a switched network in two ways: by using multiple physical interfaces or through a single interface configured as a trunk. These two connection methods are shown in Figure 2-9. The diagram on the left in this figure illustrates a router with three physical connections to the switch; each physical connection carries traffic from only one VLAN.

Figure 2-9 *A Router, Using Either Multiple Physical Interfaces or a Trunk, Is Required for Communication Among VLANs*

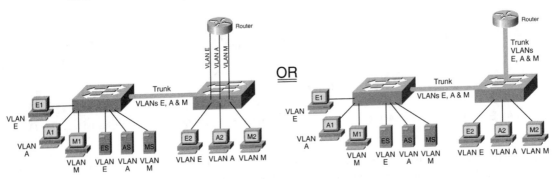

The diagram on the right in Figure 2-9 illustrates a router with one physical connection to the switch. The interfaces on the switch and the router have been configured as trunks; therefore, multiple logical connections exist between the two devices. When a router is connected to a switch through a trunk, it is sometimes called a "router on a stick," because it has only one physical interface (a stick) to the switch.

Each interface between the switch and the Layer 3 device (whether physical interfaces or logical interfaces within a trunk) is in a separate VLAN (and therefore in a separate subnet for IP networks).

Multilayer Switching and Cisco Express Forwarding

Now that you have an understanding of VLANs, the following sections introduce the two different ways that Layer 3 switching is implemented within Cisco switches—multilayer switching and Cisco Express Forwarding.

Multilayer Switching

Multilayer switching, as its name implies, allows switching to take place at different protocol layers. Switching can be performed only on Layers 2 and 3, or it can also include Layer 4.

MLS is based on network flows.

KEY POINT

A *network flow* is a unidirectional sequence of packets between a source and a destination. Flows can be very specific. For example, a network flow can be identified by source and destination IP addresses, protocol numbers, and port numbers as well as the interface on which the packet enters the switch.

The three major components of MLS are as follows[3]:

- **MLS Route Processor (MLS-RP)**—The MLS-enabled router that performs the traditional function of routing between subnets

- **MLS Switching Engine (MLS-SE)**—The MLS-enabled switch that can offload some of the packet-switching functionality from the MLS-RP

- **Multilayer Switching Protocol (MLSP)**—Used by the MLS-RP and the MLS-SE to communicate with each other

MLS can be implemented in the following two ways:

- **Within a Catalyst switch**—Here both the MLS-RP and the MLS-SE are resident in the same chassis. An example of an internal MLS-RP is a Route Switch Module (RSM) installed in a slot of a Catalyst 5500 Series switch.

- **Using a combination of a Catalyst switch and an external router**—An example of a router that can be an external MLS-RP router is a Cisco 3600 Series router with the appropriate IOS software release and with MLS enabled.

> **NOTE**   Not all Catalyst switches and routers support MLS. Refer to specific product documentation on the Cisco website for device support information for switches[4] and routers.[5]

KEY POINT   MLS allows communication between two devices that are in different VLANs (on different subnets) and that are connected to the same MLS-SE and that share a common MLS-RP. The communication bypasses the MLS-RP and instead uses the MLS-SE to relay the packets, thus improving overall performance.[6]

Figure 2-10 is an example network that illustrates MLS operation.

Figure 2-10   *The MLS-SE Offloads Work from the MLS-RP*

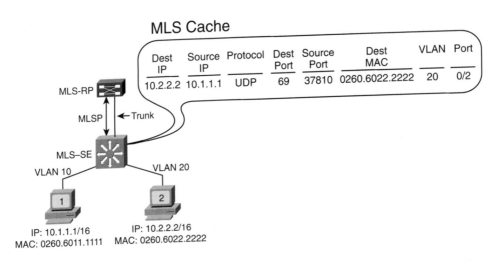

In Figure 2-10, the MLS-RP and MLS-SE communicate using MLSP. The SE learns the MAC addresses of the RP (one for each VLAN that is running MLS). When device 1 (10.1.1.1/16) wants to send a packet to device 2 (10.2.2.2/16), device 1 creates a frame with the destination MAC address of its default gateway, the router, which in this case is the RP. The SE receives the frame, sees that it is for the RP, and therefore examines its MLS cache to see whether it has a match for this flow. In the case of the first packet in the flow, no match exists, so the SE forwards the frame to the RP. The SE also puts the frame in its MLS cache and marks the frame as a *candidate entry*.

The MLS-RP receives the frame, decapsulates (unwraps) the frame, and examines the packet. The RP then examines its routing table to see whether it has a route to the destination of the packet; assuming that it does, the RP creates a new frame for the packet after decrementing the IP header

Time to Live (TTL) field and recalculating the IP header checksum. The source MAC address of this frame is the MAC address of the RP; the destination MAC address of this frame is the MAC address of the destination device (or next-hop router). The RP then sends the frame through the SE.

The MLS-SE receives the frame and compares it to its MLS cache; the SE recognizes that the frame is carrying the same packet as a candidate entry and is on its way back from the same RP. The SE therefore completes the MLS cache entry using information from the frame; this entry is now an *enabler entry*. The SE also forwards the frame out of the appropriate port toward its destination.

When a subsequent packet in the same flow enters the switch, the SE examines its MLS cache to see whether it has a match. This time it does have a match, so it does not forward the frame to the RP. Instead, the SE rewrites the frame using the information in the MLS cache, including decrementing the TTL field, recalculating the IP header checksum, and using the MAC address of the RP as the source MAC address; the resulting frame looks as though it came from the RP. The SE then forwards the frame out of the appropriate port toward its destination.

NOTE   Network flows are unidirectional. Therefore, if device 1 and device 2 both send packets to each other, two flows would be recorded in the MLS cache, one for each direction.

NOTE   In Figure 2-10, the MLS cache is shown as having a "protocol" field. In the output of the display on the Catalyst switches this field is called a "port" field, even though it represents the protocol field in the IP header.

The MLS-SE also keeps traffic statistics that can be exported to other utilities to be used, for example, for troubleshooting, accounting, or other functions.

Cisco Express Forwarding

Cisco Express Forwarding (CEF), like MLS, aims to speed the data routing and forwarding process in a network. However, the two methods use different approaches.

CEF uses two components to optimize the lookup of the information required to route packets: the Forwarding Information Base (FIB) for the Layer 3 information and the adjacency table for the Layer 2 information.[7]

CEF creates an FIB by maintaining a copy of the forwarding information contained in the IP routing table. The information is indexed so that it can be quickly searched for matching entries as packets are processed. Whenever the routing table changes, the FIB is also changed so that it always contains up-to-date paths. A separate routing cache is not required.

The adjacency table contains Layer 2 frame header information, including next-hop addresses, for all FIB entries. Each FIB entry can point to multiple adjacency table entries, for example, if two paths exist between devices for load balancing.

After a packet is processed and the route is determined from the FIB, the Layer 2 next-hop and header information is retrieved from the adjacency table and a new frame is created to encapsulate the packet.

Cisco Express Forwarding can be enabled on a router (for example, on a Cisco 7500 Series router) or on a switch with Layer 3 functionality (such as the Catalyst 8540 switch).

NOTE Not all Catalyst switches support Cisco Express Forwarding. Refer to specific product documentation on the Cisco website[8] for device support information.

Switching Security

In the past few years, switches have become equipped with features that make them more intelligent, allowing them to provide an active role in network security.

Cisco documentation refers to Catalyst integrated security (CIS). However, the term CIS refers only to built-in functionality that is native to the Catalyst switches, not to the security features inherent in the modules that can be installed in the switches (for example, firewall blades and so forth). Thus, in this book, we have categorized these two types of switch security as follows:

- **Catalyst native security**—Those features built into the switch itself

- **Catalyst hardware security**—Features of hardware that can be installed in the switch

These categories are described in the following sections.

NOTE Refer to Chapter 4, "Network Security Design," for general information on network security.

Catalyst Native Security

Cisco switches have many native attributes that can be used to secure a network.

Some attributes are related to the secure management of the switch itself. One example is the use of secure shell (SSH), rather than Telnet, when remotely managing the switch. Another example is disabling unused switch ports so that the network cannot be accessed through them.

Secure Shell

SSH is a protocol that is similar to Telnet, but SSH uses encryption for security. SSH usually uses TCP port 22.

Catalyst native security can protect networks against serious threats originating from the exploitation of MAC address vulnerabilities, ARP vulnerabilities, and Dynamic Host Configuration Protocol (DHCP) vulnerabilities. (Both ARP and DHCP are covered in Appendix B.) Table 2-1 shows some examples of the protection provided by the built-in intelligence in Catalyst switches.

Table 2-1   *Examples of Built-In Intelligence to Mitigate Attacks*

Attack	Native Security (Built-In Intelligence) to Mitigate Attacks
DHCP Denial of Service (DoS) A DHCP DoS attack can be initiated by a hacker. As well as taking down the DHCP server, the attack could also be initiated from a server that is pretending to be a legitimate DHCP server. This rogue server replies to DHCP requests with phony DHCP information.	**Trusted-State Port** The switch port to which the DHCP server is attached can be set to a "trusted" state. Only trusted ports are allowed to pass DHCP replies. Untrusted ports are only allowed to pass DHCP requests.
MAC Flooding A hacker targets the switch's MAC address table, to flood it with many addresses.	**MAC Port Security** The switch can be configured with a maximum number of MAC addresses per port. The switch can also be configured with static MAC addresses that identify the specific addresses that it should allow, further constraining the devices allowed to attach to the network.

Table 2-1 *Examples of Built-In Intelligence to Mitigate Attacks (Continued)*

Attack	Native Security (Built-in Intelligence) to Mitigate Attacks
Redirected Attack A hacker wanting to cover his tracks and complicate the network forensics investigation might decide to compromise an intermediary target first. The hacker would then unleash his attack to the intended target from that intermediary victim.	**Private VLAN (PVLAN)** The flow of traffic can be directed by using PVLANs. In the example shown in Figure 2-11, a PVLAN is defined so that traffic received on either switch port 2 or 3 can exit only by switch port 1. Should a hacker compromise server A, he would not be able to directly attack server B because the traffic can only flow between port 1 and port 2, and between port 1 and port 3. Traffic is not allowed to flow between port 2 and port 3.

Figure 2-11 *Using a Switch to Create a PVLAN*

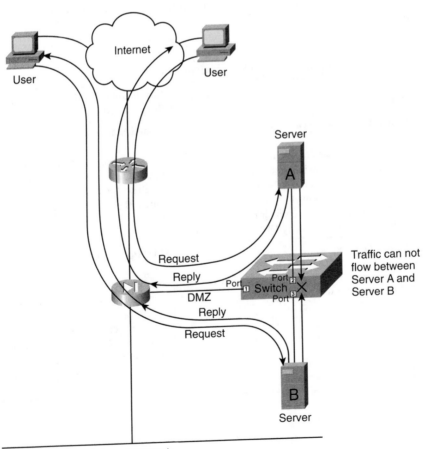

Catalyst Hardware Security

Cisco switches can provide security, flexibility, and expandability to networks. As an example, the Catalyst 6500 Series switches can be equipped with modules that are full-fledged security devices themselves. Some example security modules are as follows:

- Cisco Firewall service module

- Cisco Internet Protocol security (IPsec) virtual private network (VPN) service module

- Cisco Intrusion Detection System (IDS)

- Cisco Secure Socket Layer (SSL)

> **NOTE**   Refer to Chapter 4 for information on IPsec, VPNs, IDSs, and SSLs.

As an example of the flexibility provided by these modules, consider that when using a Cisco Firewall service module, any port on a Catalyst 6500 switch can operate as a firewall. An example of the expandability of the modules is the use of the IPsec VPN module. This module can terminate up to 8000 VPN connections (known as *VPN tunnels*) simultaneously and can create 60 new tunnels per second; up to 10 of these modules can be installed in a Catalyst 6500 switch.

Switching Design Considerations

Chapter 1, "Network Design," introduces the hierarchical network design model and the Enterprise Composite Network Design model. Recall that the three functions that comprise the hierarchical network design model are the access layer, the distribution layer, and the core layer. The Enterprise Composite Network Model is the name given to the architecture used by the Cisco SAFE blueprint; it supports larger networks than those designed with only the hierarchical model and clarifies the functional boundaries within the network. Three functional areas exist within this model: Enterprise Campus, Enterprise Edge, and Service Provider Edge. Each of these functional areas contains network modules, which in turn can include the hierarchical layers.

Switches within the Enterprise Campus are in all three of the hierarchical layers. Layer 2 and/or Layer 3 switches can be used, depending on a number of factors.

For the access layer, design considerations include the following:

- The number of end-user devices to be supported

- The applications that are being used—this defines some of the features required in the switches, as well as the performance and bandwidth needed

- The use of VLANs, including whether trunks are required between switches

- Redundancy requirements

For the distribution layer, design factors include the following:

- The number of access switches to be aggregated

- Redundancy requirements

- Features required for specific applications to be supported

- Required interfaces to the core layer

- For Layer 3 switches, the routing protocols to be supported and whether sharing of information among multiple routing protocols is required. (Routing protocols are discussed in detail in Chapter 3.)

The role of the core layer is to provide a high-speed backbone. Thus, the key requirement is the performance needed to support all the access and distribution data. The number of ports to the distribution layer, and the protocols (for example, routing protocols) that need to be supported on those ports, are also important considerations. Redundancy in the core is a typical requirement, to meet the availability needs of the network.

Cisco current campus design recommendations include the following:[9]

- Layer 2 switches can be used at the access layer, with Layer 3 switches at the distribution and core layers.

- VLANs should not spread across the campus, because this can slow network convergence.

- The core and distribution layers can be combined into one layer (called a *collapsed backbone*) for smaller networks. Larger campuses should have a separate distribution layer to allow the network to grow easily.

- Redundancy in the core, between the core and distribution layers, and between the distribution and access layers is also recommended. Redundancy can also be used within these layers as required.

Figure 2-12 illustrates a sample small network design that uses Layer 2 switches in the access layer of the campus Building and Server modules. This network features a collapsed backbone in Layer 3 switches. Redundancy is incorporated between all layers.

Figure 2-12 *A Small Network Can Include a Collapsed Backbone*

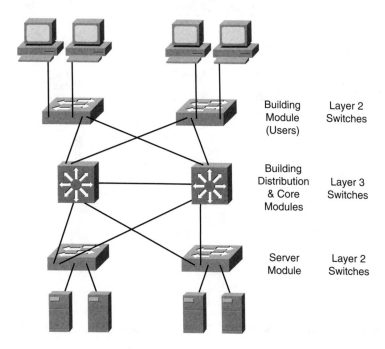

Figure 2-13 illustrates an example of a larger network design. Two buildings are shown, each with Layer 2 access switches and Layer 3 distribution switches. These buildings are then redundantly connected to the Layer 3 core. The Server module is shown with Layer 2 access switches connected directly to the core; distribution switches can be added if additional functionality or performance is required.

Figure 2-13 *A Larger Network Has Separate Core and Distribution Switches*

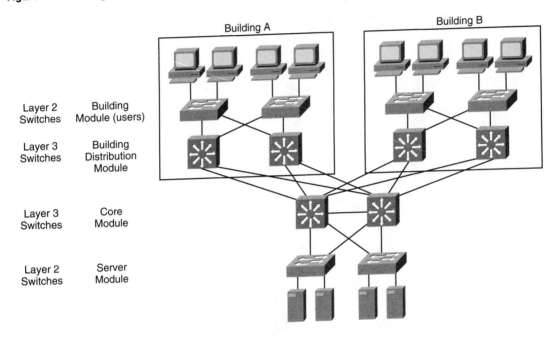

Layer 2 Switches — Building Module (users)

Layer 3 Switches — Building Distribution Module

Layer 3 Switches — Core Module

Layer 2 Switches — Server Module

Summary

In this chapter, you learned about Layer 2 and Layer 3 switching network design, including the following topics:

- How switches improve the performance of your network

- The two types of switches: Layer 2 and Layer 3

- The two implementations of Layer 3 switching within Cisco switches: multilayer switching and Cisco Express Forwarding

- How the STP is critical in a Layer 2 switched environment to prevent loops

- The usefulness of VLANs in defining logical broadcast domains

- The features in switches that can be used to increase the security of your network

- How switches fit into the design models

Endnotes

[1] Webb, *Building Cisco Multilayer Switched Networks,* Indianapolis, Cisco Press, 2001, p. 165.

[2] "Virtual LANs/VLAN Trunking Protocol (VLANs/VTP)," http://www.cisco.com/en/US/tech/tk389/tk689/tsd_technology_support_protocol_home.html.

[3] "Troubleshooting IP Multilayer Switching," http://www.cisco.com/en/US/products/hw/switches/ps700/products_tech_note09186a00800f99bc.shtml.

[4] Cisco switch products home page, http://www.cisco.com/en/US/products/hw/switches/index.html.

[5] Cisco router products home page, http://www.cisco.com/en/US/products/hw/routers/index.html.

[6] "Troubleshooting IP Multilayer Switching," http://www.cisco.com/en/US/products/hw/switches/ps700/products_tech_note09186a00800f99bc.shtml.

[7] "Cisco Express Forwarding Overview," http://www.cisco.com/univercd/cc/td/doc/product/software/ios122/122cgcr/fswtch_c/swprt1/xcfcef.htm.

[8] Cisco switch products home page, http://www.cisco.com/en/US/products/hw/switches/index.html.

[9] "Hierarchical Campus Design At-A-Glance," http://www.cisco.com/application/pdf/en/us/guest/netsol/ns24/c643/cdccont_0900aecd800d8129.pdf.

ISBN: 1-58705-240-7

Content Networking Fundamentals

A comprehensive introduction to the theory and
practical applications of content networking

ciscopress.com

Silvano Da Ros

Chapter Goals

In this chapter, you will cover the following topics to learn how to present and transform content:

- **Introducing Markup Languages**— You can use markup languages to format and describe your content.

- **Transforming and Formatting Content**—Powerful tools are available to you for transforming and formatting content.

CHAPTER 7

Presenting and Transforming Content

Introducing Markup Languages

You can use markup languages to manage structured documents in a standard format. To "mark up" a document means to imbed text within the content of the document in order to perform procedures on the data and convey information about it. Today's markup languages form their bases on **procedural markup** languages of the 1960s, when typesetters used proprietary coding for fine control over the font, size, and spacing of printed copy, with the intention of formatting documents destined for paper. For example, some book publishers required authors to submit their manuscript using proprietary procedural markup tags embedded in the text. Procedural coding leaves the task of formatting to the publisher who uses proprietary software to process the tags embedded in the document. This enables the author to concentrate on the content of the document.

Figure 7-1 gives a sample excerpt from the beginning of this book.

Figure 7-1 *A Sample Book Excerpt*

Content Networking Fundamentals, Silvano D. Da Ros

Chapter 1 – Introducing Content Networks

Chapter 1 Goals

1.)   To state the purposes of content networking.
2.)   To inform the reader of the major protocols of content networking.
3.)   To create a framework for configuring content networks.

The Purposes of Content Networking
        The purpose of content networking is to accelerate your applications...

The Protocols
        Each content networking device runs numerous networking protocols...

Configuring Content Networking
        You can configure content networking devices using the command-line interface (CLI) or web interface...

> **NOTE** Common word processing packages, such as Microsoft Word or Corel WordPerfect, use procedural markup internally to format documents. Each package has its own set of proprietary procedural markup tags for formatting, which is why you normally require a conversion tool to read a document created by one package in the other.

To produce the formatting in Figure 7-1 using procedural markup, you can insert the imaginary procedural marks *!SkipLine=n!*, *!Center!*, *!Bold!*, and *!Indent=n!* in to the text to provide the correct formatting instructions to a word processor, browser, or printer. As you can see from Figure 7-2, the procedural markup tags specify a particular procedure that is to be applied to the text that it references.

Figure 7-2 *A Basic Procedural Markup Example*

```
!Center!!Bold!Content Networking Fundamentals, Silvano D. Da Ros!/Bold!!/Center!
!SkipLine=2!
!Bold!Chapter 1 — Introducing to Content Networks!/Bold!
!SkipLine=1!
!Bold!Chapter 1 Goals!/Bold!
!SkipLine=1!
1.)!Indent=1!To state the purposes of content networking.
2.)!Indent=1!To inform the reader of the major protocols of content networking.
3.)!Indent=1!To create a framework for configuring content networks.
!SkipLine=1!
!Bold!The Purposes of Content Networking!/Bold!
!Indent=1!The purpose of content networking is to accelerate your applications...
!SkipLine=1!
!Bold!The Protocols!/Bold!
!Indent=1!Each content networking device runs numerous networking protocols...
!SkipLine=1!
!Bold!Configuring Content Networking!/Bold!
!Indent=1!You can configure content networking devices using the command-line
interface (CLI) or web interface...
```

Descriptive markup languages, or generic coding, differs from procedural markup languages by describing the structure of the document, leaving the parsers (programs used to display, print, or store the information) to perform the desired procedure. For example, you can use exactly the same text document for printing, monitor display, or even Braille. In contrast, with procedural markup, you would require a separate document for each.

Procedural markup languages have the following disadvantages over descriptive languages for publishing documents on the web:

- **Inflexible**—The number of commands indicating how the text should be formatted (that is, skip line, indent, and so on) is often cumbersome for effective usage. For example, internally, most word processors contain thousands of tags, which are transparent to you. This number of tags is unmanageable for use in web publishing.

- **Requires Multiple Document Formats**—Procedural markups are inflexible because, if you require different styles of documents, the text needs to be marked up again for each style. For example, if a document destined for a printer needs to be displayed to a monitor, a new marked-up document is necessary, because even the slightest offset of margins requires reformatting.

Stanley Rice and William Tunnicliffe first conceived of the separation of content from its formatting in 1967. The first formal descriptive markup language was GenCode and was the first general markup specification for the typesetting industry. Gencode recognized the need of different codes for different types of documents. Together, Rice and Tunnicliffe formed the Graphic Communications Association (GCA) Gencode Committee to further develop their ideas into a nonproprietary generic coding markup standard.

IBM then took the ideas behind GenCode to produce Generalized Markup Language (GML—also the initials of its creators, Charles Goldfarb, Edward Mosher, and Raymond Lorie) in 1969, to organize IBM's legal documents into a searchable form. GML automated functions performed specifically on IBM's legal documents. The ANSI Computer Languages group expanded GML in 1980 into the Standard Generalized Markup Language (SGML) for the Processing of Text Committee. In 1984, the International Standards Organization (ISO) joined the ANSI committee to publish the SGML standard based on its sixth working draft in 1986 as an international norm (ISO 8879). The first important users of the standard were the US Internal Revenue Service (IRS) and Department of Defense (DoD).

Figure 7-3 illustrates how to mark up the example described previously using SGML.

Figure 7-3 *A Basic Structural Markup Example Using SGML*

```
<Book title="Content Networking Fundamentals" author="Silvano D. Da Ros">
<Chapter>
<ChapterTitle>Chapter 1 — Introducing Content Networks</ChapterTitle>
<ChapterGoals title="Chapter 1 Goals" >
<Goal>To state the purposes of content networking.</Goal>
<Goal>To inform the reader of the major protocols of content networking.</Goal>
<Goal>To create a framework for configuring content networks.</Goal>
</ChapterGoals>
</Chapter>
<Section title= "The Purposes of Content Networking " >
The purpose of content networking is to accelerate your applications...
</Section>
<Section title= "The Protocols" >
Each content networking device runs numerous networking protocols...
</Section>
<Section title= "Configuring Content Networking" >
You can configure content networking devices using the command-line interface (CLI)
or web interface...
</Section>
</Book>
```

The tags shown in Figure 7-3 group the document into elements. For example, you can use the tags <Book>, <Chapter>, and <Goal> to group the document into elements. Each piece of content has the general form of a start-tag (for example, "<Book>") followed by the content, and ending with the end-tag (for example, </Book>). The title of the <Book> element is an attribute of the element as opposed to being an element itself.

Because the elements, attributes, and overall structure of Figure 7-3 are specific to the application, you should formally define them for the application. This need for formally declaring elements, attributes, and structure gave birth to the Document Type Definition (DTD) file, against which you can validate markup language files. DTD files define the syntax of the markup language. That is, it declares all tags within the markup file and specifies the order with which they should appear, which ones are optional or repeatable, and that they are properly nested. You can use DTD files to establish portability and interoperability and exchange data between organizations with different file formats.

The DTD file for the SGML sample in Figure 7-3 is in Table 7-1. The <!ELEMENT> tag defines each element, preceded by the <ATTLIST> tag, if the element contains any attributes (for example, title and author).

Table 7-1   *A Sample Book.dtd DTD File*

DTD Information	Description
<!ELEMENT book (chapter+)> <!ATTLIST book title CDATA #REQUIRED author CDATA #IMPLIED>	The Book element contains one or more chapter elements. The + indicates that one or more elements may exist. The Book element contains attributes for the required book's title and optional (IMPLIED) author name.
<!ELEMENT chapter (chaptertitle,chaptergoals?,section+)>	Each chapter contains one chapter title, an optional "Chapter Goals" area (as indicated by a question mark), and one or more Sections elements.
<!ELEMENT chaptertitle (#PCDATA)>	The Chapter Title contains parsable character data (meaning it can contain tags within the data), which require special parsing to be rendered properly.
<!ELEMENT chaptergoals (goal+)> <!ATTLIST chaptergoals title CDATA #REQUIRED>	The Chapter Goals area contains one or more Goals Elements.
<!ELEMENT goal (#PCDATA) >	Each goal is parsable data.

Table 7-1   *A Sample Book.dtd DTD File (Continued)*

DTD Information	Description
<!ELEMENT section (subsection*)> <!ATTLIST section title CDATA #REQUIRED>	A section contains a title attribute, optional parsable character data, and zero or more sub-sections.
<!ELEMENT subsection (subsubsection*)> <!ATTLIST subsection title CDATA #REQUIRED>	A subsection contains a title attribute and zero or more subsubsections.
<!ELEMENT subsubsection (#PCDATA)> <!ATTLIST subsubsection title CDATA #REQUIRED>	A subsubsection contains a title attribute and parsable text.

Hypertext Markup Language

HTML was developed as a simple means to publish hyperlinked documents in a standard fashion. HTML enables you to avoid proprietary formats, and thus promote interoperability between the various devices expected to connect to the web. At the time, SGML was considered too bulky and complicated for such a "simple" environment. In general, HTML is an application of SGML, and includes a minor subset of simple tags for organizing content on the web.

> **NOTE**   You can use DTD files to define not only applications of certain markup languages but entire markup languages themselves. For example, just as in the book example above, HTML has its own SGML-compliant structure and subset of tags, which are used to mark up hypertext on the WWW.

In 1990, Tim Berners-Lee, then working at the Organsation Européenne pour la recherche nucléaire (CERN), published the first version of the HTML DTD (that is, HTML 1.0). Tim developed the first prototype browser, supporting HTML transported in HTTP over a TCP/IP network, resulting in the birth of the World Wide Web. The computer community received HTML 1.0 with welcoming arms, and many text-based browsers, such as Viola, Cello, and Lynx, became available shortly after its release.

The IETF published HTML version 2 as RFC 1866 in 1994. Version 2.0 included many new features and fixes to version 1.0, such as support for images and forms. The National Center for Supercomputing Applications (NCSA) developed the first graphical browser for HTML 2.0, then called Mosaic, in late 1993. The developers of Mosaic soon decided that leaving NCSA to form Netscape would be a profitable endeavor.

> **NOTE**   Numerous parties with vested interests in web protocols formed the W3C consortium in 1993 to take web standardization into a nonprofit and unincorporated setting. Soon after work began on HTML version 3.0 at W3C.

In 1993, Netscape developed HTML+ for its Mosaic browser, based on HTML version 2.0, but it included many additional practical features over HTML version 2.0. Numerous competitive companies followed suite with various browsers with support for HTML version 2.0, the largest being Microsoft with Internet Explorer. Although the two largest browser companies developed browsers with close interpretation of the HTML spec, they each developed new and incompatible tags. The browser manufacturers quickly diverged from one another, creating a highly competitive browser market. As a result, the differences between HTTP 2.0 and 3.0 and Netscape's HTML+ were so vast that W3C decided to avoid standardizing 3.0 and instead to include the version 3.0 and HTML+ updates in version HTML 3.2, among various fixes and other new features. Thus, HTTP 3.2 was released in 1997 and included the generally accepted practices at the time, or as general as possible given the major explosion of web applications developed with HTML. HTML 4.0 and 4.0.1 are the most recent versions of documents. The HTML 4.0.1 specification comprises three separate DTDs maintained and published by W3C.

HTML is an excellent markup language for displaying content for humans to read on a screen and for navigation between documents. However, even though the use of HTML is widespread, it soon proved to be insufficient in abstraction and structure for today's increasingly complex content-based applications. Like its procedural markup predecessor, presentation and formatting were given higher priority during the drafting of the HTML DTD than structure and organization, especially since the popularization of style sheets within HTML.

> **NOTE**   You can use style sheets to further separate content from the presentation of content of web documents written in HTML or Extensible HTML (XHTML). You will learn about Cascading Style Sheets (CSS) and XHTML later in this chapter.

Although HTML is a structural markup language based on SGML, the HTML tags do not sufficiently describe the content, and the specification is very loose in terms of syntax and structure as compared to SGML. Due to the explosion of the web, content providers quickly thirsted for control over formatting that was similar to that used with printed copy. Browser developers in conjunction with W3C responded with numerous HTML presentational controls. As HTML matured, its procedural markup features were replaced by mechanisms, such as converting text to images, using proprietary HTML extensions, and style sheets, as simple ways to separate presentation from content without severely changing the markup language specification.

Example 7-1 shows how an HTML file is structured.

Example 7-1 *A Sample HTML Document to Print "Hello World" to a Web Browser*

```
<HTML>
<HEAD>
<TITLE>Hello World Page/TITLE>
</HEAD>
<BODY>
Hello World!
</BODY>
</HTML>
```

To fully overcome the limitations of HTML, people recently favor more robust descriptive markup languages coupled with separate presentational markup languages as successors to HTML. In order to bridge the gap between the structured, self-descriptive nature of SGML and the usability of HTML for visual, interactive web applications, the W3C created the XML family of markup languages to simplify HTML.

Extensible Markup Language

Like HTML, Extensible Markup Language (XML) is an application of the SGML protocol, but includes more of the semantic aspects of SGML. XML is a true structural markup language in that it does not do anything to the data but just describe it. In contrast to HTML, which achieved a certain level of structure with abstractions such as headings, paragraphs, emphasis, and numbered lists, in XML you can create custom XML tags to describe content (for example, Book, Section, and Goals are custom XML tags). HTML has only a specific set of tags available to describe content (e.g., Header, Body, and so on), and vast numbers of tags to perform actions on the data.

NOTE In contrast to the way you use HTML, you use XML to carry data, not both data and presentation information. In order to present the data, you must use a style sheet or transform the XML document into HTML or XHTML. You will learn how to present XML later in this chapter.

XML was published as a W3C Recommendation in early 1998. Much of the out-of-date features are excluded from XML. For example, SGML typewriter directives are no longer pertinent today. XML also extends SGML with its internationalization features and typing of elements using XML schemas.

With HTML, user agents can accept any syntax and try to make sense out of it, without giving errors. User agents are therefore difficult to write because an enormous number of erroneous pages exist on the web. The validation of XML is much more deliberate, easing the pressure on user agent developers to perform the complex error correction required on poorly written HTML. The downfall is that users must conform to the strict rules imposed by XML to avoid errors in their documents.

> **NOTE** The term *user agent* refers to any program that fetches, parses, and optionally displays web pages. Search engine robots are user agents, which is why you will not often see the term *web browser* used in most web texts, journals, and standardization documents to refer to all such agents.

Drawing on the ability to create custom elements in XML, numerous associated XML-based languages are available to you for extending the basic functionality of XML. Each requires special applications to recognize and perform actions on their respective custom-defined elements.

- **Extensible StyleSheet Language (XSL) and Extensible Stylesheet Transformation (XSLT)**—You can use the XSL and XSLT languages to display and transform XML documents, for Cisco IP phones, WAP cell phones, and PDAs.

- **Extensible StyleSheet Language-Format Object (XSL-FO)**—You can use XSL-FO to format documents for print, such as Adobe PDF files and barcodes.

- **XPath**—Use XPath to specify locations within XML documents, similar to the way files are organized on a standard computer file system. XPath is not an application of XML, but it is a major component in XSLT. You will see how XPath works with XSLT later in this chapter.

- **XLink**—Use XLink for hyperlinking between XML documents. XLink is similar to HTML links but includes many extensions, such as bidirectional, typed, one-to-many and many-to-many links. You can also use XLink to download links automatically or on user request.

- **XQuery**—You can perform queries on XML files using XQuery, similar to the way in which you use Structure Query Language (SQL) queries in database systems.

- **Synchronized Multimedia Integration Language SMIL**—Use SMIL for the multimedia structured markup. You will learn about SMIL in Chapter 9, "Introducing Streaming Media."

- **Scalable Vector Graphics (SVG)**—Use SVG for structuring graphics.

- **Resource Description Framework (RDF)**—Use RDF for structured metadata markup.

- **MathML**—You can use MathML for mathematical equation structured markup.

Figure 7-4 shows the sample document described previously in Figure 7-1, structured in XML. Notice that the simple SGML example discussed previously in Figure 7-3 is identical when written XML, except for the required "?xml version" header.

Figure 7-4 *Sample XML File*

```
<?xml version="1.0"?>
<!DOCTYPE book SYSTEM "book.dtd">
<Book title="Content Networking Fundamentals" author="Silvano D. Da Ros">
<Chapter>
<ChapterTitle>Chapter 1 – Introducing Content Networks</ChapterTitle>
<ChapterGoals> title="Chapter 1 Goals" >
<Goal>To state the purposes of content networking.</Goal>
<Goal>To inform the reader of the major protocols of content networking.</Goal>
<Goal>To create a framework for configuring content networks.</Goal>
</ChapterGoals>
</Chapter>
<Section title= "The Purposes of Content Networking " >
The purpose of content networking is to accelerate your applications...
</Section>
<Section title= "The Protocols" >
Each content networking device runs numerous networking protocols...
</Section>
<Section title= "Configuring Content Networking" >
You can configure content networking devices using the command-line interface
(CLI) or web interface...
</Section>
</Book>
```

NOTE   XML with correct syntax is *well-formed XML*. XML validated against a DTD is *valid XML*. You can optionally specify the DTD to validate an XML file against in the header of the XML document, as show in Figure 7-4. You can also use XML Schemas as an XML-based alternative to the standard DTDs. Relax NG is the schema language by OSI.

Extensible Hypertext Markup Language

Extensible HTML (XHTML) is the next step in the evolution of web documents, and its creation was motivated by the need to deliver content to many different types of devices, such as mobile phones, PDAs, and web kiosks. As the name suggests, it is a combination of XML and HTML. More specifically, the XHTML DTDs are a reformulation of the three HTML 4.0 DTDs, as an application of XML (recall that HTML 4.0 is conversely an application of SGML). In other words, the HTML DTDs where rewritten within the XML DTD, creating the new XHTML DTD. With the new definitions, the old HTML syntax must follow the same strict rules as XML. This leads the way to a more standardized language, as user agents gradually transition to XHTML.

NOTE   Because documents in XHTML conform to both XML and HTML 4, you can view them in user agents supporting either type.

Although HTML may never totally retire as a web markup language, it will become much more extensible and standardized under the guise of XML. It will be extensible in that you can create your own tags and standardized in that user agents concern themselves with the standards of the XML specification, not the complex HTML error-correction methods stemming from a lack of standard syntax. Important differences between HTML and XHTML are

- You must nest XHTML elements properly.

- XHTML documents must be well-formed.

- Tag names must be in lowercase.

- You must close all XHTML elements.

Wireless Application Protocol Markup Languages

New business potential in mobile browsing has fostered the development in Wireless Application Protocol (WAP). You can use WAP to supply web content to mobile devices, such as cell phones, pagers, and PDAs. Just as the W3C is responsible for web protocols, the WAP Forum is responsible for its wireless protocol counterparts. The WAP 1.0 protocol is composed of the following specifications:

- **Wireless Markup Language (WML) 1.0 language**—Use WML structural markup language for WAP content rendering. WML is an application of XML and as such strictly adheres to the XML specification.

- **WMLScript language**—A scaled-down scripting language for wireless devices, similar to JavaScript or VBscript for HTML client or server scripting or both.

- **Wireless Telephony Application Interface (WTAI)**—API for making phone calls from data connections.

WAP is an application of XML. Using the analogy of playing cards, WML pages are called decks, and contain one or more cards. WAP devices download all the cards at once but are displayed one at a time to the user. Figure 7-5 illustrates how to publish an online book in WML.

Figure 7-5   *A Sample WML File*

```
<?xml version="1.0" encoding="UTF-8"?>
<!DOCTYPE wml PUBLIC "-//WAPFORUM//DTD WML 1.3//EN" "http://www.wapforum.org/DTD/wml13.dtd">
<wml>
  <card id="ch1" title="Chapter 1 - Introducing Content Networks">
    <p>Chapter 1 Goals<br/>
      1. To state the purposes of content networking.<br/>
      2. To inform the reader of the major concepts of content networking.<br/>
      3. To detail the underlying protocols of content networking.<br/>
    </p>
  </card>

  <card id="ch2" title="Chapter 2 - Exploring the Network Layers">
    <p>Chapter 2 Goals<br/>
      1. To inform the reader of Layers 1 through 4 of the OSI model.<br/>
      2. To give the reader an overview of Ethernet, ARP, and IP routing.<br/>
      3. To illustrate basic TCP operation.<br/>
    </p>
  </card>
</wml>
```

Figure 7-6 shows how you can navigate between individual cards, or chapters, using the WAP device controls.

Figure 7-6   *Navigating a WML Document on a WAP Device*

The W3C specifies a subset of XHTML 1.1 for small devices, called XHTML Basic. However, the WAP Forum created WAP 2.0 to include the XHTML Basic features plus some of the features from the full XHTML 1.1 specification, called the XHTML Mobile Profile (XHTMLMP), or Wireless Markup Language 2.0 (WML 2.0). WAP 2.0 was motivated by advancements in wireless transmission technologies, such as GSM, GPRS, G2.5, and G3.

WAP 2.0 also introduced support for special WAP versions of TCP/IP protocols in order to leverage the same languages and tools for mobile and standard web content (alternatively, WAP 1.0 uses the WAP protocol stack and does not support connectivity to TCP/IP networks). The wTCP/IP protocol supports TCP/IP, HTTP for content transport, and PKI for content security. Additionally, the power of CSS is available to you in WAP 2.0-enabled devices for the possibility to control a document's layout, including the text fonts, text attributes, borders, margins, padding, text alignment, text colors, and background colors to name a few. WAP 2.0 also supports XSLT transformation to transform between WML 1.0 and WML 2.0 documents.

Transforming and Formatting Content

You can use XSL to transform, filter, sort, and format your content. The XSL family consists of XSLT, XPath, and XSL-FO. Use XSLT for transforming XML documents, XPath for defining parts of an XML document, and XSL-FO for formatting XML documents.

You have two options to transform your XML documents for the purpose of publishing them to the web:

- **Transforming XML to XHMTL/HMTL**—You can translate your XML documents into HTML or XHTML and apply CSS's to the documents for display to a web browser.

- **Transforming XML to XSL-FO**—You can translate your XML documents directly into XSL-FO. You can then use a third-party program to convert the standard XSL-FO into HTML/XMTL/CSS (as mentioned previously), Braille, bar-codes, Adobe PDF, PostScript, SVG, Abstract Windowing Toolkit (AWT), or Maker Interchange Format (MIF).

NOTE You can apply XSL stylesheets to your content within your network using the Cisco Application Oriented Network (AON) network modules for the Catalyst 6500 series switches and Cisco 2600/2800/3700/3800 Series routers. For more information on the AON, refer to its product documentation on Cisco.com.

Transforming XML to XHMTL/HMTL

Consider an application where you would like to publish an outline of this book on the web. The outline will contain the book title, author name, and chapter titles followed by the goals within each chapter. The content of each chapter's sections and subsections will not be included in the outline but assume that the entire book is available and marked up with the elements discussed previously in the simple DTD in Table 7-1. Figure 7-7 gives the sample XML file containing the outline of the first two chapters.

Figure 7-7   *A Sample Book Outline XML File*

```
<?xml version="1.0" encoding="UTF-8"?>        The <?xml> element defines the XML version and
                                              character encoding for the XML file.
<!DOCTYPE cnbookoutline SYSTEM "book.dtd">    The DTD file is used to validate the structure of the XML.
<book title="Content Networking Fundamentals" author="Silvano D. Da Ros" >
  <chapter>
    <chaptertitle>Chapter 1 - Introducing Content Networks</chaptertitle>
    <chaptergoals title="Chapter 1 Goals" >
      <goal>To state the purposes of content networking.</goal>
      <goal>To inform the reader of the major concepts of content networking.</goal>  The chapter
      <goal>To detail the underlying protocols of content networking.</goal>          goals element
    </chaptergoals>                                                                   consists of one
    <section title="" />                                                              or more goals
  </chapter>
  <chapter>
    <chaptertitle>Chapter 2 - Exploring the Network Layers</chaptertitle>
    <chaptergoals title="Chapter 2 Goals" >                                           The <chapter>
      <goal>To inform the reader of Layers 1 through 4 of the OSI model.</goal>        element contains
      <goal>To give the reader an overview of Ethernet, ARP, and IP routing.</goal>   the structure of
      <goal>To illustrate basic TCP operation.</goal>                                 each chapter.
    </chaptergoals>                                                                   Note, the chapter
    <section title="" />                                                              title is includes as
  </chapter>                                                                          an element, as
</book>                                                                               opposed to an
                         The root element is <book> and                              attribute, unlike
                         envelopes the source tree structure.                        the<book>
                                                                                     element.
```

Because you define custom element names in XML, name conflicts may occur when the same name from different DTDs is used to describe two different types of elements. You can use XML namespaces to provide unique element names within an XML document. In Figure 7-8, the namespace is the string "xsl:" that prefixes all of the XSL elements. You are required to use a namespace to differentiate elements among languages. The particular application that parses the document will know what to do with the specific elements based on the prefix. For example, an XSLT parser will look for the xsl: namespace URI and perform the intended actions based on the elements in the document. Alternatively, a XSL-FO parser will see the "fo:" namespace and perform the appropriate actions using the respective elements.

Parsers do not use the URL of the namespace to retrieve a DTD or schema for the namespace—the URL is simply a unique identifier within the document. According to W3C, the definition of a namespace simply defines a two-part naming system and nothing else. However, you must define namespaces of individual markup languages with a specific URL for the parsing application to take action on tags within the context of the language. For example, you must define the XSLT namespace with the URL "http://www.w3.org/1999/XSL/Transform" in your documents. Additionally, you must define the XSL-FO namespace with "http://www.w3.org/1999/XSL/Format." That said, many simple XML parsing applications do not require namespaces in order to differentiate elements; they simply treat all elements as within the same namespace. However, this chapter uses namespaces strictly for illustration purposes.

In Figure 7-8, the namespace for XSL is defined for the XSLT parser to recognize the XSL specific elements **value-of**, **for-each**, and **number**. An XSLT parser inputs the XSLT file and the XML source file. It processes these two files and outputs an HTML file as a well-formed XML document. There are many other XSLT elements available to you, but you should know at least these three to understand the content transformations in this section.

Figure 7-8 *Sample XSLT File Transforming XML to HTML*

```
<?xml version="1.0" encoding="UTF-8"?>
<xsl:stylesheet version="2.0" xmlns:xsl="http://www.w3.org/1999/XSL/Transform"
xmlns:fo="http://www.w3.org/1999/XSL/Format" >

<!-- Template to commence processing at the start of the XML document -->
<xsl:template match="/">

  <!-- Output the HTML headers -->
  <html>

    <head>
      <!-- Output the CSS stylesheet definition to the head -->
      <LINK REL="stylesheet" TYPE="text/css" HREF="cnbook.css"/>

      <!-- Output the book title and author names -->
      <h1> <xsl:value-of select="book/@title"/> </h1>
      <h1> <xsl:value-of select="book/@author"/> </h1>
    </head>

    <body>
    <!-- eBook Content -->
      <xsl:for-each select="book/chapter">
        <h2> <xsl:value-of select="chaptertitle"/> </h2>
        <h3> <xsl:value-of select="chaptergoals/@title"/> </h3>
        <xsl:for-each select="chaptergoals/goal">
          <p>
          <xsl:value-of select="."/>
          <xsl:number value="position()"/>
          </p>
        </xsl:for-each>
      </xsl:for-each>
    </body>
  </html>
</xsl:template>
</xsl:stylesheet>
```

The HTML head of the result tree document. The CSS style sheet is output to the HTML file here. See the next section for details. The book title and name are output here as well.

The main body of the document contains the control structures for scanning the source tree (XML)

Loops through the individual 'goal' elements and displays the position and goal text.

Main for-each loop for iterating through the chapters. This loop displays the chapter title, and goals.

The HTML document contains a header and a body section.

The XSL stylesheet element requires the template child element with a match clause to indicate where to start scanning the source document. Tell '/' tells the parser to start at the root element of the source tree, in this case, the root is the <book> element.

The XSL stylesheet element defines the namespace URI and XSL version for the xsl element.

The first line in Figure 7-8 defines the XML version and encoding scheme. The second line defines the namespace for the XSL elements within the document. The XSL element "template" imposes a logical template for the whole document. The parser outputs the <head> and <html> tags without modification. The two <h1> tags within the <head> section are output containing the title and author name attributes from the source file.

> **NOTE** The elements <h1>, <h2>, and <h3> have specific implied formats when read by browsers in HTML. However, you can adjust the implied formats of these tags using CSS, as discussed in the next section.

The XSLT language organizes the XML elements into a tree structure, using XPath, similar to the way in which a standard computer file system organizes files. You reference the node elements or attributes by specifying the entire path, starting at the current location in the tree. In this case, the root element contains the desired attribute, so you should use path "book/@title." The "@" character indicates to the parser to select an attribute as opposed to an element.

The parser then reads the content of the book from the XML source file. The **for-each** element iterates through each of the elements given within the **select** attribute. Within the outer **for-each** element, the parser first outputs the chapter goals title and then begins another **for-each** loop to iterate through the list of chapter goals. Figure 7-9 gives the output from the XSLT translation file in Figure 7-8. The text view is the exact text output by the XSLT file, and the browser view is how the HTML looks from an HTML 4.0-based web browser's interpretation of the tags.

Figure 7-9 *Output HTML from XSLT Transformation*

HTML View

```
<html>
  <head>
    <h1>Content Networking Fundamentals</h1><h1>Silvano D. Da Ros</h1>
  </head>
  <body>
    <h2>Chapter 1 - Introducing Content Networks</h2>
      <h3>Chapter 1 Goals</h3>
        <p>1. To state the purposes of content networking.</p>
        <p>2. To inform the reader of the major concepts of content networking.</p>
        <p>3. To detail the underlying protocols of content networking.</p>
    <h2>Chapter 2 - Exploring the Network Layers</h2>
      <h3>Chapter 2 Goals</h3>
        <p>1. To inform the reader of Layers 1 through 4 of the OSI mode.l</p>
        <p>2. To give the reader an overview of Ethernet, ARP, and IP routing.</p>
        <p>3. To illustrate basic TCP operation.</p>
  </body>
</html>
```

A Typical Browser View

Content Networking Fundamentals

Silvano D. Da Ros

Chapter 1 - Introducing Content Networks

Chapter 1 Goals

1. To state the purposes of content networking.
2. To inform the reader of the major concepts of content networking.
3. To detail the underlying protocols of content networking.

Chapter 2 - Exploring the Network Layers

Chapter 2 Goals

1. To inform the reader of Layers 1 through 4 of the OSI mode.l
2. To give the reader an overview of Ethernet, ARP, and IP routing.
3. To illustrate basic TCP operation.

NOTE To transform the XML source file into a WML file instead, you require a new XSL transformation file. Instead of outputting HTML tags, you output WML tags, leaving the overall flow of the XSLT file the same.

Using Cascading Style Sheets

You can use CSSs to separate the formatting of a web document from the content in the document. Style sheets are useful because you can locate them in files that are separate from the content, allowing for multiple formats for the same content. For example, you can create two versions of your website: a standard style and a style for the visually impaired containing clearer images and larger font. Another example is the format specific to the different series of Cisco IP phones. Each series of IP phone has a different size display and requires special consideration with respect to content placement.

The concept of CSSs gives your authors the ability to blend different style sheets into the same document, as opposed to using completely separate styles for different groups of end users or different displays. For example, the author of a Cisco.com page can apply three different style sheets for a page within the Cisco TAC website. The first style sheet may impose the Cisco corporate look and feel. The second style sheet may apply to the standard TAC presentation, and the third may apply a format for the series of TAC documents that the author is writing for, such as network troubleshooting topics.

You can use the CSS file in Example 7-2 to format the HTML generated in Figure 7-9.

Example 7-2 *Sample CSS File for Formatting a Standard HTML Document*

```
body { background-color: #FFFFFF; }
h1 { font-family: Arial, sans-serif; font-size: 20px; color: #660000; text-align: center}
h2 { font-family: Arial, sans-serif; font-size: 16px; color: #660000 }
h3 { font-family: Arial, sans-serif; font-size: 14px; color: #003333; }
p { font-family: Arial, sans-serif; font-size: 12px; color: #003333;}
```

Alternatively, you can generate HTML using XSLT to include CSS classes. Figure 7-10 illustrates how you can use XSLT to generate HTML with CSS classes, to provide a robust formatting solution to your XML documents.

Figure 7-10 *XSLT for Generating HTML with Embedded CSS Classes*

```
<?xml version="1.0" encoding="UTF-8"?>
<xsl:stylesheet version="1.0" xmlns:xsl="http://www.w3.org/1999/XSL/Transform" >
  <!-- Template to commence processing at the start of the XML document -->
  <xsl:template match="/">
    <!-- Output the HTML headers -->
    <html>
      <head>
      <LINK REL="stylesheet" TYPE="text/css" HREF=" cnbook.css"/>
      </head>
      <body>
      <div class="container">
      <div class="header"><xsl:value-of select="book/@title"/> <br/>
      By: <xsl:value-of select="book/@author"/></div>
      <div class="content">
      <!-- eBook Content -->
      <xsl:for-each select="book/chapter">
        <h2 class="chaptitle"> <xsl:value-of select="chaptertitle"/> </h2>
        <h3 class="goalstitle"> <xsl:value-of select="chaptergoals/@title"/> </h3>
        <p class="goal">
        <xsl:for-each select="chaptergoals/goal">
          <xsl:number value="position()" format="1. "/>
          <xsl:value-of select="."/>
        <br/>
        </xsl:for-each>
        </p>
      </xsl:for-each>
      </div>
      <div class="footer">Copyright &#xA9; 2006 CiscoPress</div>
      </div>
      </body>
    </html>
  </xsl:template>
</xsl:stylesheet>
```

The CSS is linked to the generated HTML document using the LINK directive

CSS classes are used to create numerous areas of the document to define the style of the document.

"container" - encompasses the entire document.

"header" - contains the top area, that will display the title name and author name.

"content" - will contain the outline content. Within the "content" area, **"chaptitle"**, **"goalstitle"**, and **"goal"** classes will further define the style of the book outline.

"footer" - will output copyright information.

The XSLT file in Figure 7-10 will generate the formatted document in Figure 7-11.

Figure 7-11   *Sample HTML Document Formatted with CSS*

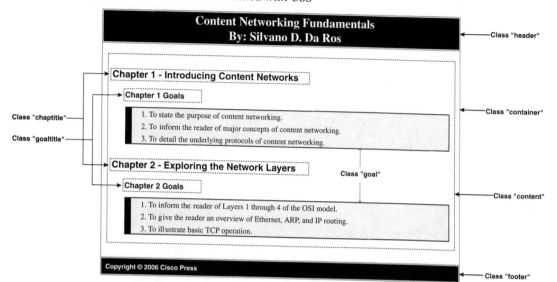

You can use the CSS file in Figure 7-12 to provide the format attributes for the classes described previously.

Style sheets are beneficial when you require rendering a large number of documents into the same style. With a standard XML format, your authors can create content and use a given set of markup tags to describe the content. If the documents require different versions, such as XHTML and HTML for online viewing or Braille and PDF for printing, you will require a separate XSL transformation file for each. At any time, you can create new versions of the content by writing a new transformation file without changing the XML source files. Moreover, you can further separate the style and formatting using CSS. In the future, if a style or layout change to the documents is required, only the style sheets require modification, not the source XML file or XSL transformation file.

Figure 7-12 *Sample CSS File Using Classes*

```
body { background-color: #FFFFFF; }

div.container
{width:100%; margin:0px; border:1px solid gray; line-height:150%;
}

div.header
{
font-family: Times;
font-size: 19px;
text-align: center;
color:white;
background-color:660000;
border:10px solid 0x660000;
line-height: 25px
}

div.footer
{
font-family: Arial;
font-size: 10px;
color:white;
background-color:003333;
border:1px solid white;
margin:0cm 0cm 0cm 0cm
}

div.content
{
border-bottom:1px solid gray;
padding:1em;
}

h1.header
{
font-family: Times, sans-serif;
font-size: 14px;
color: #FFFFFF;
text-align: left;
padding:0; margin:0;
}

h1.title, h1.author
{
font-family: Times, sans-serif;
font-size: 19px;
color: #FFFFFF;
text-align: center;
line-height: 5px}
```

```
p.divhead
{
font-family: Times, sans-serif;
font-size: 20px;
color: #FFFFFF;
text-align: left;
}

h2.chaptitle
{
font-family: Arial, sans-serif;
font-size: 14px;
color: #000000 ;
}

h3.goalstitle
{
font-family: Arial, sans-serif;
font-size: 12px;
color: #000000;
line-height: 1px;
margin-left: 1cm
}

p.goal
{
font-family: Times, sans-serif;
font-size: 11px;
border-color: #003333;
background:EEEFEE;
border-style: solid;
border-left-width: 10px;
border-top-width: 1px;
border-bottom-width: 1px;
border-right-width: 1px;
margin-left: 1cm;
padding-left: 15px;
line-height: 18px
}
```

Transforming XML to XSL-FO

Now that you have a solid understanding of XML, XSL, and CSSs, you can tackle the more complex and highly powerful style sheet formatting language called XSL Format Objects (XSL-FO). Like CSS, you can use XSL-FO to format XML data for output. However, unlike CSS, XSL-FO is XML-based, and you can use it to further mark up XML by including descriptive formatting elements. Once marked up with XSL-FO, the formatted XML files can be output into various formats using third-party XSL-FO processors. The output formats can include any of the online display markup languages discussed in this chapter, such as HTML, XHTML, and WML. However, the most common use of XSL-FO is to produce typeset documents for print in Adobe PDF format.

The XSL-FO in Example 7-3 is the general format for an XSL-FO formatted file. Notice that the "fo:" namespace precedes all the XSL-FO elements in the document.

Example 7-3   *The General Format for an XSL-FO Document.*

```
<?xml version="1.0" encoding="ISO-8857-1"?>
<fo:root xmlns:fo="http://www.w3.org/1999/XSL/Format">

<fo:layout-master-set>
  <fo:simple-page-master master-name="A4">
    <!-- Page template goes here -->
  </fo:simple-page-master>
</fo:layout-master-set>

<fo:page-sequence master-reference="A4">
  <!-- Page content goes here -->
</fo:page-sequence>
</fo:root>
```

The <fo:layout-master-set> element declares the page layout for the document. For your book outline project, you need only a single-page layout. All XSL-FO documents are broken into three areas, **region-before**, **region-body**, and **region-after**, but you can rename them to HEADER, CONTENT, and FOOTER in this example for clarity. Within our page outline, called BOOK-OUTLINE, we define the characteristics of each region. When supplying the content of the page, you reference the outline BOOK-OUTLINE, and the particular regions in which the content will reside.

The last part of the document specifies the actual content for output. The **page-sequence** element specifies the format for each page in your output document and references BOOK-OUTLINE for the placement and structure of content on the page. In the book outline example, the HEADER region contains the book title and author name, the CONTENT region contains the book outline, and the FOOTER region contains the copyright information. The HEADER and FOOTER content do not change. As such, you should define the HEADER and FOOTER content with static-content elements. If the data in this example happened to span multiple printed pages, the header and footer data would not change. Conversely, if content is not destined for print as in previous examples in this chapter, the header and footer remain at the top and bottom of the page. For content that changes from page-to-page, use the <fo:flow> element to output the content. The <block> element specifies each area within a flow. Attributes of the <block> element give the specific formatting for each block. For example, the block containing the content for the chapter goals would contain the formatting attributes in Example 7-4.

Example 7-4   *Sample "Chapter Goal" XSL-FO Block*

```
<fo:block
 background-color="#EEEFEE"
 margin="30px"
 border="1px solid #003333"
 border-left="15px solid #003333"
 text-indent="40px"
 line-height="25px"
 font-family="Times"
 font-size="11pt"
 color="black">
</fo:block>
```

The attributes in Example 7-4 produce the indentation, fonts, and colors that you see in the final output in Figure 7-13. To simplify Figure 7-13, none of the format attributes are included in the XSL-FO output. As an exercise, you can add format attributes based on those provided in Example 7-3 and the CSS example in Figure 7-13 to produce the same results.

Figure 7-13   *Sample XML Document Formatted with XSL-FO and Generated into an Adobe PDF Document Using a XSL-FO Processor*

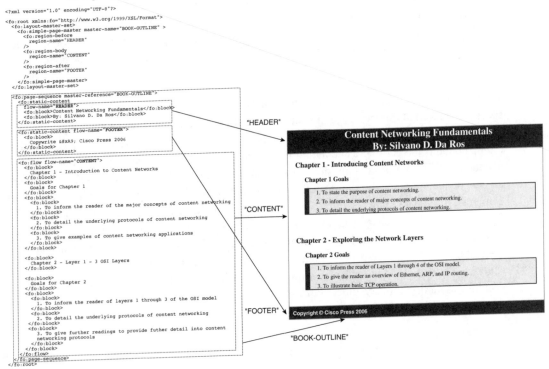

In Figure 7-13, the XSL-FO document includes the content from the source XML file. In order to automatically populate the content from a source XML file, you can use the XSLT document in Example 7-5. The XSLT elements from the previous examples are in bold—the parser generates the non-bolded text as the XSL-FO output in Figure 7-13.

Example 7-5   *XSL File That Generates XSL-FO with Embedded XML Content*

```
<?xml version="1.0" encoding="UTF-8"?>
<xsl:stylesheet version="1.0" xmlns:xsl="http://www.w3.org/1999/XSL/Transform"
    xmlns:fo="http://www.w3.org/1999/XSL/Format" >

  <xsl:template match="/">

    <fo:root xmlns:fo="http://www.w3.org/1999/XSL/Format">
      <fo:layout-master-set>
        <fo:simple-page-master master-name="BOOK-OUTLINE" >
          <fo:region-before
            region-name="HEADER" />
          <fo:region-body margin-top="60px"
            region-name="CONTENT" />
          <fo:region-after extent="30px"
            region-name="FOOTER" />
        </fo:simple-page-master>
      </fo:layout-master-set>

      <fo:page-sequence master-reference="BOOK-OUTLINE">
        <fo:static-content
          flow-name="HEADER">
          <fo:block><xsl:value-of select="book/@title"/></fo:block>
          <fo:block>By: <xsl:value-of select="book/@author"/></fo:block>
        </fo:static-content>
        <fo:static-content flow-name="FOOTER">
          <fo:block>
            Copyright &#xA9; Cisco Press 2005
          </fo:block>
        </fo:static-content>
      </fo:page-sequence>
      <fo:flow flow-name="CONTENT">
        <xsl:for-each select="book/chapter">
          <fo:block
            <xsl:value-of select="chaptertitle"/>
          </fo:block>
          <fo:block>
            <xsl:value-of select="chaptergoals/@title"/>
          </fo:block>

          <fo:block>
            <xsl:for-each select="chaptergoals/goal">
```

continues

Example 7-5 *XSL File That Generates XSL-FO with Embedded XML Content (Continued)*

```
                    <fo:block>
                      <xsl:number value="position()" format="1. "/>
                      <xsl:value-of select="."/>
                    </fo:block>
                  </xsl:for-each>
                </fo:block>
              </xsl:for-each>
            </fo:flow>
          </fo:root>
        </xsl:template>
</xsl:stylesheet>
```

Summary

In this chapter, you learned how to present and transform printed and online content using markup languages. Procedural markup languages are inflexible, information retrieval is difficult, and they require multiple documents for files that require different formats. Descriptive markup languages separate document formatting from document content. This chapter discussed the following descriptive markup languages:

- HTML

- Extensible Markup Language (XML)

- Extensible HTML (XHTML)

- Wireless Application Protocol (WAP) Markup Languages including Wireless Markup Language 1.0 (WML) and XHTML Mobile Profile (XHTMLMP).

- You also learned how to transform XML content into XHTML and HTML using XSLT. Once you transform XML into either of these two markup languages, you can format the content for display using CSSs. As an alternative, you learned how to transform XML into XSL-FO. XSL-FO is a standard formatting output with which you can use XSL-FO processors to parse and output to online or printable form.

Review Questions

1. What are the disadvantages of using procedural markup languages?

2. What is PDATA?

3. What is the purpose of the Document Type Definition (DTD) file and XML schemas?

4. What are the benefits of XHTML over HTML?

5. What are your two options for transforming XML content into a displayable or printable form?

6. What is an XML namespace?

7. What is the benefit of CSS?

8. What is the purpose of the **position**() function in the XSLT examples in this chapter?

Recommended Reading

Erik T. Ray, *Learning XML*, O'Reilly, 2003

Thomas Powell, *HTML & XHTML: The Complete Reference*, McGraw-Hill Osborne Media, 2003

Michael Kay, *XSLT 2.0 Programmer's Reference*, Wrox, 2004

http://www.w3c.org

http://www.w3schools.com

CISCO SYSTEMS

ISBN: 1-58705-160-5

Storage Networking Protocol Fundamentals

A comparative analysis of Ethernet, TCP/IP, and Fibre Channel in the context of SCSI

ciscopress.com

James Long

Upon completing this chapter, you will be able to:

- List all of the flow control and QoS mechanisms related to modern storage networks
- Describe the general characteristics of each of the flow control and QoS mechanisms related to modern storage networks

CHAPTER 9

Flow Control and Quality of Service

The chapters in Part I, "The Storage Networking Landscape," and Part II, "The OSI Layers," introduce the flow control and QoS mechanisms used in modern storage networks. Building upon those chapters, this chapter provides a comprehensive inventory of the flow control and QoS mechanisms used by Ethernet, IP, TCP, Internet SCSI (iSCSI), Fibre Channel (FC), Fibre Channel Protocol (FCP), and Fibre Channel over TCP/IP (FCIP). Readers are encouraged to review the flow control and QoS discussion at the beginning of Chapter 5, "The OSI Physical and Data Link Layers," before reading this chapter. Additionally, readers are encouraged to review the frame/packet format descriptions and delivery mechanism discussions in the chapters in Part II, "The OSI Layers," before reading this chapter. Finally, readers are encouraged to review the data transfer optimization discussions in Chapter 8, "The OSI Session, Presentation, and Application Layers," before reading this chapter.

Conceptual Underpinnings of Flow Control and Quality of Service

To fully understand the purpose and operation of flow-control and QoS mechanisms, first readers need to understand several related concepts. These include the following:

- The principle of operation for half-duplex upper layer protocols (ULPs) over full-duplex network protocols
- The difference between half-duplex timing mechanisms and flow-control mechanisms
- The difference between flow control and Quality of Service (QoS)
- The difference between the two types of QoS algorithms
- The relationship of delivery acknowledgement to flow control
- The relationship of processing delay to flow control
- The relationship of network latency to flow control
- The relationship of retransmission to flow control
- The factors that contribute to end-to-end latency

As previously mentioned, SCSI is a half-duplex command/response protocol. For any given I/O operation, either the initiator or the target may transmit at a given point in time. The SCSI communication model does not permit simultaneous transmission by both initiator and target within the context of a single I/O operation. However, SCSI supports full-duplex communication across multiple I/O operations. For example, an initiator may have multiple I/O operations outstanding simultaneously with a given target and may be transmitting in some of those I/O operations while receiving in others. This has the affect of increasing the aggregate throughput between each initiator/target pair. For this to occur, the end-to-end network path between each initiator/target pair must support full-duplex communication at all layers of the OSI model.

Readers should be careful not to confuse half-duplex signaling mechanisms with flow-control mechanisms. Communicating FCP devices use the Sequence Initiative bit in the FC Header to signal which device may transmit at any given point in time. Similarly, iSCSI devices use the F bit in the iSCSI Basic Header Segment (BHS) to signal which device may transmit during bidirectional commands. (iSCSI does not explicitly signal which device may transmit during unidirectional commands.) These mechanisms do not restrict the flow of data. They merely control the timing of data transmissions relative to one another.

Flow control and QoS are closely related mechanisms that complement each other to improve the efficiency of networks and the performance of applications. Flow control is concerned with pacing the rate at which frames or packets are transmitted. The ultimate goal of all flow-control mechanisms is to avoid receive buffer overruns, which improves the reliability of the delivery subsystem. By contrast, QoS is concerned with the treatment of frames or packets after they are received by a network device or end node. When congestion occurs on an egress port in a network device, frames or packets that need to be transmitted on that port must be queued until bandwidth is available. While those frames or packets are waiting in queue, other frames or packets may enter the network device and be queued on the same egress port. QoS policies enable the use of multiple queues per port and determine the order in which the queues are serviced when bandwidth becomes available. Without QoS policies, frames or packets within a queue must be transmitted according to a simple algorithm such as First In First Out (FIFO) or Last In First Out (LIFO). QoS mechanisms enable network administrators to define advanced policies for the transmission order of frames or packets. QoS policies affect both the latency and the throughput experienced by a frame or packet. The QoS concept also applies to frames or packets queued within an end node. Within an end node, QoS policies determine the order in which queued frames or packets are processed when CPU cycles and other processing resources become available.

All QoS algorithms fall into one of two categories: queue management and queue scheduling. Queue management algorithms are responsible for managing the number of frames or packets in a queue. Generally speaking, a frame or packet is not subject to being dropped after being admitted to a queue. Thus, queue management algorithms primarily deal with queue admission policies. By contrast, queue scheduling algorithms are responsible for selecting the next frame or packet to be transmitted from a queue. Thus, queue scheduling algorithms primarily deal with bandwidth allocation.

End-to-end flow control is closely related to delivery acknowledgement. To understand this, consider the following scenario. Device A advertises 10 available buffers to device B. Device B then transmits 10 packets to device A, but all 10 packets are transparently dropped in the network. Device B cannot transmit any more packets until device A advertises that it has free buffers. However, device A does not know it needs to send another buffer advertisement to device B. The result is a deadlock condition preventing device B from transmitting additional frames or packets to device A. If the network notifies device B of the drops, device B can increment its transmit buffers for device A. However, notification of the drops constitutes negative acknowledgement. Device A could send a data packet to device B containing in the header an indication that 10 buffers are available in device A. Although this does not constitute an acknowledgement that the 10 packets transmitted by device B were received and processed by device A, it does provide an indication that device B may transmit additional packets to device A. If device B assumes that the first 10 packets were delivered to device A, the result is an unreliable delivery subsystem (similar to UDP/IP and FC Class 3). If device B does not assume anything, the deadlock condition persists. Other contingencies exist, and in all cases, either a deadlock condition or an unreliable delivery subsystem is the result. Because the goal of flow control is to avoid packet drops due to buffer overrun, little motivation exists for implementing end-to-end flow control on unreliable delivery subsystems. So, end-to-end flow control is usually implemented only on reliable delivery subsystems. Additionally, end-to-end flow-control signaling is often integrated with the delivery acknowledgement mechanism.

End-to-end flow control is also closely tied to frame/packet processing within the receiving node. When a node receives a frame or packet, the frame or packet consumes a receive buffer until the node processes the frame or packet or copies it to another buffer for subsequent processing. The receiving node cannot acknowledge receipt of the frame or packet until the frame or packet has been processed or copied to a different buffer because acknowledgement increases the transmitting node's transmit window (TCP) or EE_Credit counter (FC). In other words, frame/packet acknowledgement implies that the frame or packet being acknowledged has been processed. Thus, processing delays within the receiving node negatively affect throughput in the same manner as network latency. For the effect on throughput to be negated, receive buffer resources must increase within the receiving node as processing delay increases. Another potential impact is the unnecessary retransmission of frames or packets if the transmitter's retransmission timer expires before acknowledgement occurs.

Both reactive and proactive flow-control mechanisms are sensitive to network latency. An increase in network latency potentially yields an increase in dropped frames when using reactive flow control. This is because congestion must occur before the receiver signals the transmitter to stop transmitting. While the pause signal is in flight, any frames or packets already in flight, and any additional frames or packets transmitted before reception of the pause signal, are at risk of overrunning the receiver's buffers. As network latency increases, the number of frames or packets at risk also increases. Proactive flow control precludes this scenario, but latency is still an issue. An increase in network latency yields an increase in buffer requirements or a decrease in throughput. Because all devices have finite memory resources, degraded throughput is inevitable if network latency continues to increase over time. Few devices support dynamic reallocation of memory to or from the receive buffer pool based on real-time fluctuations in network latency (called jitter), so the maximum expected RTT, including jitter, must be used to calculate the buffer requirements to sustain optimal throughput. More buffers increase equipment cost. So, more network latency and more jitter results in higher equipment cost if optimal throughput is to be sustained.

Support for retransmission also increases equipment cost. Aside from the research and development (R&D) cost associated with the more advanced software, devices that support retransmission must buffer transmitted frames or packets until they are acknowledged by the receiving device. This is advantageous because it avoids reliance on ULPs to detect and retransmit dropped frames or packets. However, the transmit buffer either consumes memory resources that would otherwise be available to the receive buffer (thus affecting flow control and degrading throughput) or increases the total memory requirement of a device. The latter is often the design choice made by device vendors, which increases equipment cost.

The factors that contribute to end-to-end latency include transmission delay, serialization delay, propagation delay, and processing delay. Transmission delay is the amount of time that a frame or packet must wait in a queue before being serialized onto a wire. QoS policies affect transmission delay. Serialization delay is the amount of time required to transmit a signal onto a wire. Frames or packets must be transmitted one bit at a time when using serial communication technologies. Thus, bandwidth determines serialization delay. Propagation delay is the time required for a bit to propagate from the transmitting port to the receiving port. The speed of light through an optical fiber is 5 microseconds per kilometer. Processing delay includes, but is not limited to, the time required to:

- Classify a frame or a packet according to QoS policies
- Copy a frame or a packet into the correct queue
- Match the configured policies for security and routing against a frame or a packet and take the necessary actions
- Encrypt or decrypt a frame or a packet
- Compress or decompress a frame or a packet
- Perform accounting functions such as updating port statistics
- Verify that a frame or a packet has a valid CRC/checksum
- Make a forwarding decision
- Forward a frame or a packet from the ingress port to the egress port

The order of processing steps depends on the architecture of the network device and its configuration. Processing delay varies depending on the architecture of the network device and which steps are taken.

Ethernet Flow Control and QoS

This section summarizes the flow-control and QoS mechanisms supported by Ethernet.

Ethernet Flow Control

As discussed in Chapter 5, "The OSI Physical and Data Link Layers," Ethernet supports reactive flow control via the Pause Operation Code (Pause Opcode). All 10-Gbps Ethernet implementations inherently support flow control and do not need to negotiate its use. 1000BASE-X negotiates flow control using the Pause bits in the Configuration ordered sets. Twisted-pair-based Ethernet implementations use the Technology Ability field to negotiate flow control. Except for 10-Gbps Ethernet implementations, three options may be negotiated: symmetric, asymmetric, or none. Symmetric indicates that the device is capable of both transmitting and receiving the Pause Opcode. Asymmetric indicates that the device is capable of either receiving or transmitting the Pause Opcode. None indicates that the Pause Opcode is not supported. All 10-Gbps Ethernet implementations support symmetric operation. A Pause Opcode may be sent before a queue overrun occurs, but many Ethernet switches do not behave in this manner.

Ethernet switches often employ "tail-drop" to manage flows. Tail-drop is not a mechanism per se, but rather a behavior. Tail-drop is the name given to the process of dropping packets that need to be queued in a queue that is already full. In other words, when a receive queue fills, additional frames received while the queue is full must be dropped from the "tail" of the queue. ULPs are expected to detect the dropped frames, reduce the rate of transmission, and retransmit the dropped frames. Tail-drop and the Pause Opcode often are used in concert. For example, when a receive queue fills, a Pause Opcode may be sent to stem the flow of new frames. If additional frames are received after the Pause Opcode is sent and while the receive queue is still full, those frames are dropped. For more information about Ethernet flow control, readers are encouraged to consult the IEEE 802.3-2002 specification.

Ethernet QoS

Ethernet supports QoS via the Priority field in the header tag defined by the IEEE 802.1Q-2003 specification. Whereas the 802.1Q-2003 specification defines the header tag format, the IEEE 802.1D-2004 specification defines the procedures for setting the priority bits. Because the Priority field is 3 bits long, eight priority levels are supported. Currently, only seven traffic classes are considered necessary to provide adequate QoS. The seven traffic classes defined in the 802.1D-2004 specification include the following:

- Network control information
- Voice applications
- Video applications
- Controlled load applications

- Excellent effort applications
- Best effort applications
- Background applications

The 802.1D-2004 specification defines a recommended set of default mappings between the seven traffic classes and the eight Ethernet priority values. In Ethernet switches that support seven or more queues per port, each traffic class can be mapped into its own queue. However, many Ethernet switches support fewer than seven queues per port. So, the 802.1D-2004 specification also defines recommendations for traffic class groupings when traffic classes must share queues. These mappings and groupings are not mandated, but they promote interoperability between Ethernet devices so that end-to-end QoS can be implemented successfully in a plug-and-play manner (even in multi-vendor environments).

Currently, no functionality is defined in the Ethernet specifications for the Pause Opcode to interact with the Priority field. So, the Pause Opcode affects all traffic classes simultaneously. In other words, an Ethernet switch that supports the Pause Opcode and multiple receive queues on a given port must send a Pause Opcode via that port (affecting all traffic classes) if any one of the queues fills. Otherwise, tail-drop occurs for the queue that filled. However, tail-drop can interact with the Priority field. Many Ethernet switches produced by Cisco Systems support *advanced tail-drop*, in which queuing thresholds can be set for each Ethernet priority level. Tail-drop then affects each traffic class independently. When a particular traffic class exceeds its queue threshold, frames matching that traffic class are dropped while the queue remains above the threshold defined for that traffic class. Other traffic classes are unaffected unless they also exceed their respective thresholds. The Pause Opcode needs to be sent only if all queues filled simultaneously. Alternately, the Pause Opcode may be sent only when one or more of the high-priority queues fill, thus avoiding tail-drop for high-priority traffic while permitting tail-drop to occur for lower-priority traffic. In this manner, the Pause Opcode can interact with the Priority field, but this functionality is proprietary and is not supported by all Ethernet switches. For more information about Ethernet QoS, readers are encouraged to consult the IEEE 802.1Q-2003 and 802.1D-2004 specifications.

IP Flow Control and QoS

This section summarizes the flow-control and QoS mechanisms supported by IP.

IP Flow Control

IP employs several flow-control mechanisms. Some are explicit, and others are implicit. All are reactive. The supported mechanisms include the following:

- Tail-drop
- Internet Control Message Protocol (ICMP) Source-Quench

- Active Queue Management (AQM)
- Explicit Congestion Notification (ECN)

Tail-drop is the historical mechanism for routers to control the rate of flows between end nodes. It often is implemented with a FIFO algorithm. When packets are dropped from the tail of a full queue, the end nodes detect the dropped frames via TCP mechanisms. TCP then reduces its window size, which precipitates a reduction in the rate of transmission. Thus, tail-drop constitutes implicit, reactive flow control.

ICMP Source-Quench messages can be used to explicitly convey a request to reduce the rate of transmission at the source. ICMP Source-Quench messages may be sent by any IP device in the end-to-end path. Conceptually, the ICMP Source-Quench mechanism operates in a manner similar to the Ethernet Pause Opcode. A router may choose to send an ICMP Source-Quench packet to a source node *in response to* a queue overrun. Alternately, a router may send an ICMP Source-Quench packet to a source node *before* a queue overruns, but this is not common. Despite the fact that ICMP Source-Quench packets can be sent before a queue overrun occurs, ICMP Source-Quench is considered a reactive mechanism because some indication of congestion or potential congestion must trigger the transmission of an ICMP Source-Quench message. Thus, additional packets can be transmitted by the source nodes while the ICMP Source-Quench packets are in transit, and tail-drop can occur even after "proactive" ICMP Source-Quench packets are sent. Upon receipt of an ICMP Source-Quench packet, the IP process within the source node must notify the appropriate Network Layer protocol or ULP. The notified Network Layer protocol or ULP is then responsible for slowing its rate of transmission. ICMP Source-Quench is a rudimentary mechanism, so few modern routers depend on ICMP Source-Quench messages as the primary means of avoiding tail-drop.

RFC 2309 defines the concept of AQM. Rather than merely dropping packets from the tail of a full queue, AQM employs algorithms that attempt to proactively avoid queue overruns by selectively dropping packets prior to queue overrun. The first such algorithm is called Random Early Detection (RED). More advanced versions of RED have since been developed. The most well known are Weighted RED (WRED) and DiffServ Compliant WRED. All RED-based algorithms attempt to predict when congestion will occur and abate based on rising and falling queue level averages. As a queue level rises, so does the probability of packets being dropped by the AQM algorithm. The packets to be dropped are selected at random when using RED. WRED and DiffServ Compliant WRED consider the traffic class when deciding which packets to drop, which results in administrative control of the probability of packet drop. All RED-based algorithms constitute implicit flow control because the dropped packets must be detected via TCP mechanisms. Additionally, all RED-based algorithms constitute reactive flow control because some indication of potential congestion must trigger the packet drop. The proactive nature of packet drop as implemented by AQM algorithms should not be confused with proactive flow-control mechanisms that exchange buffer resource information before data transfer occurs, to completely avoid frame/packet drops. Note that in the most generic sense, sending an ICMP Source-Quench message before queue overrun ocurs based on threshold settings could be considered a form of AQM. However, the most widely accepted definition of AQM does not include ICMP Source-Quench.

ECN is another method of implementing AQM. ECN enables routers to convey congestion information to end nodes explicitly by marking packets with a congestion indicator rather than by dropping packets. When congestion is experienced by a packet in transit, the congested router sets the two ECN bits to 11. The destination node then notifies the source node (see the TCP Flow Control section of this chapter). When the source node receives notification, the rate of transmission is slowed. However, ECN works only if the Transport Layer protocol supports ECN. TCP supports ECN, but many TCP implementations do not yet implement ECN. For more information about IP flow control, readers are encouraged to consult IETF RFCs 791, 792, 896, 1122, 1180, 1812, 2309, 2914, and 3168.

IP QoS

IP QoS is a robust topic that defies precise summarization. That said, we can categorize all IP QoS models into one of two very general categories: stateful and stateless. Currently, the dominant stateful model is the Integrated Services Architecture (IntServ), and the dominant stateless model is the Differentiated Services Architecture (DiffServ).

The IntServ model is characterized by application-based signaling that conveys a request for flow admission to the network. The signaling is typically accomplished via the Resource Reservation Protocol (RSVP). The network either accepts the request and admits the new flow or rejects the request. If the flow is admitted, the network guarantees the requested service level end-to-end for the duration of the flow. This requires state to be maintained for each flow at each router in the end-to-end path. If the flow is rejected, the application may transmit data, but the network does not provide any service guarantees. This is known as best-effort service. It is currently the default service offered by the Internet. With best-effort service, the level of service rendered varies as the cumulative load on the network varies.

The DiffServ model does not require any signaling from the application prior to data transmission. Instead, the application "marks" each packet via the Differentiated Services Codepoint (DSCP) field to indicate the desired service level. The first router to receive each packet (typically the end node's default gateway) conditions the flow to comply with the traffic profile associated with the requested DSCP value. Such routers are called conditioners. Each router (also called a hop) in the end-to-end path then forwards each packet according to Per Hop Behavior (PHB) rules associated with each DSCP value. The conditioners decouple the applications from the mechanism that controls the cumulative load placed on the network, so the cumulative load can exceed the network's cumulative capacity. When this happens, packets may be dropped in accordance with PHB rules, and the affected end nodes must detect such drops (usually via TCP but sometimes via ICMP Source-Quench). In other words, the DiffServ model devolves into best-effort service for some flows when the network capacity is exceeded along a given path.

Both of these QoS models have strengths and weaknesses. At first glance, the two models would seem to be incompatible. However, the two models can interwork, and various RFCs have been published detailing how such interworking may be accomplished. For more information about IP QoS, readers are encouraged to consult IETF RFCs 791, 1122, 1633, 1812, 2205, 2430, 2474, 2475, 2815, 2873, 2963, 2990, 2998, 3086, 3140, 3260, 3644, and 4094.

TCP Flow Control and QoS

This section summarizes the flow-control and QoS mechanisms supported by TCP.

TCP Flow Control

TCP flow control is a robust topic that defies precise summarization. TCP implements many flow-control algorithms, and many augmentations have been made to those algorithms over the years. That said, the primary TCP flow-control algorithms include slow start, congestion avoidance, fast retransmit, and fast recovery. These algorithms control the behavior of TCP following initial connection establishment in an effort to avoid congestion and packet loss, and during periods of congestion and packet loss in an effort to reduce further congestion and packet loss.

As previously discussed, the TCP sliding window is the ever-changing receive buffer size that is advertised to a peer TCP node. The most recently advertised value is called the receiver window (RWND). The RWND is complemented by the Congestion Window (CWND), which is a state variable within each TCP node that controls the amount of data that may be transmitted. When congestion is detected in the network, TCP reacts by reducing its rate of transmission. Specifically, the transmitting node reduces its CWND. At any point in time, a TCP node may transmit data up to the Sequence Number that is equal to the lesser of the peer's RWND plus the highest acknowledged Sequence Number or the CWND plus the highest acknowledged Sequence Number. If no congestion is experienced, the RWND value is used. If congestion is experienced, the CWND value is used. Congestion can be detected implicitly via TCP's acknowledgement mechanisms or timeout mechanisms (as applies to dropped packets) or explicitly via ICMP Source-Quench messages or the ECE bit in the TCP header.

When ECN is implemented, TCP nodes convey their support for ECN by setting the two ECN bits in the IP header to 10 or 01. A router may then change these bits to 11 when congestion occurs. Upon receipt, the destination node recognizes that congestion was experienced. The destination node then notifies the source node by setting to 1 the ECE bit in the TCP header of the next transmitted packet. Upon receipt, the source node reduces its CWND and sets the CWR bit to 1 in the TCP header of the next transmitted packet. Thus, the destination TCP node is explicitly notified that the rate of transmission has been reduced. For more information about TCP flow control, readers are encouraged to consult

IETF RFCs 792, 793, 896, 1122, 1180, 1323, 1812, 2309, 2525, 2581, 2914, 3042, 3155, 3168, 3390, 3448, 3782, and 4015.

TCP QoS

TCP interacts with the QoS mechanisms implemented by IP. Additionally, TCP provides two explicit QoS mechanisms of its own: the Urgent and Push flags in the TCP header. The Urgent flag indicates whether the Urgent Pointer field is valid. When valid, the Urgent Pointer field indicates the location of the last byte of urgent data in the packet's Data field. The Urgent Pointer field is expressed as an offset from the Sequence Number in the TCP header. No indication is provided for the location of the first byte of urgent data. Likewise, no guidance is provided regarding what constitutes urgent data. An ULP or application decides when to mark data as urgent. The receiving TCP node is not required to take any particular action upon receipt of urgent data, but the general expectation is that some effort will be made to process the urgent data sooner than otherwise would occur if the data were not marked urgent.

As previously discussed, TCP decides when to transmit data received from a ULP. However, a ULP occasionally needs to be sure that data submitted to the source node's TCP byte stream has actually be sent to the destination. This can be accomplished via the push function. A ULP informs TCP that all data previously submitted needs to be "pushed" to the destination ULP by requesting (via the TCP service provider interface) the push function. This causes TCP in the source node to immediately transmit all data in the byte stream and to set the Push flag to one in the final packet. Upon receiving a packet with the Push flag set to 1, TCP in the destination node immediately forwards all data in the byte stream to the required ULPs (subject to the rules for in-order delivery based on the Sequence Number field). For more information about TCP QoS, readers are encouraged to consult IETF RFCs 793 and 1122.

iSCSI Flow Control and QoS

This section summarizes the flow-control and QoS mechanisms supported by iSCSI.

iSCSI Flow Control

The primary flow-control mechanism employed by iSCSI is the Ready To Transfer (R2T) Protocol Data Unit (PDU). iSCSI targets use the R2T PDU to control the flow of SCSI data during write commands. The Desired Data Transfer Length field in the R2T PDU header controls how much data may be transferred per Data-Out PDU sequence. The R2T PDU is complemented by several other mechanisms. The MaxOutstandingR2T text key controls how many R2T PDUs may be outstanding simultaneously. The use of implicit R2T PDUs (unsolicited data) is negotiated via the InitialR2T and ImmediateData text keys. When unsolicited data is supported, the FirstBurstLength text key controls how much data may be transferred in or with the SCSI Command PDU, thus performing an equivalent function to the Desired Data Transfer Length field. The MaxRecvDataSegmentLength text key controls how much data may be transferred in a single Data-Out or Data-In PDU. The MaxBurstLength text key controls how much data may be transferred in a single PDU sequence (solicited or unsolicited). Thus, the FirstBurstLength value must be equal to or less than the MaxBurstLength value. The MaxConnections text key controls how many TCP connections may be aggregated into a single iSCSI session, thus controlling the aggregate TCP window size available to a session. The MaxCmdSN field in the Login Response BHS and SCSI Response BHS controls how many SCSI commands may be outstanding simultaneously. For more information about iSCSI flow control, readers are encouraged to consult IETF RFC 3720.

iSCSI QoS

iSCSI depends primarily on lower-layer protocols to provide QoS. However, iSCSI provides support for expedited command processing via the I bit in the BHS of the Login Request PDU, the SCSI Command PDU, and the TMF Request PDU. For more information about iSCSI QoS, readers are encouraged to consult IETF RFC 3720.

FC Flow Control and QoS

This section summarizes the flow-control and QoS mechanisms supported by FC.

FC Flow Control

The primary flow-control mechanism used in modern FC-SANs (Class 3 fabrics) is the Buffer-to-Buffer_Credit (BB_Credit) mechanism. The BB_Credit mechanism provides link-level flow control. The FLOGI procedure informs the peer port of the number of BB_Credits each N_Port and F_Port has available for frame reception. Likewise, the Exchange Link Parameters (ELP) procedure informs the peer port of the number of BB_Credits each E_Port has available for frame reception. Each time a port transmits a frame, the port decrements the BB_Credit counter associated with the peer port. If the BB_Credit counter reaches zero, no more frames may be transmitted until a Receiver_Ready (R_RDY) primitive signal is received. Each time an R_RDY is received, the receiving port increments the BB_Credit counter associated with the peer port. Each time a port processes a received frame, the port transmits an R_RDY to the peer port. The explicit, proactive nature of the BB_Credit mechanism ensures that no frames are ever dropped in FC-SANs because of link-level buffer overrun. However, line-rate throughput can be very difficult to achieve over long distances because of the high BB_Credit count requirement. Some of the line cards available for FC switches produced by Cisco Systems support thousands of BB_Credits on each port, thus enabling long-distance SAN interconnectivity over optical networks without compromising throughput. When FC-SANs are connected over long-distance optical networks, R_RDY signals are sometimes lost. When this occurs, throughput drops slowly over a long period. This phenomenon can be conceptualized as *temporal droop*. This phenomenon also can occur on native FC inter-switch links (ISLs), but the probability of occurrence is much lower with local connectivity. The FC-FS-2 specification defines a procedure called BB_Credit Recovery for detecting and recovering from temporal droop. For more information about FC flow control, readers are encouraged to consult the ANSI T11 FC-FS-2 and FC-BB-3 specifications.

FC switches produced by Cisco Systems also support a proprietary flow control feature called FC Congestion Control (FCC). Conceptually, FCC mimics the behavior of ICMP Source-Quench. When a port becomes congested, FCC signals the switch to which the source node is connected. The source switch then artificially slows the rate at which BB_Credits are transmitted to the source N_Port. Cisco Systems might submit FCC to ANSI for inclusion in a future FC standard.

FC QoS

FC supports several QoS mechanisms via fields in the FC header. The DSCP sub-field in the CS_CTL/Priority field can be used to implement differentiated services similar to the IP DiffServ model. However, the FC-FS-2 specification currently reserves all values other than zero, which is assigned to best-effort service. The Preference subfield in the CS_CTL/Priority field can be used to implement a simple two-level priority system. The FC-FS-2 specification requires all Class 3 devices to support the Preference subfield. No requirement exists for every frame within a sequence or Exchange to have the same preference value. So, it is theoretically possible for frames to be delivered out of order based on inconsistent values in the Preference fields of frames within a sequence or Exchange. However, this scenario is not likely to occur because all FC Host Bus Adapter (HBA) vendors recognize the danger in such behavior. The Priority subfield in the CS_CTL/Priority field can be used to implement a multi-level priority system. Again, no requirement exists for every frame within a sequence or Exchange to have the same priority value, so out-of-order frame delivery is theoretically possible (though improbable). The Preemption subfield in the CS_CTL/Priority field can be used to preempt a Class 1 or Class 6 connec-tion to allow Class 3 frames to be forwarded. No modern FC switches support Class 1 or Class 6 traffic, so the Preemption field is never used. For more information about FC QoS, readers are encouraged to consult the ANSI T11 FC-FS-2 specification.

FCP Flow Control and QoS

This section summarizes the flow-control and QoS mechanisms supported by FCP.

FCP Flow Control

The primary flow-control mechanism employed by FCP is the FCP_XFER_RDY IU. FCP targets use the FCP_XFER_RDY IU to control the flow of SCSI data during write commands. The FCP_BURST_LEN field in the FCP_XFER_RDY IU header controls how much data may be transferred per FCP_DATA IU. The FCP_XFER_RDY IU is complemented by a variety of other mechanisms. The Class 3 Service Parameters field in the PLOGI ELS header determines how many FCP_XFER_RDY IUs may be outstanding simultaneously. This is negotiated indirectly via the maximum number of concurrent sequences within each Exchange. The use of implicit FCP_XFER_RDY IUs (unsolicited data) is negotiated via the WRITE FCP_XFER_RDY DISABLED field in the PRLI Service Parameter Page.

When unsolicited data is supported, the First Burst Size parameter in the SCSI Disconnect-Reconnect mode page controls how much data may be transferred in the unsolicited FCP_DATA IU, thus performing an equivalent function to the FCP_BURST_LEN field. The Maximum Burst Size parameter in the SCSI Disconnect-Reconnect mode page controls how much data may be transferred in a single FCP_DATA IU (solicited or unsolicited). Thus, the First Burst Size value must be equal to or less than the Maximum Burst Size value. FCP does not support negotiation of the maximum number of SCSI commands that may be outstanding simultaneously because the architectural limit imposed by the size of the CRN field in the FCP_CMND IU header is 255 (versus 4,294,967,296 for iSCSI). For more information about FCP flow control, readers are encouraged to consult the ANSI T10 FCP-3 and ANSI T11 FC-LS specifications.

FCP QoS

FCP depends primarily on lower-layer protocols to provide QoS. However, FCP provides support for expedited command processing via the Priority field in the FCP_CMND IU header. For more information about FCP QoS, readers are encouraged to consult the ANSI T10 FCP-3 specification.

FCIP Flow Control and QoS

This section summarizes the flow-control and QoS mechanisms supported by FCIP.

FCIP Flow Control

FCIP does not provide any flow-control mechanisms of its own. The only FCIP flow-control functionality of note is the mapping function between FC and TCP/IP flow-control mechanisms. FCIP vendors have implemented various proprietary features to augment FCIP performance. Most notable are the FCP_XFER_RDY IU spoofing techniques. In some cases, even the FCP_RSP IU is spoofed. For more information about FCIP flow control, readers are encouraged to consult IETF RFC 3821 and the ANSI T11 FC-BB-3 specification.

FCIP QoS

FCIP does not provide any QoS mechanisms of its own. However, RFC 3821 requires the FC Entity to specify the IP QoS characteristics of each new TCP connection to the FCIP Entity at the time that the TCP connection is requested. In doing so, no requirement exists for the FC Entity to map FC QoS mechanisms to IP QoS mechanisms. This may be optionally accomplished by mapping the value of the Preference subfield or the Priority subfield in the CS_CTL/Priority field of the FC header to an IntServ/RSVP request or a DiffServ DSCP value. FCIP links are not established dynamically in response to received FC frames, so the FC Entity needs to anticipate the required service levels prior to FC frame reception. One method to accommodate all possible FC QoS values is to establish one TCP connection for each of the seven traffic classes identified by the IEEE 802.1D-2004 specification. The TCP connections can be aggregated into one or more FCIP links, or each TCP connection can be associated with an individual FCIP link. The subsequent mapping of FC QoS values onto the seven TCP connections could then be undertaken in a proprietary manner. Many other techniques exist, and all are proprietary. For more information about FCIP QoS, readers are encouraged to consult IETF RFC 3821 and the ANSI T11 FC-BB-3 specification.

Summary

The chapter reviews the flow-control and QoS mechanisms supported by Ethernet, IP, TCP, iSCSI, FC, FCP, and FCIP. As such, this chapter provides insight to network performance optimization. Application performance optimization requires attention to the flow-control and QoS mechanisms at each OSI Layer within each protocol stack.

Review Questions

1 What is the primary function of all flow-control mechanisms?

2 What are the two categories of QoS algorithms?

3 What is the name of the queue management algorithm historically associated with tail-drop?

4 Which specification defines traffic classes, class groupings, and class-priority mappings for Ethernet?

5 What is the name of the first algorithm used for AQM in IP networks?

6 What are the names of the two dominant QoS models used in IP networks today?

7 What is the name of the TCP state variable that controls the amount of data that may be transmitted?

8 What is the primary flow-control mechanism employed by iSCSI?

9 What are the names of the two QoS subfields currently available for use in FC-SANs?

10 What is the primary flow-control mechanism employed by FCP?

11 Are FCIP devices required to map FC QoS mechanisms to IP QoS mechanisms?

ISBN: 1-58705-240-7

Firewall Fundamentals

An introduction to network and computer firewall security

Wes Noonan

Ido Dubrawsky

ciscopress.com

CHAPTER 1

Introduction to Firewalls

Depending on whom you talk to, a firewall is either the cornerstone of their organization's security infrastructure, or it is a device that has woefully failed to live up to expectations. How can one device have such a contrast in perceptions? The biggest reason for this is a misunderstanding of what a firewall is and is not, and what a firewall can and cannot do.

This chapter looks at what a firewall is and how a firewall works to illustrate what are the reasonable expectations for a firewall. This chapter also examines the threats that exist and motivations of attackers to explore how firewalls can—and most important, cannot—protect against those threats.

What Is a Firewall?

When most people think of a firewall, they think of a device that resides on the network and controls the traffic that passes between network segments, such as the firewall in Figure 1-1 (a network-based firewall). However, firewalls can also be implemented on systems themselves, such as with Microsoft Internet Connection Firewall (ICF), in which case they are known as host-based firewalls. Fundamentally, both types of firewalls have the same objective: to provide a method of enforcing an access control policy. Indeed, at the simplest definition, firewalls are nothing more than access control policy enforcement points.

Figure 1-1 *A Network Firewall Enforcing Access Controls*

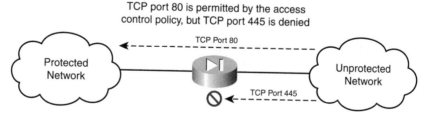

Firewalls enable you to define an access control requirement and ensure that only traffic or data that meets that requirement can traverse the firewall (in the case of a network-based firewall) or access the protected system (in the case of a host-based firewall). Figure 1-1 illustrates how you can use a network-based firewall to allow only traffic that is permitted to access protected resources.

What Can Firewalls Do?

Chapter 2, "Firewall Basics," and all of Part II, "How Firewalls Work," examine the details of how different types of firewalls work; before delving into more detail, however, you need to understand from a broad design perspective what firewalls can and cannot do. All firewalls (or at least all firewalls that you should be considering implementing) share some common traits and functionality that help define what a firewall can do.

Fundamentally, firewalls need to be able to perform the following tasks:

- Manage and control network traffic

- Authenticate access

- Act as an intermediary

- Protect resources

- Record and report on events

Firewalls Manage and Control Network Traffic

The first and most fundamental functionality that all firewalls must perform is to manage and control the network traffic that is allowed to access the protected network or host. Firewalls typically do so by inspecting the packets and monitoring the connections that are being made, and then filtering connections based on the packet-inspection results and connections that are observed.

Packet Inspection

Packet inspection is the process of intercepting and processing the data in a packet to determine whether it should be permitted or denied in accordance with the defined access policy. Packet inspection can look at any or all of the following elements in making a filtering determination:

- Source IP address

- Source port

- Destination IP address

- Destination port

- IP protocol

- Packet header information (that is, sequence numbers, checksums, data flags, payload information, and so on)

An important thing to keep in mind about packet inspection is that, to make a filtering decision, the firewall must inspect every single packet in every direction and on all interfaces, and access control rules must exist for every packet that will be inspected. This requirement can present a problem when it comes time to define an access control rule to address the return traffic from a permitted request.

Connections and State

For two TCP/IP hosts to communicate with one another, they must establish some sort of connection with each other. Connections serve two purposes. First, the hosts can use the connection to identify themselves to each other. This identification ensures that systems do not inadvertently deliver data to hosts that are not involved in the connection. Firewalls can use this connection information to determine what connections between hosts are allowed by the access control policy and thus determine whether data should be permitted or denied.

Second, connections are used to define the manner in which two hosts will communicate with each other. For Transmission Control Protocol (TCP), this type of connection is known as a connection-oriented session. For User Datagram Protocol (UDP) and Internet Control Message Protocol (ICMP), this type of connection is known as a connectionless session. Although connectionless session would seem to be contradictory in this context (how can a connection be connectionless?), connectionless session simply means that the hosts do not undertake any special mechanisms to ensure reliable data delivery, unlike TCP, which does undertake special mechanisms (specifically sequencing) to ensure that data is reliably delivered. Connections allow the hosts to know what the rules of etiquette for communications are. For example, when Host A makes a request for data from Host B using a protocol such as TCP, Host B responds with the data that was requested, not with a new connection request or with data other than what was requested.

This defined structure of a connection can be used to determine the state of the communications between two hosts. The easiest way to think of state is to think of a conversation between two people. If Bob asks John a question, the proper response is for John to answer the question. Thus, at the point that Bob has asked his question, the state of the conversation is that it is waiting for a response from John.

Network communication follows a similar format for tracking the state of a conversation. When Host A attempts to communicate with Host B, Host A initiates a connection request. Host B then responds to the connection request, and in doing so defines how the two hosts will keep track of what data needs to be sent and when it should be sent. So if Host A initiates a request, it can be assumed that the state of the conversation at that time is waiting for a response from Host B. Figure 1-2 illustrates this process in detail:

1. HostA initiates a connection to HostB.

2. HostB responds to the connection request from HostA.

3. HostA finalizes the connection with HostB, allowing for the passing of data.

4. HostA begins transmitting the required data to HostB.

5. HostB responds as required, either with the requested data, or to periodically acknowledge the receipt of data from HostA.

Figure 1-2 *Connections Between Hosts*

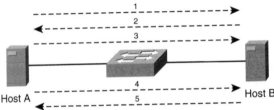

Host A   Host B

Firewalls can monitor this connection state information to determine whether to permit or deny traffic. For example, when the firewall sees the first connection request from HostA (Step 1), it knows that the next data it should see is the acknowledgment of the connection request from HostB (Step 2). This is typically done by maintaining a state table that tracks what the state of all the conversations traversing the firewall are in. By monitoring the state of the conversation, the firewall can determine whether data being passed is expected by the host in question, and if it is, it is permitted accordingly. If the data being passed does not match the state of the conversation (as defined by the state table), or if the data is not in the state table, it is dropped. This process is known as stateful inspection.

Stateful Packet Inspection

When firewalls combine stateful inspection with packet inspection, it is known as stateful packet inspection. This is the inspection of packets not only based on packet structure and the data contained in the packet, but also based on what state the conversation between hosts is in. This inspection allows firewalls to filter not only based on what the contents of the packet are, but also based on the connection or state in which the connection is currently in (and thus provides a much more flexible, maintainable, and scalable filtering solution).

A benefit of stateful packet inspection over the packet inspection discussed previously is that after a connection has been identified and permitted (after being inspected accordingly), it is generally not necessary to define a rule to permit the return communications because the firewall knows by state what an accepted response should be. This buys you the security of being able to perform inspection of the commands and data contained within the packet to determine whether a connection will be permitted, and then automatically have the firewall track the state of the conversation and dynamically permit traffic that is in accordance with the state of the conversation. This process is done without needing to explicitly define a rule to permit the responses and subsequent communications. Most firewalls today function in this manner.

> **NOTE**   For more information about TCP/IP packet structure and TCP/IP-based communications, see Chapter 3, "TCP/IP for Firewalls."

Firewalls Authenticate Access

A common mistake that people make when evaluating firewalls is to consider packet inspection of the source IP address and port as being the same as authentication. Sure, packet inspection allows you to restrict what source hosts are able to communicate with your protected resources, but that does not ensure that the source host should be allowed to communicate with your protected resources. After all, it is a relatively trivial task to spoof an IP address, making one host appear to be an entirely different host and thus defeating inspection based on source address and port.

To eliminate this risk, firewalls also need to provide a means of authenticating access. TCP/IP was built on the premise of open communications. If two hosts know each others' IP addresses and are connected to each other, they are allowed to communicate. Although this was a noble design at the time, in today's world you may not want just anyone to be able to communicate with systems behind your firewall.

Firewalls can perform authentication using a number of mechanisms. First, the firewall can require the input of a username and password (often known as extended authentication or xauth). Using xauth, the user who attempts to initiate a connection is prompted for a username and password prior to the firewall allowing a connection to be established. Typically, after the connection has been authenticated and authorized by the security policy, the user is no longer prompted for authentication for that connection.

Another mechanism for authentication of connections is through the use of certificates and public keys. A benefit of certificates over xauth is that the authentication process can typically occur with no user intervention, provided the hosts have been properly configured with certificates and the firewall and hosts are using a properly configured public key infrastructure. A benefit of this approach is that it scales much better for large implementations.

Finally, authentication can be handled through the use of pre-shared keys (PSKs). PSKs are less complex to implement than certificates, while at the same time allowing for the authentication process to occur without user intervention. With PSKs, the host is provided a predetermined key that is used for the authentication process. A drawback of this system is that the PSK rarely changes and many organizations use the same key value for multiple remote hosts, thus undermining the security of the authentication process. If possible, certificate-based authentication or xauth should be used over (or in addition to) PSKs.

By implementing authentication, the firewall has an additional method of ensuring that the connection should be permitted. Even when the packet would be permitted based on inspection and the state of the connection, if the host cannot authenticate successfully with the firewall, the packet will be dropped.

Firewalls Act as an Intermediary

When people are concerned that a direct meeting would be too risky for them, they commonly use intermediaries to act on their behalf, and thus protect them from the risk of direct interaction. In the same vein, a firewall can be configured to act as an intermediary in the communications process between two hosts. This intermediary process is commonly referred to as acting as a proxy.

A proxy functions by effectively mimicking the host it is trying to protect. All communications destined for the protected host occurs with the proxy, which to the remote host appears to be the protected host. Indeed, the remote host has no way of knowing that it is not actually talking directly to the protected resource. The proxy receives packets destined for the protected host, strips out the relevant data, and builds a brand new packet that is then forwarded to the protected host. The protected host responds to the proxy, which simply reverses the process and forwards the response to the originating host. In doing so, the proxy (in this case, a firewall) acts as an intermediary to insulate the protected host from threats by ensuring that an external host can never directly communicate with the protected host.

In many cases, this function as a proxy is complemented by using a firewall that is capable of inspecting the actual application data to ensure that it is legitimate and nonmalicious data. When functioning in this manner, the firewall is known as working as an application proxy, because it is proxying the actual application functionality. This allows the firewall to inspect the actual application data itself (for example, allowing it to differentiate between legitimate HTTP traffic and malicious HTTP traffic) before presenting the data to the protected resource. For more detailed information about application proxies, see Chapter 2.

Firewalls Protect Resources

The single most important responsibility of a firewall is to protect resources from threat. This protection is achieved through the use of access control rules, stateful packet inspection, application proxies, or a combination of all to prevent the protected host from being accessed in a malicious manner or being made susceptible to malicious traffic. Firewalls are not an infallible method of protecting a resource however, and you should never rely exclusively on the firewall to protect a host. If an unpatched host (that is, a host that is lacking security updates that would protect it from being exploited) is connected to the Internet, a firewall may not be able to prevent that host from being exploited, especially if the exploit uses traffic that the firewall has been configured to permit. For example, if a packet-inspecting firewall permits HTTP traffic to an unpatched web server, a malicious user could leverage an HTTP-based exploit to compromise the web server because the web server is not patched against this new exploit. The unpatched web server renders the firewall useless as a protection device in this case. This is because the firewall cannot differentiate between malicious and nonmalicious HTTP requests, especially if the firewall does not function as an application proxy, and thus will happily pass the malicious HTTP data to the protected host. For this reason, protected resources should always be kept patched and up-to-date, in addition to being protected by a firewall.

Firewalls Record and Report on Events

The simple reality is that regardless of what you do to protect resources with a firewall, you cannot stop every malicious act or all malicious data. From simple misconfigurations of the firewall to new threats and exploits the firewall cannot protect against yet, you have to be prepared to deal with a security event that the firewall was not able to prevent. As a result, all firewalls should have a method of recording all communications (in particular access policy violations) that occur to enable the administrator to review the recorded data in an attempt to ascertain what transpired.

You can record firewall events in a number of ways, but most firewalls use two methods, either syslog or a proprietary logging format. By using either method of logging, the firewall logs can be interrogated to determine what may have transpired during a security event. In addition to the forensic analysis benefits of recording events, this data can also frequently be used when troubleshooting a firewall to help determine what may be the cause of the problem that is occurring.

Some events are important enough that merely logging them is not a good enough policy. In addition to logging the event, the firewall also needs to have a mechanism of alarming when a policy has been violated. Firewalls should support a number of types of alarms:

- **Console notification**—This is the simple process of presenting a notification to the console. The drawback of this alarm method is that it requires someone to be actively monitoring the console to know an alarm has been generated.

- **SNMP notification**—Simple Network Management Protocol (SNMP) can be used to generate traps that are sent to a network management system (NMS) that is monitoring the firewall.

- **Paging notification**—When an event occurs, the firewall can be configured to send a page to an administrator. This page can be numeric or alphanumeric, depending on the type of pager carried by the administrator.

- **E-mail notification**—Similar to paging notification, but the firewall simply sends an e-mail to the appropriate e-mail address.

By having a method of recording and reporting events, your firewall can provide an incredibly detailed level of insight as to what is currently occurring, or what may have previously occurred in the event that a forensic analysis must be performed.

What Are the Threats?

One of my favorite quotes is from Sun Tzu's *The Art of War*:

> If you know the enemy and know yourself, you need not fear the result of a hundred battles. If you know yourself but not the enemy, for every victory gained you will also suffer a defeat. If you know neither the enemy nor yourself, you will succumb in every battle.

To this end, it is not good enough to merely know what a firewall does or how a firewall works. You need to understand the threats that exist, to ensure that you can effectively protect your environment from the threats.

Threats that most IT organizations need to deal with include the following:

- Targeted versus untargeted attacks

- Viruses, worms, and trojans

- Malicious content and malware

- Denial-of-service (DoS) attacks

- Zombies

- Compromise of personal information and spyware

- Social engineering

- New attack vectors

- Insecure/poorly designed applications

Targeted Versus Untargeted Attacks

On the surface, the difference between a targeted and untargeted attack may seem pretty unimportant. As the saying goes, an attack is an attack, regardless of source. While in the midst of an attack, whether the attack is targeted or not may fall down the list of priorities. However, it is important to define the difference because it could impact the ultimate level of response required to address the attack.

Untargeted attacks are attacks that are not directly motivated by the resources being attacked. In other words, the attacker is not necessarily being motivated to attack *your* resources, as much as the attacker is probably trying to gain access to *any* server that might be susceptible, and your server just so happened to fall in their sights. This is a common attack method for defacement-style attacks. In many cases, the attacker has not chosen to target your website because you own it, as much as they are trying to find websites running on certain versions of web server software, and you just so happened to be running that web server software. As a result, untargeted attacks typically do not have as much effort and motivation behind them and can be easier to defend against than a targeted attack is. In many cases, merely dropping the malicious traffic is enough to effectively defend against an untargeted attack and cause the attacker to move on to easier hunting grounds.

Targeted attacks, on the other hand, present an additional twist to the attack. For whatever reason, the attacker is interested in the resources and data you have, and has made a conscious and concerted effort to try to gain access to those resources. This makes a targeted attack of more concern than an untargeted attack, because in general it means that the attacker is going to continue to attempt to gain access to those resources, despite your efforts to protect them. Therefore, you must be even more vigilant in attempting to stop and ultimately catch the attacker so that the legal authorities can take the appropriate action. Indeed, if you suspect that your environment is under a targeted attack, it is a good idea to get the authorities involved sooner than later, because often attackers will not stop until they have been locked up by the appropriate legal authorities.

Viruses, Worms, and Trojans

It seems like as long as there have been computer systems, there has been someone willing to make malicious software to attack them. Although the terms *virus*, *worm*, and *trojan* are often used interchangeably to refer to malicious software, each term has its own distinct qualities and attributes that you need to understand.

Viruses are pieces of malicious code that typically are attached to legitimate software. For example, an attacker might make a game for use on a computer that includes the virus code as part of the game code. As the game is passed from computer to computer, typically through user intervention such as e-mail or sharing discs, the virus is able to spread, infecting computers that run the game software. Viruses have differing degrees of severity, ranging from merely annoying messages and content, to destructive code designed to erase or otherwise cause the loss of data or system functionality. The key attribute to a virus is that it cannot execute and spread by itself; it requires user intervention to allow it to function and infect other systems.

Worms are similar to viruses (sometimes even considered a subclass, or evolution of the traditional virus), with one major difference. Worms are self-replicating and can spread and infect systems with no help from a human user after they have been initially unleashed. In many cases, worms take advantage of system exploits in their propagation process, utilizing the exploit to allow the worm to infect a new system. Another common method of propagation is to utilize the e-mail client on an infected host to e-mail the worm to additional targets. This nature of a worm allows it to be much more devastating than a traditional virus because an infected host can effectively spread the infection to hundreds of thousands of systems at once, allowing the spread of the worm to grow exponentially after the initial host has been compromised. This propagation can be so disruptive as to actually cause an inadvertent denial of service against resources in some cases. For example, Code Red spread by attempting to connect to a large number of remote hosts, which in turn caused the routers connected to the networks that those remote hosts resided on to issue a corresponding amount of Address Resolution Protocol (ARP) requests in an attempt to connect to the remote hosts. Because of the sheer quantity of requests and the nature of how ARP functions (ARP is covered in more detail in Chapter 3), many routers were unable to handle the sheer volume of traffic and therefore stopped being able to forward legitimate data.

Trojans take the idea of malicious viruses and worms to a new level. Rather than functioning as a virus or worm, the objective of a trojan is to appear as a piece of useful software that has a hidden function, typically to gain access to the resources on the infected system. For example, many trojans will install back-door software (such as BackOrifice) on the infected system, allowing the designer of the trojan to be able to connect to and access the infected system.

Viruses, worms, and trojans can be difficult to defend against using firewalls alone, and generally require either the integration of virus-scanning software on the firewall itself or the use of third-party products in conjunction with a firewall.

Malicious Content and Malware

Malicious content is simply data that was written with a nefarious purpose in mind. In most cases, malicious content requires the user to undertake some action that allows the protected system to be exposed to the content. This action may be accessing a website or simply viewing an e-mail that contains the content. The users, by virtue of the fact that they undertook the risky action, inadvertently allow their systems to become compromised by the malicious content. Often, the malicious content is active scripting functionality that allows arbitrary code to be executed by the client web browser or e-mail client, thus allowing the malicious content to perform functions ranging from accessing/destroying client data to installing viruses, worms, trojans, back doors, or just about any malware (malicious software) the attacker desires.

Malware (malicious software) simply builds on the basic premise of malicious content and includes any software that has a nefarious purpose in mind. Malicious software includes software such as viruses, worms, and trojans, although those three types of malware warrant their own distinct discussions because of the specialized nature and impact of each.

Unlike most threats this book covers, malicious content and malware generally requires the user on the protected network or resource to purposely or inadvertently perform some action to allow the content to be executed. As a result, protecting against malicious content and malware frequently requires the firewall to be able to monitor and control traffic that may originate from a protected network or host, typically through the use of egress filters on the firewall itself and content-filtering software used in conjunction with the firewall.

Denial of Service

A DoS attack entails a threat that simply prevents legitimate traffic from being able to access the protected resource. A common DoS is one that causes the services or server itself to crash, thus rendering the service being provided inaccessible. This attack is commonly done by exploiting buffer overflows in software and protocols or by sending data to the host that the host does not know how to respond to, thus causing the host to crash.

A variant of the DoS that has gained traction and is much more difficult to protect against is the distributed DoS (DDoS). With a DDoS, the end purpose is the same, but the method of attack differs. DDoS attacks typically utilize thousands of hosts to attack a target, thus increasing the amount of traffic exponentially. The objective of the DDoS is to overload the target with so many bogus requests that the target cannot respond to legitimate requests. Consequently, the difference between a DoS and a DDoS is generally the number of hosts engaging in the attack and the fact that the attackers are distributed across these systems as opposed to attacks coming from a single attacker. In fact, many DDoS attacks are nothing more than a DoS that is being executed on a much larger scale.

One well-known method of performing a DDoS is what is known as a SYN flood. A SYN flood in and of itself is not necessarily a DDoS. A SYN flood functions by presenting a target host with thousands of connection requests that are not allowed to complete successfully. The target must wait a determined amount of time for the connection to be successfully completed, thus utilizing network traffic buffers to store the partially created connections. When these buffers fill up with these partially created connections, the target can no longer accept new connection requests, and therefore begins dropping new traffic. What makes it particularly potent as a DDoS attack, however, is when thousands of hosts undertake the SYN flood, thus exponentially increasing the amount of traffic the targeted host must deal with. If one host attempts a SYN flood, it might not be able to generate enough connection requests to cause the DoS, but when 1000 (or more) other hosts join in, suddenly the targeted host can be quickly become inundated. Another method of performing a DDoS is to simply saturate the target with so much data, legitimate or otherwise, that the amount of traffic exceeds the capacity of the network bandwidth. This type of DDoS is particularly difficult to protect against because by the time DDoS traffic is on the network, it is already too late to stop it. The only effective way to protect against this type of DDoS is to rely on an upstream partner with more bandwidth than you have to filter the malicious traffic prior to it traversing your network segments. More mundane forms of DoS, particularly a DoS that attempts a SYN flood, can be protected against by implementing the appropriate rules on the firewall.

Zombies

Zombies are systems that have been infected with software (typically trojans or back doors) that puts them under the control of the attacker. The zombies can then be used at some point in the future to launch an attack, frequently a DoS attack against the ultimate target of the attacker.

The most effective way to protect against zombies is to prevent a system from being used as a zombie in the first place. You can do so by implementing egress filtering (filtering of traffic from a protected network) at the firewall as well as content filtering to ensure that even if a system is somehow turned into a zombie, it cannot be used to execute the final attack. In this sense, it is the responsibility of the firewall administrator to not only ensure that the firewall protects the organization's resources, but also to ensure that the firewall protects others from the organization's internal systems.

Compromise of Personal Information and Spyware

Personal information, in particular financial information, is the holy grail of many attackers. With that information, an attacker can either use or sell the data to someone who will use it to engage in all sorts of financial-based frauds. Literally millions of dollars of fraudulent purchases are made every year using personal information that was obtained illegally.

Financial information is only one component in the compromise of personal information. Another risk is the compromise of private medical data. This information, if made public, could result in people being illegally discriminated against. For example, an insurance company that has full and unfettered access to a patient's medical data might not be willing to insure the subject.

The compromise of personal information has led to a slew of legislation, the most well known being the Health Insurance Portability and Accountability Act of 1996 (HIPAA), which requires companies and organizations to take steps to ensure that personal information is not exposed to unauthorized access. From a corporate perspective, this means that the systems that collect this kind of data need to be insulated and protected to ensure that only authorized access to the data is permitted. The penalties for failing to protect personal information range from legal penalties to the loss of business and trust from the users of your systems.

A variation of the compromise of personal information is the compromise of proprietary or confidential information of a company or organization. This compromise could include the loss of source code or trade secrets as well as more mundane items such as company strategies and future business initiatives, allowing your competitors to gain an unfair advantage in business operations and competition.

In all of the previous methods, firewalls can be used to segment and isolate the critical systems, allowing greater control over who and what types of access to the protected resources will be allowed.

The compromise of information is not restricted solely to the realm of business. Individuals also risk the loss of their personal information through the use of malicious software such as spyware. Spyware functions in many ways like a trojan and allows the designer of the spyware to track everything from what websites an individual frequents to the purchases (and potentially the credit cards used) that the user makes. Spyware is much more difficult to control using network firewalls because in most cases the spyware is distributed throughout the environment. Many personal firewalls have included spyware-detection and -removal functionality as a component of their firewall suite, however, and therefore these can be an effective solution to the problem of how to protect personal information on a local computer.

Social Engineering

Whereas brute-force hacking a system gets all the sex appeal, social engineering is the surgical strike to the carpet-bombing mentality of a traditional hack. Social engineering attempts to compromise what is often the weakest link in an organization's security, the wetware (or people).

A social-engineering attack typically involves attackers attempting to pretend to be someone they are not, sometimes a user in need of help, sometimes an administrator attempting to help a user in need, and then trying to get the information they need from their target. For example, someone might contact users asking whether they are having any computer problems (most all users have *some* problem). The attacker might then seem to be trying to help the users troubleshoot the problem by asking them their password so they can attempt to log in as the user and see whether they experience the same problem. If a user provides that password, the attacker can then attempt to use it to gain access to other resources. Let's assume that your virtual private network (VPN) requires user authentication. With this information, a remote attacker might then be able to successfully log on to your VPN concentrator, and thus gain access to the internal network.

Because of the nature of a social-engineering attack, all the firewalls in the world will not do anything to prevent the attack from being successful. Rather, the best defense against social engineering is a well-trained user community and staff (you would be amazed at how many IT administrators will turn passwords over to a "service provider" trying to help troubleshoot a problem) that knows what is and is not acceptable information that should be shared either over the phone or in person.

New Attack Vectors

A current buzz is the threat of the zero-day event or exploit. The zero-day event is a security vulnerability that is exploited on the same day it is discovered—before vendors can respond with the appropriate patch or solution. Although the zero-day event has not happened yet, the time between when vulnerabilities are discovered and exploited has continued to get shorter and shorter.

The decreasing time from vulnerability to exploitation presents a problem because most technologies today take a rather reactionary response to attacks. As new vulnerabilities are discovered and published, vendors often must figure out the solution and attempt to deliver it before the attack is attempted. During this time period, after a vulnerability has been discovered but before a solution is available, systems are completely vulnerable and susceptible to attack and exploit. As an administrator, the only effective way to deal with new attack vectors is to ensure that you have an aggressive patch management solution in place, and that you apply patches and access control rule updates in a timely fashion, thus reducing that period of vulnerability.

Insecure/Poorly Designed Applications

The ugly truth that few software vendors want to admit is that a sizeable number of successful attacks result from insecure and poorly designed applications. In some cases, the application was designed well at the time, but the times changed and the application did not. In other cases, the application is just badly designed and implemented.

Regardless of the reason, insecure and poorly designed applications are one of the most difficult threats to address. Unfortunately, we are all at the mercy of the software vendors to patch their systems; if they have not or will not undertake this, the best we can do is attempt to work around the insecurity or design flaw, or use a different vendor's products.

Application proxies can be an effective solution to this problem, because the application proxy can typically be configured to recognize malicious traffic that attempts to exploit the application insecurity, and thus protect the system running the insecure application. Another potential solution is to use the firewall to prevent connections to the vulnerable system that are not necessary for the system to perform its job. For example, if the protected system is running a web server that is insecure, but the web server does not need to be accessed from an external source, you can configure the firewall to prevent access to the web server, while allowing access to any other applications the protected system is running.

What Are the Motives?

There is no shortage of motives behind the threats that attackers come up with. Perhaps the most dangerous motive is the conscious decision to break the law, typically in an effort to gain some financial or monetary gain. Often, criminals develop attacks and exploits with the sole purpose of gaining illegal access to systems, typically for the purpose of monetary gain. This gain could come from obtaining personal information and committing fraud with that information, gaining access to data and blackmailing the victim into paying for that data, or stealing trade secrets from a competitor's system or undermining the financial stability of the company.

A less-driven, but still dangerous motive is the simple desire to cause mischief and wreak havoc on an environment. Mischief covers everything from bored teenagers looking to do something they consider exciting and interesting, to the disgruntled ex-employee who is just looking to cause trouble for his former employer. One of the most difficult aspects of attackers motivated by mischief is that often the attacks they engage in have logical reason, especially if the attacker falls into the category of the bored person just looking for something interesting to do. Many times, their attempts at what they consider mundane and harmless activities can inadvertently cause significant problems or outages. Many virus writers fall into this category, not realizing just how much damage their innocuous virus can cause if someone is able to modify it slightly.

Another angle for motivation is simple ego. Attackers are convinced that they are smarter than you, the defender, and an easy way to prove it is to compromise the system. They can then run off to their chat rooms and brag about how they were able to get the best of the company they targeted.

However, the most troublesome motive comes from attackers with multiple motives. In this case, the attacker is frequently so driven by boredom, ego, and criminal behavior that nothing short of legal intervention can stop the attacker. Indeed, a number of attacks that may have started as untargeted attacks against an environment have escalated with bad consequences when attackers realized that what they did has been patched. Their ego cannot handle that they were stopped, and they become willing to undertake more risky—and more costly—activities to prove that they are superior.

Motives are not solely the realm of the attacker, however. As administrators, we have to know what our motivation is in protecting our resources. Ensure not only that you are protecting your resources, but that you are doing so in the proper manner. Although it is human nature when presented with an attack to want to lash out and strike back at attackers to teach them a lesson, that is not our place or our role. In fact, in the case of zombies, the system that you decide to strike back against often becomes an unwitting victim not only of the original hacker's attack on their system, but of your attack in an effort to teach the hacker not to mess with your systems. As cliché as it sounds, there are good guys and bad guys, and as administrators we need to make sure that our motives and undertakings remain on the side of the good guys.

Security Policies

As mentioned previously, firewalls are nothing more than access control policy enforcement points. Consequently, a firewall is only as effective as the firewall security policy (as opposed to the enterprise security policy) that dictates how the firewall will be used. Firewall security policies are discussed in great detail in Chapter 10, "Firewall Security Policies," but we can look at the fundamentals of what kinds of firewall security policies exist and how to build an effective security policy now.

The first step to a good security policy is to perform a risk analysis to determine what the threats to the protected system are. After doing this, you can develop a strategy and policy for protecting the system from those threats with your firewalls. A key thing to understand when you develop this strategy is that you may not be able to protect against or prevent everything. The reasons for this range from technological limitations (technically the recommendation cannot be done) to practical limitations (it would not be practical to undertake the recommendation) to financial limitations (you do not have the money in the budget to undertake the recommendation). As a result, you need to approach the subject from the perspective of seeking to minimize the risk associated with the threat. In some cases, that means you can reduce the risk to zero (for example, if you use a firewall to prevent all access to a system). In other cases, you can only reduce the risk to a level that is acceptable by management. For example, management may not decide that they can afford to spend the money required to implement the security solution recommended. In this instance, it is absolutely critical to convey in an honest and accurate manner what the level of risk will be. The reason for this is that after an incident occurs, it becomes real convenient for people to suddenly "forget" that they agreed to that level of risk in the first place. This is the time that it comes in handy to be able to produce a signed document that proves everyone agreed that the level of risk that was settled on was appropriate.

Examples of Security Policies

You have two primary security policies to use as a baseline in designing your security policy. The first is the closed security policy, also known as the minimalist security policy. The other is an open security policy, also known as generally a bad idea.

The closed security policy is based on the premise that by default all access is denied, and only access that is explicitly required will be permitted. The benefit of this approach is that the security policy will be designed only to allow access that has been explicitly granted. This security policy is frequently implemented when dealing with granting access from an untrusted source to a protected system (sometimes referred to as ingress filtering). The drawback of this system is the same as its strength, however. Because the default action is to deny traffic, it can be a time-consuming process to identify, configure, and maintain the list of exceptions that must be permitted.

At the other end of the spectrum is the open security policy. It takes the exact opposite approach, by default granting all access and denying only the traffic that is explicitly configured to be denied. This type of security policy is frequently implemented for granting access from a trusted network to external systems (sometimes referred to as egress filtering). The benefit of this system is that it generally takes little to no configuration to allow systems to traverse the firewall and access resources. As a result, *many* firewalls by default apply this methodology to traffic that is sourced from the internal network to external networks such as the Internet. Although convenient, it is incredibly insecure because the firewall will allow legitimate and malicious traffic out with equal ease. Consequently, it is not recommended that you implement a firewall that is configured in this manner. Although more convenient, the risk is simply too great for most environments.

Firewalls and Trust

After the decision has been made to allow some traffic through the firewall, the administrator has effectively made the decision (intentional or not) to trust the traffic that will be permitted. This decision is part of defining an acceptable level of risk. A firewall typically does not exist to stop all traffic. If it did, you would be better served just to disconnect the system from the network entirely. Instead, the firewall exists to allow some traffic while stopping other traffic.

In these situations, you have to realize and accept that by permitting certain traffic, you are trusting that the traffic is safe and acceptable. However, this does not mean that by deciding to permit traffic you are effectively removing any security a firewall can provide. Simply put, just because you trust certain types of traffic does not mean you have to trust the traffic in its entirety and in every way.

In the continued pursuit of mitigating and minimizing risk, you can configure the firewall to authenticate connections that will access the trusted resource, adding an additional level of security and risk management to the access that is being granted. Doing so ensures that before access to the protected resource will be granted, the requesting system must be authenticated as a legitimate user of the resource.

Another option is to use the firewall as an application proxy, serving as an intermediary for providing access to the protected resource. As discussed previously in this chapter, this can help mitigate and minimize risk by ensuring that all access to the protected resource must go through the proxy, allowing the proxy to ensure that the data being transmitted is not malicious or harmful.

The biggest thing to remember about firewalls and trust is that no matter how much you trust the access being granted, it has to go through the firewall before gaining access to the protected resource as opposed to just bypassing or not using a firewall at all.

Determining If You Need a Firewall

It is convenient (and accurate) to say that you always need a firewall if you are connecting to the Internet. Firewalls should not be relegated exclusively to the realm of providing access to and protection from Internet-based resources. Instead, you should consider implementing a firewall any time a resource needs to be protected, regardless of where the protected resource is located, or where the requesting traffic will be coming from. Firewalls can, and in many cases should, be used to control access to important servers or different subnets within the corporate network. For example, if two branch offices should never need access to each other's resources, you should consider a firewall to enforce that policy and ensure that such access is never granted.

To help determine where you can implement a firewall, define what the cost of the data you are trying to protect is. This cost includes a number of variables. One variable to consider is the cost of restoring or repairing the data. An additional variable is the cost of lost work and downtime as a result of the data being inaccessible to employees. Yet another variable is the cost in lost revenue or income that might come as a result of the loss of data.

A common way of quantifying this kind of cost is known as determining the single loss expectancy (SLE) and annual loss expectancy (ALE). SLE is the expected monetary loss every time an incident occurs. The ALE is the expected monetary loss over the course of a year. The ALE is calculated by multiplying the annual rate of occurrence (ARO) by the SLE. The ARO is the probability that something will occur during a given year. The easiest way to understand how to calculate and determine this information is to go through a fictional scenario.

Suppose that your external web server is compromised and that web server is used to process incoming requests that 100 data processors work on. The first thing to do is to define the SLE, and doing that requires that you define the variables mentioned previously. First, you need to define the cost of restoring or repairing the data. This cost can range from the time it takes someone to reboot a server and apply a patch or to restore the server from a tape backup. For this scenario, assume that the cost to recover from this compromise is $500. Next, the loss of the web server and subsequent inability of the workers to do anything productive needs to be factored into the equation. Assuming the employees are paid $12 an hour (average salary of a data-entry clerk in the Houston, Texas, area) and the server is down for a half a day being rebuilt, the cost to the company in just lost time for the users of the web server is $4800. Finally, the cost of loss of revenue or income needs to be factored into the equation. There are a number of ways to determine this, which the accounting department should be able to help in defining. For example, if the application in question generates a certain amount of money per transaction, and the average number of transactions per day is known, you can easily determine the number of lost transactions, and thus revenue, for a given period of time. For example, suppose that the loss of revenue is $1000. This gives you a grand total of $6300, which is the SLE of the given scenario.

On the surface, considering that an enterprise-class firewall with failover can be had for less than $6000 (Cisco PIX 515E unrestricted license with failover), it would seem to make perfect sense that if a firewall could have prevented the incident, that there should be no question about whether a firewall should have been purchased and implemented. However, it is not quite that simple. With the benefit of hindsight, you can easily see that the firewall was worth the cost. Rarely do we have the benefit of hindsight when it is time to determine what to spend money on, which is where the ALE comes into play.

Defining the ALE is a little bit trickier than defining the SLE because it almost always requires you to make some educated guesses as to what the ARO is. For example, it is impossible to say with certainty that an event will occur a certain number of times a year or even a certain number of times over the course of many years. The ARO is more of a method of making an educated calculation based on historic data and information to determine what the expected probability of an occurrence is. For example, suppose that in reviewing insurance data the probability of a serious fire is once every 25 years. This does not guarantee that a fire will happen in any given year, or even at all during that time, but it does allow you to put a value to the probability that a fire will occur, in this case 1/25 or 0.04 percent in any given year. When the ARO is multiplied by the SLE, you can get the ALE.

Reviewing the scenario, suppose that the ARO is defined as 1 or greater. In that case, you can easily justify spending $6000 on a firewall that could prevent the loss ($6300), because it will pay for itself by preventing a single incident. What if the ARO is less than 1 (which it frequently is)? At that point, it can be tougher to make the case that a firewall should be implemented, because the cost of the firewall may not be less than the ALE. In this case, however, keep in mind that the ALE is the expected loss, not the actual loss, and although the cost of the solution may be less than the ALE, it may still be financially viable and a worthwhile endeavor. Conversely, if the probability that an event will occur is so low, the cost of the solution may never be justified. Of course, as the saying goes in technology, it is always difficult to get money for security before an event occurs. . .but after an event does occur, the pocketbooks open right up to prevent a recurrence.

Another variable is the cost of starting over. This variable is particularly important for smaller companies, because the majority of smaller companies that experience a week of downtime as a result of a security incident are rarely able to recover from that outage, and subsequently go out of business.

The cost of legal repercussions as a result of the data loss or compromise is another real cost that you must consider. The simple reality is that we live in a litigious society, and if a company is negligent in adequately protecting their data, especially if they maintain consumer data, there will be no shortage of lawyers seeking monetary compensation for the security incident. I would not want to be on the jury of a company being sued that admitted that they decided not to use a firewall, or do anything else to protect their resources, and were subsequently hacked.

Whereas the corporate user has many justifications for protecting their resources, home users tend not to share such concerns. Some home users might think, "What do I have that I need to protect?" and not come up with anything important. This is a deceptive line of thinking, however. The home user might be unaware of data that needs protection. We have all seen the news regarding identity theft and the loss of financial information; and if home users have used their computer to make online transactions or store their financial data, protecting that data can go a long way toward preventing them from becoming a victim of these types of crimes and events. Even going beyond protecting financial data, however, many home users maintain data such as personal or family information that they probably would not want to be made publicly available. Also, although home users might legitimately not have any data of any consequence that they believe they need to protect, if they leave their system unprotected it can relatively easily be used by someone else to engage in malicious activity, particularly by using the system as a zombie, and use a home user's computer to attack other systems on the Internet. Therefore, home users really have an obligation to implement a firewall (in addition to making sure that they run current antivirus and antispyware/malware software and keep their systems patched and up-to-date) not only to protect themselves, but to protect others from their systems being used as part of an attack.

Summary

Firewalls, regardless of how complex in design and implementation, have a simple responsibility to act as security policy enforcement points. Firewalls can do this by inspecting the data that is received and tracking the connections that are made to determine what data should be permitted and what data should be denied. In addition, firewalls can act as an intermediary and proxy requests to the protected host while at the same time providing a means of authenticating access to better ensure that only approved access is granted. Finally, firewalls can report and alert on events related to all of these processes to allow you, the administrator, to know what is going on with your firewall and the systems it is protecting.

Any number of motivations drive people to develop threats to our systems. By examining the threats and the appropriate responses, you can develop a security policy that minimizes the risk presented by a threat through the proper implementation and configuration of a firewall. Although a firewall cannot prevent all attacks, it is one of the best methods of protecting resources; and when in doubt, there is a good chance that a firewall can help make your resources even more secure than if there were no firewall at all.

CISCO SYSTEMS

ISBN: 1-58705-207-5

IPsec Virtual Private Network Fundamentals

ciscopress.com

James Henry Carmouche

CHAPTER 3

Basic IPsec VPN Topologies and Configurations

In this chapter, we will review several common deployments of IPsec virtual private networks (VPN). We will begin by reviewing the typical site-to-site IPsec model over a dedicated circuit between two endpoints, then discuss some of the design implications as that dedicated circuit grows to include an entire routed domain. We will discuss aggregation of many site-to-site IPsec VPNs at an aggregation point, or hub IPsec router, in a standard hub-and-spoke design and extend the IPsec aggregation concept to include Remote Access VPN (RAVPN) design considerations. Figure 3-1 illustrates a loose process that may be helpful when configuring a crypto endpoint for basic IPsec operations. Though effective IPsec VPN design drives the complexity of configuration far beyond what is depicted in Figure 3-1, most of the basic topologies we will discuss will relate to this procedure on a fundamental level.

Figure 3-1 *High-Level Configuration Process for IPsec VPN*

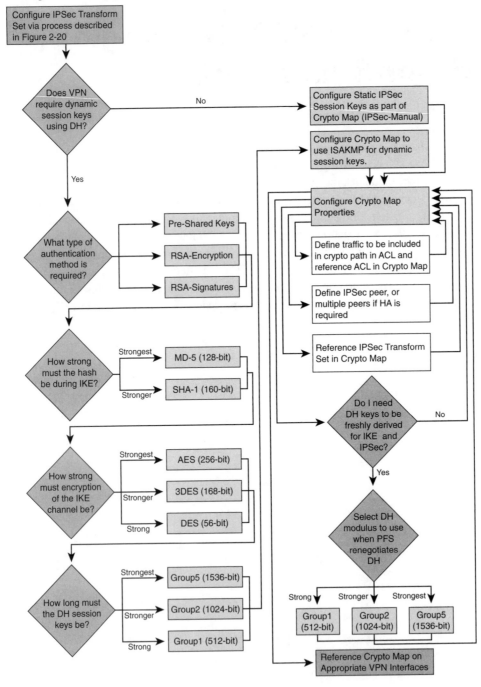

Each of the following deployments requires the configuration of IPsec in a point-to-point fashion in one way or another. As such, each of the topologies discussed share common configuration tasks to establish the IPsec tunnel:

Step 1   Decide how strong the IPsec transform must be and what mode the tunnel must use (Define IPsec Transform Set).

Step 2   Decide how the session keys must be derived and if IKE is necessary (create Internet Security Association and Key Management Protocol policy or session keys within crypto map)

Step 3   If IKE is required, decide on ISAKMP policy parameters (create Internet Security Association and Key Management Protocol policy), addressing the following tasks in your configuration:

- Authentication method (select one of the following):

  Assign key and peer if pre-shared.

  Create and share RSA public keys if RSA-encr.

  Authenticate and enroll with CA if RSA-sig.

- Diffie-Hellman Key Modulus (Group #.

- Hash used for IKE authentication

- Encryption method used for IKE channel

Step 4   Identify and assign IPsec peer and any High-Availability requirements (Create crypto map).

NOTE   In this chapter, topologies will include only limited discussions of IPsec High-Availability (HA) design concepts. IPsec HA design and examples are discussed in greater detail in Chapters 5-9.

Step 5   Define traffic sets to be encrypted (Crypto ACL Definition and Crypto Map Reference).

Step 6   Identify requirement for PFS and reference PFS group in crypto map if necessary.

Step 7   Apply crypto map to crypto interfaces.

Site-to-Site IPsec VPN Deployments

The most basic form of IPsec VPN is represented with two VPN endpoints communicating over a directly-connected shared media, or dedicated circuit, which closely resembles bulk encryption alternatives at Layer 1 and 2 of the OSI stack (see Table 1-1 for VPN technologies and the OSI stack). This scenario, while simple to deploy and manage, can be cost prohibitive and does not yield many of the benefits of IPsec VPN connectivity over a routed domain (multiple Layer 3 hops between endpoints).

Indeed, because IPsec is a Layer 3 VPN technology, it was designed to function across multiple Layer 3 hops in order to circumvent many of the scalability and manageability issues in previous VPN alternatives. As such, IPsec deployed over a routed domain will also provide further scalability, flexibility, and availability over and beyond the simple dedicated-circuit model. In this section, we will explore design concepts related to both topologies and the corresponding configuration and verification processes required.

Site-to-Site VPN Architectural Overview for a Dedicated Circuit

Site-to-site IPsec VPNs are typically deployed when two or more autonomous systems wish to communicate with each other over an untrusted media when confidential exchange of data is required. Consider the situation described in Figure 3-2, where three autonomous systems wish to communicate using dedicated T-1 circuits between each other.

Figure 3-2 *Site-to-Site IPsec VPN Topology using Dedicated T-1 Circuits for Communications*

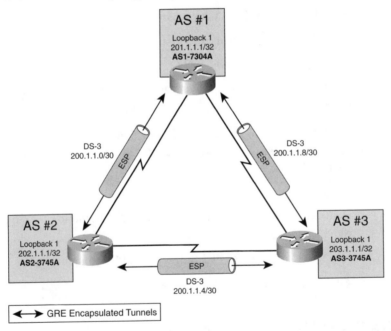

It is important to note that, assuming that each autonomous system (AS) does not act as a transit AS, there is only one path between each AS. Therefore, in this specific case, there is no benefit to configuring redundant peering options or sourcing IPsec tunnel endpoints from highly available

IP addresses (such as a loopback address). In this simple site-to-site topology, it is most common to source IPsec VPN tunnel endpoints on the physical interfaces (DS-3 in this case) themselves. This type of topology does not leave room for much in the way of IPsec HA design, and therefore, it is relatively simple to deploy. We will now explore the configuration steps necessary to establish the basic site-to-site IPsec VPN described earlier, and then we will outline some common techniques used to verify the establishment and operation of the IPsec VPN tunnel.

Cisco IOS Site-to-Site IPsec VPN Configuration

The configuration in the following examples were all built using the process described in Figure 3-1, and pertain to the topology depicted in Figure 3-2. Some design considerations for these particular IPsec VPNs are as follows:

- Tunnel mode is used to keep the original IP header confidential.

- The routers are capable of handling 256-bit AES ESP transforms in hardware. Hash-based Message Authentication Codes (HMAC) are implemented in the transform to ensure integrity in the cipher block chain of encrypted packets traversing the IPsec security association (SA).

- The DH group is 5 in order to accommodate the large key material needed by the AES transform.

- There is no certification authority (CA), and the administrators want to use hardware acceleration, which rules out the RSA-encrypted nonces method of authentication. So, pre-shared keys are used for Internet Security Association and Key Management Protocol (ISAKMP) authentication.

- Strong authentication is required during ISAKMP, so the hash is SHA-1 and the symmetric transform for the IKE SA is 3DES.

- It is desirable to have the IPsec session keys derived independently (as opposed to derived from) the ISAKMP DH shared secret keys. As such, perfect forward secrecy (PFS) is enabled. Again, the group is 5 to generate the appropriate key material for the IPsec transform (AES).

NOTE The preceding VPN considerations describe a relatively strong cryptographic suite. As such, computation resources on the routers must be somewhat substantial to accommodate them. It is important that one weigh the amount of available computational resources against the organization's performance and security requirements before building IPsec VPN configurations.

Example 3-1 provides a configuration for the AS1-7301A in Figure 3-2. This router's configuration employs all of the elements necessary to accommodate a site-to-site IPsec VPN, including the IPsec transform, crypto ACL, and IPsec peer. In this case, AS1-7301A uses two site-to-site IPsec VPNs, to AS#2 and AS#3, respectively. This is accomplished by using two process IDs within the same crypto map (AS1VPN 10 and AS1VPN 20). AS1VPN, process 10, protects traffic from AS1 to AS2, as defined in crypto ACL 101. AS1VPN, process 20, protects traffic form AS1 to AS3 (Example 3-1, line 14), as defined in crypto ACL 102 (Example 3-1, line 15).

Example 3-6 *Site-to-Site VPN Configuration on AS1-7301A*

```
1   AS1-7304A#show running-config
2   !
3   crypto IPsec transform-set ivdf3-1 esp-aes esp-sha-hmac
4   crypto map AS1VPN 10 IPsec-isakmp
5    set peer 200.1.1.2
6    set transform-set ivdf3-1
7    match address 101
8    set pfs group5
9   crypto map AS1VPN 20 IPsec-isakmp
10   set peer 200.1.1.10
11   set transform-set ivdf3-1
12   match address 102
13   set pfs group5
14  access-list 101 permit ip 211.0.0.0 0.255.255.255 212.0.0.0 0.255.255.255
15  access-list 102 permit ip 211.0.0.0 0.255.255.255 213.0.0.0 0.255.255.255
16  !
17  interface HSSI1/0
18   ip address 200.1.1.1 255.255.255.252
19   encapsulation HDLC
20   crypto map AS1VPN
21  interface HSSI2/0
22   ip address 200.1.1.9 255.255.255.252
23   encapsulation HDLC
24   crypto map AS1VPN
```

Example 3-2 provides the configuration for the IPsec VPN gateway for AS2, AS2-3745A. Like AS1-7304A, AS2-3745A uses a single crypto map with two process IDs to protect traffic flows to AS1 and AS3. AS2VPN, 10 Protects Traffic to AS1 (endpoint 200.1.1.1), references ACL101 for crypto-protected traffic and IPsec transform "ivdf3-1". AS2VPN, 20 Protects Traffic to AS3 (endpoint 200.1.1.6), references ACL102 for crypto-protected traffic and IPsec transform "ivdf3-1". AS2-3745 uses a relative strong transform, AES cipher with SHA1 HMAC authentication. PFS is also configured to refresh the symmetric transform key each time an IPsec SA is negotiated.

Example 3-7 *Site-to-Site VPN Configuration on AS2-3745A*

```
1   AS2-3745A#show running-config
2   !
3   crypto IPsec transform-set ivdf3-1 esp-aes esp-sha-hmac
4   crypto map AS2VPN 10 IPsec-isakmp
5    set peer 200.1.1.1
```

Example 3-7 *Site-to-Site VPN Configuration on AS2-3745A (Continued)*

```
6   set transform-set ivdf3-1
7   match address 101
8   set pfs group5
9  crypto map AS2VPN 20 IPsec-isakmp
10  set peer 200.1.1.6
11  set transform-set ivdf3-1
12  match address 102
13  set pfs group5
14 access-list 101 permit ip 212.0.0.0 0.255.255.255 211.0.0.0 0.255.255.255
15 access-list 102 permit ip 212.0.0.0 0.255.255.255 213.0.0.0 0.255.255.255
16 !
17 interface HSSI1/0
18  ip address 200.1.1.2 255.255.255.252
19  encapsulation HDLC
20  crypto map AS2VPN
21 interface HSSI2/0
22  ip address 200.1.1.5 255.255.255.252
23  encapsulation HDLC
24  crypto map AS2VPN
```

Example 3-3 provides the configuration for the IPsec VPN gateway for AS3, AS3-3745A. Like
AS1-7304A and AS2-3745A, AS3-3745A uses a single crypto map with two process IDs to
protect traffic flows to AS1 and AS3. AS3VPN, 10 Protects Traffic to AS1 (endpoint 200.1.1.9),
references ACL101 for crypto-protected traffic and IPsec transform "ivdf3-1". AS3VPN, 20
Protects Traffic to AS3 (endpoint 200.1.1.5), references ACL102 for crypto-protected traffic and
IPsec transform "ivdf3-1". AS2-3745 uses a relative strong transform, AES cipher with SHA1
HMAC authentication. PFS is also configured to refresh the symmetric transform key each time
an IPsec SA is negotiated.

Example 3-8 *Site-to-Site VPN Configuration on AS3-3745A*

```
1   AS3-3745A#show run
2   !
3   crypto IPsec transform-set ivdf3-1 esp-aes esp-sha-hmac
4   crypto map AS3VPN 10 IPsec-isakmp
5    set peer 200.1.1.9
6    set transform-set ivdf3-1
7    match address 101
8    set pfs group5
9   crypto map AS3VPN 20 IPsec-isakmp
10   set peer 200.1.1.5
11   set transform-set ivdf3-1
12   match address 102
13   set pfs group5
14  access-list 101 permit ip 213.0.0.0 0.255.255.255 211.0.0.0 0.255.255.255
```

continues

Example 3-8 *Site-to-Site VPN Configuration on AS3-3745A (Continued)*

```
15 access-list 102 permit ip 213.0.0.0 0.255.255.255 212.0.0.0 0.255.255.255
16 !
17 interface HSSI1/0
18  ip address 200.1.1.10 255.255.255.252
19  encapsulation HDLC
20  crypto map AS3VPN
21 interface HSSI2/0
22  ip address 200.1.1.6 255.255.255.252
23  encapsulation HDLC
24  crypto map AS3VPN
```

Verifying Cisco IOS Site-to-Site IPsec VPN Operation

Now that we have configured a full mesh of IPsec VPN tunnels between AS#1, AS#2, and AS#3, we must take some basic precautionary measures to guarantee that the VPN is operating successfully:

Step 1   Verify the establishment of ISAKMP SAs.

Step 2   Verify the establishment of IPsec SAs.

Step 3   Verify that basic network connectivity has been established over the VPN.

Step 4   Verify that the crypto engine is actively participating in IPsec and that protected traffic is being encrypted and decrypted.

Step 5   Check physical interface statistics for errors.

Examples 3-4 through 3-7 provide examples of these verification tasks on AS1-7304A in Figure 3-2. First, we verify that an ISAKMP SA has been successfully established. Example 3-4 confirms that there are indeed two ISAKMP SAs established to AS2-3745A and AS3-3745A. Note that these SAs are in "QM_IDLE" state, meaning that the ISAKMP SA is authenticated and can be used for subsequent Quick Mode (Phase 2) exchanges. The ISAKMP SA can exist in a number of other states. These states are described in Table 3-1 for ISAKMP SA negotiation in Main Mode.

Table 3-1   *ISAKMP SA States for IKE Main Mode SA Negotiation*

IKE SA State (Main Mode)	Description
MM_NO_STATE	The ISAKMP SA has been created, but nothing else has happened yet. It is "larval" at this stage—there is no state.
MM_SA_SETUP	The peers have agreed on parameters for the ISAKMP SA.
MM_KEY_EXCH	The peers have exchanged Diffie-Hellman public keys and have generated a shared secret. The ISAKMP SA remains unauthenticated.
MM_KEY_AUTH	The ISAKMP SA has been authenticated. If the router initiated this exchange, this state transitions immediately to QM_IDLE, and a Quick Mode exchange begins.

Though the SA described in Example 3-4 was negotiated using Main Mode, Aggressive Mode could have been used instead. Table 3-2 presents the ISAKMP SA states and their descriptions for SAs negotiated with Aggressive Mode. Note that in Table 3-2, there are inherently less states described for Aggressive Mode, because Aggressive Mode involves fewer message exchanges than does Main Mode.

Table 3-2   *ISAKMP SA States for IKE Aggressive Mode Negotiation*

IKE SA State (Aggressive Mode)	Description
AG_NO_STATE	The ISAKMP SA has been created, but nothing else has happened yet. It is "larval" at this stage—there is no state.
AG_INIT_EXCH	The peers have done the first exchange in Aggressive Mode, but the SA is not authenticated.
AG_AUTH	The peers have done the first exchange in Aggressive Mode, but the SA is not authenticated.

Example 3-9   *Verification of ISAKMP SAs for AS1-7304A*

```
AS1-7304A#show crypto isakmp sa
dst            src            state          conn-id slot
200.1.1.10     200.1.1.9      QM_IDLE              2   0
200.1.1.1      200.1.1.2      QM_IDLE              1   0
```

Once we can verify that Phase 1 SAs are established (by examining the output listed in Example 3-4), we are then ready to verify the establishment of IPsec SAs. Example 3-5 provides output needed to verify several important elements of Phase 2 SA establishment:

- The IPsec VPN Peer Address for the SA (200.1.1.2 for AS1VPN process 10 and 200.1.1.10 for AS1VPN process 20).

- The crypto-protected IPsec address sets specified in the Crypto ACLs for this SA (211.0.0.0/8->212.0.0.0/8 for AS1VPN process 10 and 211.0.0.0/8->213.0.0.0/8 for AS1VPN process 20).

- Inbound SA information, including IPsec transform used, crypto map used, initialization value (IV), and replay information. Note that there are fields for ESP, PCP, and Authentication Header (AH)—only the ESP fields are populated because there is no AH specified in the transform set for this IPsec SA.

- Outbound SA information, including IPsec Transform used, crypto map used, IV, and replay information. Note that there are fields for both ESP, PCP, and AH—only the ESP fields are populated as there is no AH specified in the transform set for this IPsec SA.

- The peering encryption/decryption activity for this security association.

> **NOTE** These statistics will change to match the crypto engine statistics listed in Example 3-7 after traffic is sent across the tunnel in Example 3-6.

Example 3-10 *Verification of IPsec SAs for AS1-7304A*

```
1   AS1-7304A#show crypto IPsec sa
2
3   interface: HSSI1/0
4       Crypto map tag: AS1VPN, local addr. 200.1.1.1
5      protected vrf:
6      local  ident (addr/mask/prot/port): (211.0.0.0/255.0.0.0/0/0)
7      remote ident (addr/mask/prot/port): (212.0.0.0/255.0.0.0/0/0)
8      current_peer: 200.1.1.2:500
9        PERMIT, flags={origin_is_acl,}
10     #pkts encaps: 0, #pkts encrypt: 0, #pkts digest: 0
11     #pkts decaps: 0, #pkts decrypt: 0, #pkts verify: 0
12     #pkts compressed: 0, #pkts decompressed: 0
13     #pkts not compressed: 0, #pkts compr. failed: 0
14     #pkts not decompressed: 0, #pkts decompress failed: 0
15     #send errors 1, #recv errors 0
16
17       local crypto endpt.: 200.1.1.1, remote crypto endpt.: 200.1.1.2
18       path mtu 1500, media mtu 1500
19       current outbound spi: 770BFB0E
20       inbound esp sas:
21        spi: 0xBAB54AEB(3132443371)
22          transform: esp-aes esp-sha-hmac ,
23          in use settings ={Tunnel, }
24          slot: 0, conn id: 2000, flow_id: 7, crypto map: AS1VPN
25
26          crypto engine type: Software, engine_id: 1
27          sa timing: remaining key lifetime (k/sec): (4439346/3318)
28          ike_cookies: 3A2297BC 4BED61BF 7571B28B 40217AB8
29          IV size: 16 bytes
30          replay detection support: Y
31
32       inbound ah sas:
33
34       inbound pcp sas:
35       outbound esp sas:
36        spi: 0x770BFB0E(1997273870)
37          transform: esp-aes esp-sha-hmac ,
38          in use settings ={Tunnel, }
39          slot: 0, conn id: 2001, flow_id: 8, crypto map: AS1VPN
40          crypto engine type: Software, engine_id: 1
41          sa timing: remaining key lifetime (k/sec): (4439347/3316)
42          ike_cookies: 3A2297BC 4BED61BF 7571B28B 40217AB8
```

Example 3-10 *Verification of IPsec SAs for AS1-7304A (Continued)*

```
43          IV size: 16 bytes
44          replay detection support: Y
45
46       outbound ah sas:
47
48       outbound pcp sas:
49
50 interface: HSSI2/0
51    Crypto map tag: AS1VPN, local addr. 200.1.1.9
52    protected vrf:
53    local  ident (addr/mask/prot/port): (211.0.0.0/255.0.0.0/0/0)
54    remote ident (addr/mask/prot/port): (213.0.0.0/255.0.0.0/0/0)
55    current_peer: 200.1.1.10:500
56     PERMIT, flags={origin_is_acl,}
57    #pkts encaps: 0, #pkts encrypt: 0, #pkts digest: 0
58    #pkts decaps: 0, #pkts decrypt: 0, #pkts verify: 0
59    #pkts compressed: 0, #pkts decompressed: 0
60    #pkts not compressed: 0, #pkts compr. failed: 0
61    #pkts not decompressed: 0, #pkts decompress failed: 0
62    #send errors 6, #recv errors 0
63
64       local crypto endpt.: 200.1.1.9, remote crypto endpt.: 200.1.1.10
65       path mtu 1500, media mtu 1500
66       current outbound spi: E60B73DB
67       inbound esp sas:
68        spi: 0x1A397721(439973665)
69          transform: esp-aes esp-sha-hmac ,
70          in use settings ={Tunnel, }
71          slot: 0, conn id: 2002, flow_id: 9, crypto map: AS1VPN
72          crypto engine type: Software, engine_id: 1
73          sa timing: remaining key lifetime (k/sec): (4594078/3450)
74          ike_cookies: BB9827E5 847ADAE6 4ED69C6A 7546D684
75          IV size: 16 bytes
76          replay detection support: Y
77
78       inbound ah sas:
79
80       inbound pcp sas:
81       outbound esp sas:
82        spi: 0xE60B73DB(3859510235)
83          transform: esp-aes esp-sha-hmac ,
84          in use settings ={Tunnel, }
85          slot: 0, conn id: 2003, flow_id: 10, crypto map: AS1VPN
86          crypto engine type: Software, engine_id: 1
87          sa timing: remaining key lifetime (k/sec): (4594079/3450)
88          ike_cookies: BB9827E5 847ADAE6 4ED69C6A 7546D684
89          IV size: 16 bytes
```

continues

Example 3-10 *Verification of IPsec SAs for AS1-7304A (Continued)*

```
90       replay detection support: Y
91
92    outbound ah sas:
93
94    outbound pcp sas:
```

In Example 3-6, we will attempt to send traffic across both IPsec VPN tunnels to the remote peers on AS2-3745A and AS3-3745A, respectively. First, we display the crypto-protected address spaces by displaying the ACLs referenced in the crypto map. Next, we send 100 ICMP echo-requests to both peers. Note that in both cases, we drop the first ICMP packet during IKE and IPsec SA negotiation.

Example 3-11 *Verification of Connectivity along the Crypto Path*

```
1  AS1-7304A#show access-list 102
2  Extended IP access list 102
3      10 permit ip host 201.1.1.1 host 202.1.1.1
4  AS1-7304A#show access-list 103
5  Extended IP access list 103
6      10 permit ip host 201.1.1.1 host 203.1.1.1
7  AS1-7304A#ping
8  Protocol [ip]:
9  Target IP address: 202.1.1.1
10 Repeat count [5]: 100
11 Datagram size [100]:
12 Timeout in seconds [2]:
13 Extended commands [n]: y
14 Source address or interface: 201.1.1.1
15 Type of service [0]:
16 Set DF bit in IP header? [no]:
17 Validate reply data? [no]:
18 Data pattern [0xABCD]:
19 Loose, Strict, Record, Timestamp, Verbose[none]:
20 Sweep range of sizes [n]:
21 Type escape sequence to abort.
22 Sending 100, 100-byte ICMP Echos to 202.1.1.1, timeout is 2 seconds:
23 Packet sent with a source address of 201.1.1.1
24
25 .!!!!!!!!!!!!!!!!!!!!!!!!!!!!!!!!!!!!!!!!!!!!!!!!!!!!!!!!!!!!!!!!!!!!!!!!
26 !!!!!!!!!!!!!!!!!!!!!!!!!!!!!!!!
27 Success rate is 99 percent (99/100), round-trip min/avg/max = 44/46/48 ms
28 AS1-7304A#ping
29 Protocol [ip]:
30 Target IP address: 203.1.1.1
31 Repeat count [5]: 100
32 Datagram size [100]:
```

Example 3-11 *Verification of Connectivity along the Crypto Path (Continued)*

```
33 Timeout in seconds [2]:
34 Extended commands [n]: y
35 Source address or interface: 201.1.1.1
36 Type of service [0]:
37 Set DF bit in IP header? [no]:
38 Validate reply data? [no]:
39 Data pattern [0xABCD]:
40 Loose, Strict, Record, Timestamp, Verbose[none]:
41 Sweep range of sizes [n]:
42 Type escape sequence to abort.
43 Sending 100, 100-byte ICMP Echos to 203.1.1.1, timeout is 2 seconds:
44 Packet sent with a source address of 201.1.1.1
45 .!!!!!!!!!!!!!!!!!!!!!!!!!!!!!!!!!!!!!!!!!!!!!!!!!!!!!!!!!!!!!!!!!!!!!!
46 !!!!!!!!!!!!!!!!!!!!!!!!!!!!!!!!!
47 Success rate is 99 percent (99/100), round-trip min/avg/max = 44/46/52 ms
```

Once we have successfully sent traffic to the remote crypto endpoints, we must then verify that it was successfully encrypted by the IPsec crypto engine. Example 3-7 provides the active IKE and IPsec SAs resident in the crypto engine for AS1-7304A. Note that the SAs with IDs 1 and 2 have not increased their packet count. This is expected, because these are the ISAKMP SAs (the same ones previously displayed in Example 3-4). Because IPsec SAs are unidirectional, we confirm that there are 4 SAs present in AS1-7304A's SADB:

■ SA ID #2000: Inbound SA to AS2-3745A

■ SA ID #2001: Outbound SA from AS2-3745A

■ SA ID #2002: Inbound SA from AS3-3745A

■ SA ID #2003: Outbound SA to AS3-3745A

We can confirm that the SA from AS1-7304A is actively encrypting echo requests to AS2-374A (99/100 corresponds to the success rate of Example 3-6) and that the SA received from AS2-3745A is actively decrypting the echo replies sent from AS2-3745A to AS1-7304A (also 99/100, corresponding to the success rate of Example 3-6). The same behavior is confirmed for the two SAs built between AS1-7304A and AS3-3745A (Example 3-7, SA ID #2002 and #2003).

Example 3-12 *Crypto Engine Verification*

```
1  AS1-7304A#show crypto engine connections active
2
3    ID Interface      IP-Address    State  Algorithm           Encrypt  Decrypt
4     1 Se0/0.12       200.1.1.1     set    HMAC_SHA+3DES_56_C        0        0
5     2 Se0/0.13       200.1.1.9     set    HMAC_SHA+3DES_56_C        0        0
6  2000 Se0/0.12       200.1.1.1     set    HMAC_SHA+AES_CBC          0       99
```

continues

Example 3-12 *Crypto Engine Verification (Continued)*

```
7  2001 Se0/0.12      200.1.1.1     set    HMAC_SHA+AES_CBC        99        0
8  2002 Se0/0.13      200.1.1.9     set    HMAC_SHA+AES_CBC         0       99
9  2003 Se0/0.13      200.1.1.9     set    HMAC_SHA+AES_CBC        99        0
```

Site-to-Site Architectural Overview over a Routed Domain

The design considerations of a site-to-site IPsec VPN change considerably once the underlying transit media changes. Consider the preceding site-to-site IPsec VPN example—how would our design change if we were to replace the existing dedicated DS-3 links between each AS with DS-3 uplinks to an Internet service provider? Network designers face the challenge of dealing with multicast traffic in the crypto switching path.

Multicast traffic, including Interior Gateway Protocal (IGP) multicast hellos and multicast data feeds, cannot be sent natively across an IPsec VPN tunnel. Instead, the multicast data must be encapsulated with unicast header (such as IP generic routing encapsulation (GRE)) before being presented to the IPsec crypto engine.

Typically, these design considerations have encouraged the use of leased-line connectivity for VPN extension and the insertion of GRE tunnels through the IPsec tunnel (commonly referred to as IPsec+GRE) to accommodate the multicast traffic associated with the routing protocol updates and hellos. The need for enterprise connectivity extension across intermediate routed domains is growing rapidly. Two common enterprise IPsec deployments that are driving this growth are corporate extranet deployments and RAVPN deployments.

Consider the following example in which a large automotive manufacturer wants to securely extend connectivity from its corporate headquarters network to a series of smaller home offices over an independently-maintained routed domain, such as the Internet. The smaller branch offices consist of a number of routed nodes and, as such, would benefit from getting Route Processor (RP) updates from the campus network. Figure 3-3 demonstrates how the addition of a site-to-site IPsec VPN across the independently maintained routed domain would preclude the smaller home offices from exchanging RP updates with the campus network at the corporate HQ.

Figure 3-3   *IPsec RAVPN Extension to Small Home Office over the Internet*

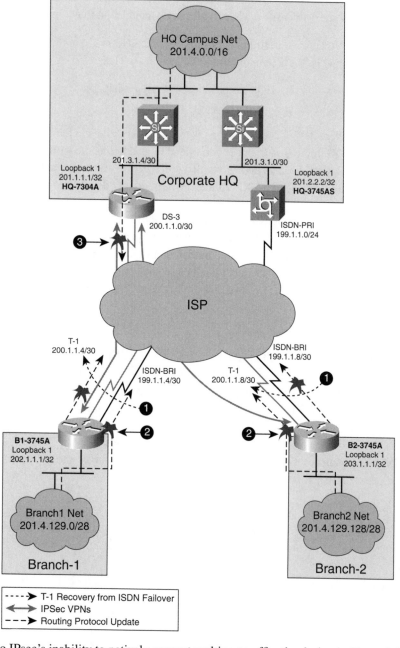

Due to IPsec's inability to natively encrypt multicast traffic, the design in Figure 3-3 presents the following design considerations:

- When the branches recover from Integrated Services Digital Network (ISDN) failover, routing protocol updates to from Branch1 and Branch2 will not be encrypted. In this scenario, IGP updates are multicast-based and will not be included in the crypto switching path.

- Any changes that occur in Branch1 Net and Branch2 Net will trigger RP update information to the corporate HQ. These updates will be sent in the clear.

- Any changes within the 'HQ Campus Net' will trigger RP updates to the branches that will be sent in the clear.

The solution to these design considerations is to add GRE tunnels to the IPsec VPN implementation. RP traffic between the corporate HQ and branch networks will then be encapsulated with GRE headers and forwarded in the crypto switching path across the ISP network. We will discuss IPsec+GRE architectures in greater detail later in this chapter.

Consider the following example in which a corporation, a large global financial organization, wants to allow extranet connectivity to its partners. The primary use of this extranet connection is to stream multicast data containing video and market information to decision makers within the global financial organization. This must be done securely, and with confidentiality. The insertion of an independently-maintained routed domain between the corporate extranet partner and the global financial organization breaks the multicast tree between the two parties, as illustrated in Figure 3-4.

The extranet model breaks multicast in two areas. First, underling media is not configured to support peripheral interface manager (PIM) or multicast routing. Therefore, even without IPsec, the multicast tree would never form properly with this deployment. Second, assuming that the multicast tree could be established, IPsec would fail to send multicast flow in ciphered format. Again, the addition of GRE to the corporate extranet would allow extension of PIM traffic across the Internet. Additionally, because the PIM updates are encapsulated in GRE prior to encryption, the PIM packets encapsulated in GRE would be processed in the crypto switching path and forwarded securely across the IPsec VPN.

NOTE   The V3PN solution outlines a VPN architecture that accommodates voice and video over IPsec. Because IP multicast is a key component of many voice and video streaming technologies, V3PN requires the use of IPsec+GRE. For more information on V3PN, please refer to the following documentation on CCO:

http://www.cisco.com/en/US/partner/netsol/ns340/ns394/ns171/ns241/networking_solutions_sub_solution_home.html

Figure 3-4 *Corporate Extranet Connection using Internet Uplinks and IPsec VPNs*

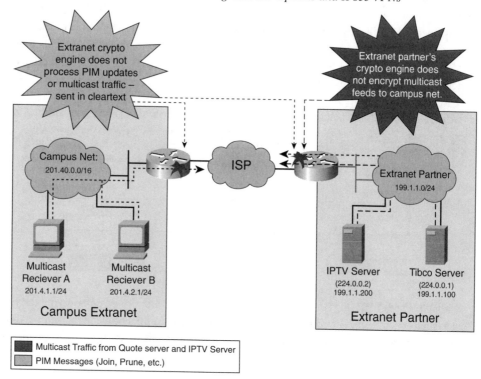

Site-to-Site IPsec VPN Deployments and GRE (IPsec+GRE)

At the core of IPsec is point-to-point functionality, which is not suited for all of today's IP communications. Indeed, many of today's voice and video applications require point-to-multipoint connectivity. As such, they leverage IP multicast techniques to selectively flood data to interested parties. Traditionally, IP multicast traffic has not effectively been passed through the crypto switching path on IPsec routers. As we have discussed, this precludes users from encrypting multicast applications such as multicast voice (hoot-n-holler), multicast video (IPTV), and routing protocols (OSPF, ISIS, RIP, EIGRP). The current solution for accommodating these types of traffic in cipher-text is IPsec+GRE.

Site-to-Site IPsec+GRE Architectural Overview

The IPsec+GRE model is used most commonly when there are traffic types that require confidentiality which are not traditionally suited for IPsec point-to-point traffic. IP multicast–based applications such as routing protocols that use multicast updates and multicast applications for streaming voice and video over IP would fall in to this category. Through the use of GRE, these multicast traffic types can be represented (encapsulated with a unicast GRE header) in a format acceptable to the IPsec crypto engine. Figure 3-5 illustrates the process of encrypting a multicast data feed with IPsec+GRE. Note that the original IP multicast header will not present an IP packet format acceptable for IPsec direct encapsulation. Because of this, GRE is used to encapsulate the multicast header and payload with a unicast header, resulting in a packet that can then be encapsulated with either ESP or AH. The GRE header and original IP multicast header will be encrypted as they are both part of the ESP-protected payload.

Figure 3-5 *Multicast packet GRE encapsulation (IP Multicast encapsulated GRE encapsulated in ESP)*

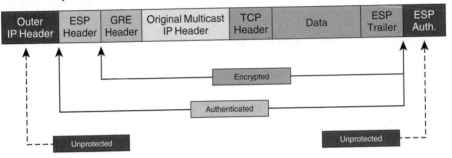

Although IPsec+GRE does provide a wider scope of confidentiality when applying the ESP encapsulation, and enables confidentiality for additional IP applications, increased maximum transmission unit (MTU) sizes of encapsulated packets become an increased design concern.

Increased Packet Size and Path MTU Considerations

Packets continue to get larger and larger as continuous layers of encapsulation are added to the original IP payload. For example, a IP encapsulated RTP packet for voice of 64-bytes in length grows to approximately 128 bytes after it is encapsulated in RTP (12 bytes), UDP (8 bytes), IP (20 bytes), and GRE (24 bytes), and to 184 bytes after the GRE-encapsulated RTP packet is encapsulated again with an ESP header, padding and authentication fields, and trailer (subtotal of approximately 56 bytes). Increasing packet sizes in this fashion also increases the chances that the packet will be fragmented after it has been encrypted, as would be the case if the encrypted packet exceeds the MTU of a link somewhere in the path between the two VPN endpoints. This can cause problems on the decrypting router, which will attempt to decrypt the fragmented packets in the process switching path (without hardware assist), causing scalability issues in terms of performance. Path MTU discovery can be deployed in conjunction with Cisco IOS's IPsec prefragmentation, enabling the encrypting router to dynamically determine the smallest MTU of the path between VPN endpoints. The encrypting VPN router is then capable of fragmenting to the appropriate MTU for the path on a per-SA basis using IPsec prefragmentation, assuring that the fragmentation of IPsec packets always occurs prior to encryption and is therefore done in the fast path.

> **NOTE**   Common fragmentation issues in IPsec VPNs are discussed in detail in Chapter 4,"
> Common IPsec VPN Issues." Available solutions for fragmenting prior to encryption, including
> path MTU discovery and IPsec prefragmentation, are also discussed in Chapter 4.

GRE and Weighted Fair Queuing

Some quality of service (QoS) techniques, such as weighted fair queuing (WFQ), perform
conversation hashing decisions based on the original source and destination IP address, which can
be ubiquified after IPsec or GRE encapsulation. While DiffServ markings are copied to the outer
IP header in tunnel mode IPsec, the original source and destination are not carried forward into
outer IP header. In order to appropriately execute hashing decisions in WFQ operations, packets
must therefore be classified prior to encapsulation. Cisco IOS supports IPsec QoS pre-classify
functionality on IOS VPN endpoints to assure that flow and conversation-based queuing decisions
can be executed accurately in IPsec VPN environments.

QoS and the IPsec Anti-replay Window

Altering the scheduling of packets before IPsec processing (as is the case with QoS pre-classify)
conflicts with sequencing schemes native to IPsec that are used for anti-replay protection. Cisco
IOS offers IPsec QoS Pre-Classify, which allows packets to be queued prior to ESP, AH, or GRE
encapsulation. Alternatively, antireplay windows can be increased to ensure that IPsec packets are
received within the antireplay window even when reordered and delayed due to queuing decisions
on nodes between IPsec VPN endpoints. When deploying QoS in vendor-diverse environments, it
is recommended that the operation be monitored to ensure that packet reordering does not conflict
with antireplay functions native to IPsec.

Site-to-Site IPsec+GRE Sample Configurations

Thus far, we have introduced the requirement of unicast presentation of data flows to the IPsec
crypto engine. In this section, we will discuss working IPsec+GRE configuration procedures,
examples, and verification techniques to use when encapsulating multicast traffic in with a unicast
header so that it can be processed with encrypted with IPsec.

Cisco IOS Site-to-Site IPsec+GRE Configuration

We will now alter the configurations that we built in Examples 3-1 through 3-3 to include GRE
encapsulation prior to the encapsulation of ESP. The IPsec transform and ISAKMP polices will
remain consistent with Examples 3-1 through 3-3, as will the some of the crypto map
configuration elements, such as the PFS and peering configurations. However, other crypto map
configuration elements, such as the crypto ACLs, will change to accommodate GRE traffic. We
will also demonstrate IOS QoS for IPsec VPNs by configuring the routers to classify packets prior
to GRE encapsulation and crypto processing. The topology used for these configurations is

depicted in Figure 3-2, but instead of native IPsec ESP tunnels, the ESP-encapsulated point-to-point GRE tunnels are used between the edge routers of AS#1, AS#2, and AS#3.

Example 3-8 illustrates some of the configuration changes made to AS1-7304A to accommodate IPsec+GRE. One of the most important differences in this configuration compared to Example 3-1 is the change in the crypto ACLs. Note that in Example 3-8, the crypto ACLs protect GRE traffic from the GRE tunnel source and destination address from AS1-7304A to AS2-3745A and AS3-3745A, respectively. This will effectively encrypt all traffic passing over the GRE tunnels from AS1-7304A to AS2-3745A and AS3-3745A.

In addition to the crypto ACL change on ASS1-7304A, several measures are taken to guarantee that encrypted packets are not fragmented. AS1-7304A's crypto engine will attempt to fragment packets to the path MTU (discovered through path MTU discovery between the two VPN endpoints) of the appropriate SA in the SADB. Additionally, AS1-7304A is configured to set the DF bit in the outer IP header of the encrypted fragments, effectively ensuring that network nodes between the two crypto endpoints are not able to fragment encrypted messages while in transit.

Example 3-13 *Site-to-Site VPN Configuration on AS1-7301A*

```
1   AS1-7304A#show run
2   !
3   crypto df-bit set
4   !
5   crypto IPsec fragmentation before-encryption
6   !
7   !
8   access-list 101 permit gre host 201.1.1.1 host 202.1.1.1
9   access-list 102 permit gre host 201.1.1.1 host 203.1.1.1
10  !
11  interface Tunnel12
12   ip address 200.1.12.1 255.255.255.252
13   qos pre-classify
14   tunnel source 201.1.1.1
15   tunnel destination 202.1.1.1
16  !
17  interface Tunnel13
18   ip address 200.1.13.1 255.255.255.252
19   qos pre-classify
20   tunnel source 201.1.1.1
21   tunnel destination 203.1.1.1
22  !
23  interface Loopback1
24   ip address 201.1.1.1 255.255.255.255
25  !
```

Example 3-9 provides the IPsec+GRE configuration for the IPsec VPN gateway for AS2. Like AS1-7304A, AS2-3745A is configured to protect all GRE-encapsulated data from a local GRE tunnel source to the appropriate GRE tunnel endpoints on AS1-7304A and AS3-3745A. AS2-3745A also is configured to prevent fragmentation after encryption and to classify packets with QoS prior to encryption.

Example 3-14 *Site-to-Site VPN Configuration on AS2-3745A*

```
1  AS2-3745A#show run
2  !
3  crypto df-bit set
4  !
5  crypto IPsec fragmentation before-encryption
6  !
7  !
8  access-list 101 permit gre host 202.1.1.1 host 201.1.1.1
9  access-list 102 permit gre host 202.1.1.1 host 203.1.1.1
10 !
11 interface Tunnel12
12  ip address 200.1.12.2 255.255.255.252
13  qos pre-classify
14  tunnel source 202.1.1.1
15  tunnel destination 201.1.1.1
16 !
17 interface Tunnel23
18  ip address 200.1.23.1 255.255.255.252
19  qos pre-classify
20  tunnel source 202.1.1.1
21  tunnel destination 203.1.1.1
22 !
23 interface Loopback1
24  ip address 202.1.1.1 255.255.255.255
25 !
```

```
Example 3-10 provides the IPsec+GRE configuration for the IPsec VPN gateway for AS3. Like
AS1-7304A, AS3-3745A is configured to protect all GRE-encapsulated data from a local GRE
tunnel source to the appropriate GRE tunnel endpoints on AS1-7304A and AS2-3745A. AS3-3745A
also is configured to prevent fragmentation after encryption and to classify packets with
QoS prior to encryption.
Example 3-10: Site-to-Site VPN Configuration on AS3-3745A
1  AS3-3745A#show run
2  !
3  crypto df-bit set
4  !
5  crypto IPsec fragmentation before-encryption
6  !
7  !
8  access-list 101 permit gre host 203.1.1.1 host 201.1.1.1
9  access-list 102 permit gre host 203.1.1.1 host 202.1.1.1
10 !
```

continues

Example 3-14 *Site-to-Site VPN Configuration on AS2-3745A (Continued)*

```
11 interface Tunnel13
12  ip address 200.1.13.2 255.255.255.252
13  qos pre-classify
14  tunnel source 203.1.1.1
15  tunnel destination 201.1.1.1
16 !
17 interface Tunnel23
18  ip address 200.1.23.2 255.255.255.252
19  qos pre-classify
20  tunnel source 203.1.1.1
21  tunnel destination 202.1.1.1
22 !
23 interface Loopback1
24  ip address 203.1.1.1 255.255.255.255
25 !
```

Verification of IPsec+GRE Tunnel Establishment

Verifying an IPsec+GRE tunnel begins with the same steps that are taken in the verification of a standard IPsec tunnel. Verification of ISAKMP and IPsec SAs must be done, and basic connectivity through the GRE tunnel must be established. However, when GRE is added to the VPN, steps must be taken to verify tunneled connectivity prior to the addition of IPsec:

- Verification of tunnel establishment

- Verification of RP (including PIM) adjacencies through the tunnel

Once these basic tunneling operations have been verified, they must be re-verified after the addition of IPsec. In addition to that re-verification, the administrator should also verify the establishment of ISAKMP SA, IPsec SA, and that traffic passed over the IPsec+GRE tunnel is actually being encrypted, as we explored in Examples 3-4 through 3-7. Example 3-8 demonstrates the non-crypto GRE verification steps on AS1-7304A (prior to the addition of the crypto map to the physical interface) and the verification of the full IPsec+GRE tunnel (after the crypto map has been applied to the physical interface). Again, note that all EIGRP traffic is kept confidential from the OSPF core via IPsec processing of all GRE traffic (which in this case includes all EIGRP traffic - 192.168.x.x/16 address space) between each endpoint. Example 3-11 illustrates several typical diagnostic steps needed to verify the establishment of a GRE tunnel and of RP adjacencies using that GRE tunnel, including:

- Verify GRE tunnel establishment and interface status.

- Verify basic connectivity through the GRE tunnel.

- Verify RP adjacencies across the GRE tunnel.

Example 3-15 *Verification of GRE Tunnels and Tunneled Routing Protocols on AS1-7304A*

```
1  AS1-7304A#show ip int brief
2  Interface            IP-Address      OK? Method Status              Protocol
3  FastEthernet0/0      unassigned      YES NVRAM  administratively down down
4  Serial0/0            unassigned      YES NVRAM  up                   up
5  Serial0/0.12         200.1.1.1       YES manual up                   up
6  Serial0/0.13         200.1.1.9       YES manual up                   up
7  Loopback0            201.1.1.1       YES manual up                   up
8  Loopback1            192.168.1.1     YES manual up                   up
9  Tunnel12             192.168.12.1    YES manual up                   up
10 Tunnel13             192.168.13.1    YES manual up                   up
11 AS1-7304A#ping 192.168.12.2
12
13 Type escape sequence to abort.
14 Sending 5, 100-byte ICMP Echos to 192.168.12.2, timeout is 2 seconds:
15 !!!!!
16 Success rate is 100 percent (5/5), round-trip min/avg/max = 32/34/36 ms
17 AS1-7304A#ping 192.168.13.2
18
19 Type escape sequence to abort.
20 Sending 5, 100-byte ICMP Echos to 192.168.13.2, timeout is 2 seconds:
21 !!!!!
22 Success rate is 100 percent (5/5), round-trip min/avg/max = 32/34/36 ms
23 AS1-7304A#show ip eigrp interfaces
24 IP-EIGRP interfaces for process 192
25
26                          Xmit Queue   Mean   Pacing Time   Multicast   Pending
27 Interface      Peers    Un/Reliable   SRTT   Un/Reliable   Flow Timer  Routes
28 Lo1              0          0/0         0        0/10          0           0
29 Tu12             1          0/0        736      71/2702       6362         0
30 Tu13             1          0/0        277      71/2702       3710         0
31 AS1-7304A#sh ip eigrp neighbors
32 IP-EIGRP neighbors for process 192
33 H   Address              Interface        Hold Uptime   SRTT   RTO  Q  Seq
34                                           (sec)         (ms)        Cnt Num
35 1   192.168.13.2         Tu13             12 00:18:36   277   5000  0  41
36 0   192.168.12.2         Tu12             12 00:19:01   736   5000  0  48
```

After we have verified the basic operation of the routing protocol adjacencies and updates over the GRE tunnels, we are ready to verify that the crypto engine is processing the GRE tunnel through which subsequent control and data plane traffic will traverse. The diagnostic output in Example 3-12 verifies that protected traffic (in this case *all* GRE traffic) is being processed by the crypto engine. This output reflects statistics after 100 pings are forwarded across each GRE (and subsequently IPsec) tunnel. Note that there are more than 100 packets processed by the crypto engine—these extra packets are GRE-tunneled packets used various control plan traffic including RP updates and adjacency maintenance.

Example 3-16 *Verification of crypto-processed traffic after crypto maps have been applied to physical interfaces that will protect all GRE traffic between the two GRE tunnel endpoints.*

```
AS1-7304A#sh crypto engine conn active

  ID Interface      IP-Address      State  Algorithm            Encrypt  Decrypt
   1 Se0/0.12       200.1.1.1       set    HMAC_SHA+3DES_56_C        0        0
   2 Se0/0.13       200.1.1.9       set    HMAC_SHA+3DES_56_C        0        0
2002 Se0/0.13       200.1.1.9       set    HMAC_SHA+AES_CBC          0      145
2003 Se0/0.13       200.1.1.9       set    HMAC_SHA+AES_CBC        146        0
2004 Se0/0.12       200.1.1.1       set    HMAC_SHA+AES_CBC          0      139
2005 Se0/0.12       200.1.1.1       set    HMAC_SHA+AES_CBC        139        0
```

TIP It is recommended that the administrator re-verify the steps taken in Example 3-11 to confirm the operation of GRE and RPs after the crypto map has been added. It is further recommended that the administrator verify the cryptographic elements added to the GRE tunnel using the techniques outlined in our discussion of site-to-site VPNs in Examples 3-4 through 3-7.

Hub-and-Spoke IPsec VPN Deployments

Most of today's enterprise class IPsec VPN deployments incorporate hub-and-spoke IPsec designs. These designs extend from the principles that we have discussed previously in this chapter, whether the situation describes the aggregation of native spoke IPsec VPNs at a hub IPsec aggregation point or the aggregation of IPsec+GRE VPNs at a hub IPsec and GRE concentrator. As the number of spoke connections increases, so do the number of design considerations surrounding the hub IPsec router. These include the following:

- **SA Scalability**—The number of security associations actively supported and dangling SA detection, elimination, and management capabilities. This is less of a concern on spokes as they will only maintain SAs relevant to hub connectivity. Hub SA maintenance becomes an issue as it must maintain an SADB comprehensive of all spoke VPN connectivity.

- **IPsec Tunnel Capacity**—In addition to the number of SAs that the endpoint's memory can accommodate, one must pay careful attention to the security policy of the tunnel itself and the impact on the CPU that this policy has. Selection of the strongest cryptographic suites comes with a cost of increased computational burden. IPsec VPN design at a hub router that concentrates IPsec VPNs with strong security policies must be sized to accommodate the computational overhead required for tunnel maintenance of the appropriate anticipated scale.

- **Crypto Path Switching Capacity**—The throughput, in packets per second (pps), of the traffic that is processed in the router's crypto (IPsec) switching path must also be considered. Or, if GRE is used, we must look at the throughput in (pps) of the GRE+IPsec switching path.

- **GRE Tunnel Maintenance Capacity**—Although most routers will support GRE encapsulation, they do not necessarily do it in the fast switching path (in hardware). When selecting a hub router that will be concentrating GRE tunnels, care must be taken to ensure that extensive GRE encapsulation and decapsulation does not limit throughput or overburden the hub's CPU.

- **Fragmentation Capabilities**—Because each spoke router in the network discovers the MTU en route to its destination, the amount of fragmented packets can potentially increase at IPsec aggregation points. Hub IPsec aggregation/concentration devices must be specified appropriately so as to handle potentially large amounts of fragmented packets sent from adjacent spoke IPsec peer endpoints.

Additionally, the urgency for HA at the hub router increases dramatically as additional spokes are reliant on the hub for connectivity to the enterprise's centrally located resources.

> **NOTE**   This section on hub-and-spoke architecture only discusses HA items directly relevant to the physical layout of the IPsec VPNs themselves. IPsec HA design optimization in IOS, ASA, and VPN3K appliances is discussed comprehensively in Chapters 6 through 10.

Hub-and-Spoke Architectural Overview

In this section, we will explore three common layouts for hub-and-spoke IPsec VPNs. The hub-and-spoke IPsec VPN model is one of the most commonly used and widely varied topologies in the IPsec VPN world today. Though the three models outlined in Figure 3-6 do not touch on all of these variations, we will use these three topologies as a framework for reviewing architectural considerations that are most commonly present in today's hub-and-spoke IPsec VPN designs.

Figure 3-6 *Hub-and-Spoke IPsec VPN Variations*

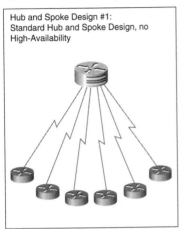
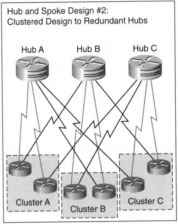
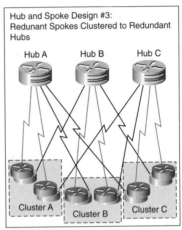

Standard Hub-and Spoke Design without High Availability

The simplest hub-and-spoke design consists of single-circuit, single-spoke connectivity to a hub router at a central facility, as described in the first design of Figure 3-6. This design, while simple from an architectural standpoint, does not allow much in the way of HA design enhancements, because this design is typically found in branch deployments that do not require high degrees of network uptime.

From a performance perspective, the design considerations are focused largely on the hub. Because the spoke devices are maintaining minimal IPsec VPN tunnels and GRE tunnels, the IPsec and GRE performance is likely to be at the platform maximum when stressed. This is not the case for the hub router, which is responsible for SA and GRE maintenance to all of the spoke routers. This poses several design issues that must be addressed at the hub:

- **SADB Scalability**—The hub router must have the appropriate amount of memory to accommodate the SADB for the whole hub/spoke deployment. Remember from our previous discussions in Chapter 2, "IPsec Fundamentals," that the number of IPsec SAs needed will be the number twice the number of IPsec connections plus one SA for each IKE channel.

- **Switching Capacity for IPsec Aggregation**—The hub router must have the appropriate amount of switching capacity (in pps) to support the performance requirements in the IPsec+GRE switching path.

- **Excessive Encrypt/Decrypt Action for Spoke-Spoke Traffic**— For spoke-spoke connectivity, the hub router will be decrypting traffic from the sending spoke and re-encrypting it before sending it to the destination spoke. For networks that have a substantial amount of spoke-spoke traffic, the hub router that has enough processing power to support substantial amounts of decrypt/re-encrypt behavior must be selected.

> **TIP** Cisco IOS offers Dynamic Multipoint VPN (DMVPN) features that support the dynamic, direct establishment of spoke-to-spoke SAs in hub-and-spoke deployments. When deployed effectively, this solution can dramatically improve the performance of hub-and-spoke IPsec VPN deployments because IPsec processing is partially transitioned from the hub router to the spokes themselves. DMVPN is discussed in greater detail in Chapter 8, "Handling Vendor Interoperability with High Availability."

- **Multicast Fanout**—In this design, the hub router is performing the multicast fanout for traffic to all of the spoke routers that are subscribed to the multicast group. For traffic profiles that have substantial amount of multicast traffic, the hub router must be capable of accommodating the appropriate amount of packet duplication, the encapsulation of those fanned-out packets in GRE, and the increased amount of IPsec processing that is required as those fanned-out packets are processed by the crypto engine.

Clustered Spoke Design to Redundant Hubs

The second design in Figure 3-6 describes the addition of two hub IPsec aggregation points into the design. This allows network designers to deploy redundancy in the spoke uplinks to the hub routers. It also allows network designers to address the design concerns raised in the first design of Figure 3-6. Deploying redundancy at the hub location of the IPsec hub-and-spoke network presents some key design advantages, including, but not limited to, the following:

- **Increased Tunnel Termination/Maintenance Capacity**—Using multiple hub routers decreases the amount of memory required for SA maintenance on a per-platform basis, because the SAs are spread across three aggregation points (as opposed being concentrated on only one). The distribution of hub processing capabilities also eases the computational burden in terms of IPsec VPN termination, GRE tunnel termination, and the decryption/re-encryption overhead of spoke-to-spoke communication discussed previously.

- **Increased Multicast Fanout Capacity**—Distributed Hub IPsec processing also presents two additional multicast fanout points to the design. This type of distribution at the multicast fanout points can dramatically improve the switching performance of the hub-and-spoke deployment, because computational resources for copying multicast packets, encapsulating them in GRE, and encrypting them are tripled at the aggregation points.

- **Load Balancing and Redundancy**—In addition to the redundancy provided to the spokes by the two redundant uplinks to their corresponding aggregation points, the correct deployment of redundant circuits allows for a primitive form of load balancing across the three aggregation points—Hubs A, B, and C. Each spoke terminates its primary uplinks on different hubs so that in a nonfailover scenario IPsec VPNs are distributed evenly across the three aggregation points. Each spoke's backup links are distributed in the same fashion, so as to provide the same load-balancing effect when there is a failover scenario at the spoke.

Redundant Clustered Spoke Design to Redundant Hubs

Design #3 in Figure 3-6 describes a topology similar to Design #2, but with redundant routers at the spoke. This is the most highly-available design discussed in this chapter, and it will lead us in to design concepts discussed in Chapters 6-10. It is also the most expensive of the three designs to deploy, as it doubles the amount of hardware to be purchased at the spoke level.

With respect to the design of the IPsec VPNs themselves, the addition of redundant spoke routers could boost performance of the IPsec VPN, especially if both IPsec tunnels were concurrently active and traffic from the spoke is load-balanced across the two redundant spoke routers. These benefits, however, although useful, are only local to the spoke itself, which is why it is more common to invest in redundancy and load-balancing improvements at the hub before adding it to the spokes. Additionally, large-scale deployment of redundant spoke routers will require more processing capability to accommodate increased IKE processing, or increased SADB capacity if a "hot" standby model is required (See Chapters 6-10 for design concepts surrounding IPsec HA in IOS).

Because of this, the primary benefit of adding an additional, redundant, router to a spoke in the greater hub/spoke design is redundancy at that particular branch. For this reason, it is most common to see only highly-available branches pursue this design, while other spokes are deployed using the framework we have discussed in Designs #1 or #2. The cost-benefit analysis of pursuing redundant uplinks and redundant routers at the spoke must be weighed carefully against the cost (both computational and monetary) of deployment. It is rare to see blanket rollouts of Designs #1, #2, or #3 shown in Figure 3-6. Instead, it is much more common to see designs that incorporate elements of all three designs on a per-spoke performance[en] and HA-requirement[en]basis.

Remote Access VPN Deployments

As workforces become increasingly mobile in nature, so changes the dynamics of a secure IP network. Remote Access VPN deployments have become the central focus of secure connectivity in enterprise mobility, allowing secure Layer 3 communications to any VPN endpoint that has an internet connection to the appropriate VPN concentrator. We've discussed some of the business drivers for enterprise adoption of RAVPN deployments during our introduction to VPNs in

Chapter 1. Now, we will explore some common architectures for delivering RAVPN services to the enterprise.

> **NOTE**   Cisco Systems Business Ready Teleworker Solutions fully outlines the business justification for RAVPN deployments. Please refer to the following resources on CCO for more information on Cisco Business Ready Teleworker Solutions:
>
> http://www.cisco.com/application/pdf/en/us/guest/netsol/ns241/c649/ ccmigration_09186a00801ea79d.pdf

RAVPN Architectural Overview

As we discussed in Chapter 1, "Introduction to VPN Technologies," the two core elements that comprise an RAVPN topology are VPN concentrators and VPN clients. These two elements communicate with one another over a predefined media at Layer 3 of the OSI Model. As such, these two entities can be connected over any media that will support Layer 3 between concentrator and client, including dial-up networks, Internet connections using DSL, and 802.11 wireless media. Because the underlying communications are relatively independent on the IPsec portion of the RAVPN, we will discuss clients and concentrators communicating with one another over a ubiquitous Internet connection, and discuss RAVPN design in greater detail in Chapter 10, "Further Architectural Options for IPsec."

RAVPN Clients

RAVPN Clients typically come in two general flavors, hardware-based clients and software-based clients. *Software-based VPN clients* run locally on the user's remote workstation or laptop, and they are used to connect to a centrally managed VPN concentrator, typically located on the enterprise campus. The strength of software-based VPN Clients is rooted in the mobility that they provide. When deployed on a user's laptop, a software-based VPN client can securely extend confidential communications from the campus to anywhere that a VPN client can access Layer 3 communications. Software-based VPN clients are therefore useful for tunneling data from centrally located campus resources to the end user. However, they do have limitations, and because of these limitations, the use of hardware-based VPN clients in some situations. Specifically, software-based VPN clients terminate VPN connectivity locally on teleworkers' laptops and do not allow for the secure networking of other Layer 3 devices at the remote end of the VPN (such as a hardware-based IP Phone) over that VPN. Additionally, software-based clients will not support the termination of GRE locally, and therefore they will not typically support multicast data flows. Hardware-based clients, though inherently less mobile, address many of the functional limitations found in software-based IPsec VPN clients.

Hardware-based VPN clients are typically found in small, remote locations that do not have dedicated connectivity to a central hub IPsec router. These devices are commonly found at home offices that have DSL- or cable-modem connectivity to the Internet. The hardware-based VPN client maintains the IPsec VPN (and GRE tunnel termination) to the concentrator, while allowing clear-text IP communications locally within the small home office or branch. Therefore, hardware-based VPN components add a networked element to the SOHO (small office, home office) or small branch environment that allows users to extend voice, video, and data securely from the campus.

In order to deliver both mobility and breadth of services to remote teleworkers, it is very common to see users deploy both software-based VPN clients and hardware-based VPN clients at the same time. Having the hardware-based VPN connectivity extends virtually all IP services available on the campus to relatively fixed remote locations. Software-based VPN communications allows users to extend communications in highly mobile scenarios. All of these services must be accommodated on the concentrator side of the VPN. For this reason, the variation in RAVPN topology is most commonly seen at the concentrator end of the design, which is what we will focus the remainder of this chapter's RAVPN discussion on.

Standalone VPN Concentrator Designs

Due to the nature of IPsec and firewalls, the placement of the VPN concentrator in a DMZ design is critical to the success of the greater RAVPN architecture. Figures 3-7 through 3-10 outline several DMZ topologies that we will use to explore common design issues which must be addressed in RAVPN implementation. Each of these designs pertains to a IPsec VPN concentrator deployment for effective termination of client IPsec VPN tunnels in an RAVPN environment.

VPN Concentrator on Outside Network with Single DMZ

The DMZ layout illustrated in Figure 3-7 is one of the most common, and most effective, designs in RAVPN/DMZ integration. This design allows for increased security, because inside traffic from the VPN concentrator is firewalled from the firewall's DMZ interface to its inside interface.

Additionally, the firewall can add an additional layer of proxy authentication AAA authentication in conjunction with an ACS server located on the inside network, offering a comprehensive authentication, authorization, and accounting solution for traffic types all the way up to Layer 7. The processing of traffic inbound from DMZ can be further inspected for network attacks using either the PIX IOS-based signature set or a compatible, more comprehensive, signature set maintained on an external Network Intrusion Detection Systems (NIDS) appliance.

As we will also see with the design in Figure 3-8, there are no IPsec-specific modifications that need to be added to the firewall ACL configuration. Likewise, there are no additional Network Address Translation (NAT) considerations to account for on the firewall. This design does, however, require marginally increased filtering capability on the firewall, as cleartext traffic from the IPsec VPN concentrator is now being processed on the DMZ interface on its way to the inside network.

Figure 3-7 *VPN Concentrator Placement in Single-DMZ Design*

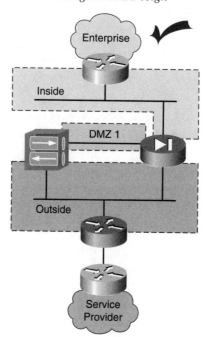

VPN Concentrator and Firewall in Parallel

Placing the VPN concentrator in parallel with the Firewall eliminates the possibility of human error when opening up holes in the Firewall ACL to allow IPsec traffic from inbound VPN clients to the concentrator (as with the design illustrated in Figure 3-10). Figure 3-8 provides an illustration of a standard DMZ design that places the VPN Concentrator in parallel with the firewall.

Additionally, this topology presents no computational overhead on the firewall for processing IPsec traffic in to the VPN concentrator. Instead, that traffic is focused solely on the VPN concentrator. Likewise, the concentrator is not burdened by non-VPN traffic, as would be the case if the concentrator were placed in series with the firewall on the outside network.

Figure 3-8 *Parallel VPN Concentrator and Firewall DMZ Design*

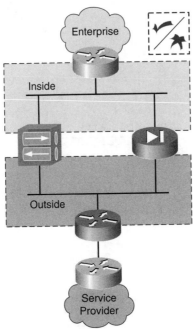

The parallel configuration described in the design of Figure 3-8 also simplifies the NAT configuration on both the firewall and DMZ. Although IPsec itself can accommodate environments where addresses are being translated, this topology eliminates the NAT processing of VPN traffic firewall and concentrator. Therefore, for RAVPN IPsec Tunnels, the need for vendor-specific IPsec extensions such as NAT-T (IPsec NAT Transparency) is avoided.

> **NOTE**   NAT can cause implementation issues in IPsec networks if not properly designed for. For more information concerning common issues related to NAT in IPsec networks, please refer to Chapter 4, "Common IPsec VPN Issues." Solutions for IPsec in NAT environments, such as IPsec NAT-T are also discussed in Chapter 4

VPN Concentrator with Dual DMZs to Firewall

Using two DMZ interfaces for inside and outside VPN traffic, as described in the design shown in Figure 3-9, can also be an effective means by which to integrate a VPN concentrator into a DMZ. This design should be deployed when increased protection of the VPN concentrator itself is desired. Designs similar to this one are also commonly found when the enterprise does not have control over the Internet gateway directly outside of the DMZ, as would be the case when the enterprise contracts with a service provider that wishes to maintain the Internet gateway itself. In such a case, the enterprise would rely on the firewall, as opposed to the Internet gateway, to switch packets to the appropriate directly connected interface. As a result, it would be the firewall's responsibility to forward VPN traffic the directly connected to DMZ1 interface and allowed, NAT'd (if necessary), enterprise traffic directly to the inside interface.

Figure 3-9 *VPN Concentrator with Dual DMZs to Firewall*

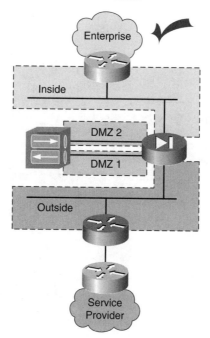

Locating the VPN concentrator's outside interface behind the DMZ inserts a layer of filtering, and authentication of IPsec traffic before the concentrator, thereby adding another layer of hardening to the design. There are also tradeoffs to the design, because the outside ACL of the firewall must be altered to allow ISAKMP, ESP, and AH traffic through to the concentrator. In addition to punching holes through the ACL to accommodate VPN traffic, this design also increases the computation overhead associated with VPN traffic on the firewall, because traffic is processed twice (once on the outside interface, and again as traffic is received from the concentrator on the second DMZ interface).

What to Avoid in DMZ/VPN Concentrator Topologies

We will use the design shown in Figure 3-10 to highlight a few things to avoid when positioning a VPN concentrator in a DMZ. The fourth design places the concentrator in a position that requires VPN traffic to be processed serially between the firewall and concentrator with little additional value. Although the concentrator is located in a more secure environment (Location A), the concentrator can be secured just as effectively by placing it in the DMZ. Additionally, when placing the concentrator in the DMZ, traffic can be sent directly from the outside interface to the concentrator itself without NAT. Alternatively the location in this design will likely require NAT, leading to a more complicated firewall configuration and increased processing overhead.

Figure 3-10 *What to Avoid in DMZ/VPN Concentrator Topologies*

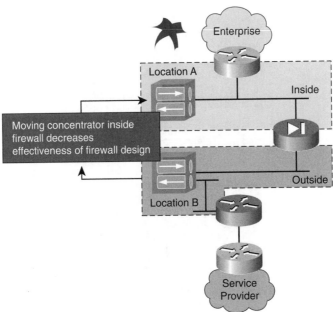

Locating the VPN concentrator serially outside of the firewall (moving the concentrator from Location A to Location B, shown in Example 3-10) can have an equally adverse effect. This type of design requires that all traffic be processed by the concentrator, as opposed to just the VPN traffic, leading to increased overhead. While this alteration eliminates the need to NAT inbound VPN traffic, it does place the concentrator in a relatively unsecured location, presenting the opportunity for denial of service (DoS) attacks for all network traffic destined to the enterprise (single point of failure).

Clustered VPN Concentrator Designs

The RAVPN designs we have discussed thus far only assume the use of a single VPN concentrator. However, all of these designs can be hardened further through the deployment of multiple concentrators in the appropriate location, commonly referred to as "clustering." The deployment of a VPN cluster offers redundancy locally at the concentrator level, and also allows for increased scalability in terms of the number of inbound IPsec VPN tunnels from VPN clients that the design can support. Figure 3-11 illustrates a typical clustered IPsec VPN concentrator deployment in a DMZ design.

Figure 3-11   *Clustered RAVPN Concentrator Deployment*

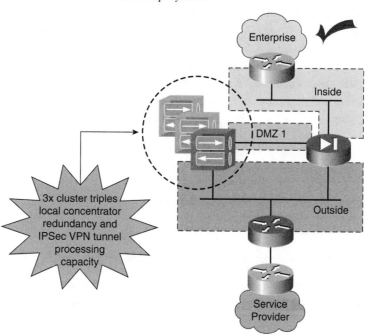

The clustered design presented in Figure 3-11 is a variation on the recommended RAVPN/DMZ shown in Figure 3-7. The altered design allows for triple redundancy relative to the original design, and it also allows the design to scale up to three times the amount of VPN tunnels during peak traffic hours for the remote access to central enterprise resources. We will discuss this design and several other effective designs for RAVPN High Availability in Chapter 9, "Solutions for Remote Access VPN High Availability."

Chapter Summary

In this chapter, we have discussed several prevalent IPsec VPN topologies, including the following:

- Site-to-site IPsec VPNs

- Site-to-site IPsec+GRE VPNs

- Hub-and-spoke IPsec VPN topologies

- Remote access VPN topologies

At this point, you should be familiar with the basic layout of the preceding topologies, because they will serve as the basis for the explanation of more advanced concepts such as local and geographic site-to-site IPsec HA and Remote Access VPN HA. Each of the preceding topologies is loosely grouped into a given design category, but you should be familiar with the design variants of each. For example, two important variations on a simple site-to-site IPsec topology are site-to-site IPsec VPN over a dedicated circuit and site-to-site IPsec VPN over a routed domain. The introduction of a routing protocol between the two crypto endpoints provides a material alteration to the VPN topology.

As with site-to-site IPsec VPN design variations, we have also covered several variations of hub-and-spoke IPsec VPN deployments, including the following:

- Standard hub-and spoke design (no hub redundancy)

- Clustered hub-and-spoke design to redundant hubs

- Clustered hub-and-spoke design to redundant hubs with redundant spokes

Our discussion in this chapter of the basic advantages to each of the preceding hub-and-spoke variations will provide useful context when discussing resilient IPsec VPN design strategies in future chapters.

Finally, we have introduced several common DMZ designs with various IPsec VPN concentrator placement alternatives. These design alternatives included the following:

- Standalone VPN concentrator DMZ design

- Parallel VPN concentrator and firewall DMZ design

- Dual DMZ VPN concentrator design

- Serial VPN concentrator placement on inside firewall interface

At this point, you should have a basic familiarity with VPN concentrator placement in a firewalled DMZ design, as well as a basic understanding of the dangers of placing IPsec VPN concentrators serially inside a firewalled domain. We raised the advantages and disadvantages of each design in preparation for discussing remote access VPN HA concepts in Chapter 9,"Solutions for Remote Access VPN High Availability."

CISCO SYSTEMS

ISBN: 1-58705-267-9

Voice over IP Fundamentals
Second Edition

A systematic approach to understanding the basics of Voice over IP

Jonathan Davidson · James Peters · Manoj Bhatia
Satish Kalidindi · Sudipto Mukherjee

ciscopress.com

VoIP: An In-Depth Analysis

To create a proper network design, it is important to know all the caveats and inner workings of networking technology. This chapter explains many of the issues facing Voice over IP (VoIP) and ways in which Cisco addresses these issues.

Communications via the Public Switched Telephone Network (PSTN) has its own set of problems, which are covered in Chapter 1, "Overview of the PSTN and Comparisons to Voice over IP," and Chapter 2, "Enterprise Telephony Today." VoIP technology has many similar issues and a whole batch of additional ones. This chapter details these various issues and explains how they can affect packet networks.

The following issues are covered in this chapter:

- Delay/latency

- Jitter

- Pulse Code Modulation (PCM)

- Voice compression

- Echo

- Packet loss

- Voice activity detection

- Digital-to-analog conversion

- Tandem encoding

- Transport protocols

- Dial-plan design

Delay/Latency

VoIP *delay* or *latency* is characterized as the amount of time it takes for speech to exit the speaker's mouth and reach the listener's ear.

Three types of delay are inherent in today's telephony networks: *propagation delay*, *serialization delay*, and *handling delay*. Propagation delay is caused by the length a signal must travel via light in fiber or electrical impulse in copper-based networks. Handling delay—also called processing delay—defines many different causes of delay (actual packetization, compression, and packet switching) and is caused by devices that forward the frame through the network.

Serialization delay is the amount of time it takes to actually place a bit or byte onto an interface. Serialization delay is not covered in depth in this book because its influence on delay is relatively minimal.

Propagation Delay

Light travels through a vacuum at a speed of 186,000 miles per second, and electrons travel through copper or fiber at approximately 125,000 miles per second. A fiber network stretching halfway around the world (13,000 miles) induces a one-way delay of about 70 milliseconds (70 ms). Although this delay is almost imperceptible to the human ear, propagation delays in conjunction with handling delays can cause noticeable speech degradation.

Handling Delay

As mentioned previously, devices that forward the frame through the network cause handling delay. Handling delays can impact traditional phone networks, but these delays are a larger issue in packetized environments. The following paragraphs discuss the different handling delays and how they affect voice quality.

In the Cisco IOS VoIP product, the Digital Signal Processor (DSP) generates a speech sample every 10 ms when using G.729. Two of these speech samples (both with 10 ms of delay) are then placed within one packet. The packet delay is, therefore, 20 ms. An initial look-ahead of 5 ms occurs when using G.729, giving an initial delay of 25 ms for the first speech frame.

Vendors can decide how many speech samples they want to send in one packet. Because G.729 uses 10 ms speech samples, each increase in samples per frame raises the delay by 10 ms. In fact, Cisco IOS enables users to choose how many samples to put into each frame.

Cisco gave DSP much of the responsibility for framing and forming packets to keep router/gateway overhead low. The Real-Time Transport Protocol (RTP) header, for example, is placed on the frame in the DSP instead of giving the router that task.

Queuing Delay

A packet-based network experiences delay for other reasons. Two of these are the time necessary to move the actual packet to the output queue (packet switching) and queuing delay.

When packets are held in a queue because of congestion on an outbound interface, the result is *queuing delay*. Queuing delay occurs when more packets are sent out than the interface can handle at a given interval.

The actual queuing delay of the output queue is another cause of delay. You should keep this factor to less than 10 ms whenever you can by using whatever queuing methods are optimal for your network. This subject is covered in greater detail in Chapter 8, "Quality of Service."

The International Telecommunication Union Telecommunication Standardization Sector (ITU-T) G.114 recommendation specifies that for good voice quality, no more than 150 ms of one-way, end-to-end delay should occur, as shown in Figure 7-1. With the Cisco VoIP implementation, *two* routers with minimal network delay (back to back) use only about 60 ms of end-to-end delay. This leaves up to 90 ms of network delay to move the IP packet from source to destination.

Figure 7-1 *End-to-End Delay*

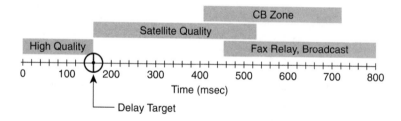

As shown in Figure 7-1, some forms of delay are longer, although accepted, because no other alternatives exist. In satellite transmission, for example, it takes approximately 250 ms for a transmission to reach the satellite, and another 250 ms for it to come back down to Earth. This results in a total delay of 500 ms. Although the ITU-T recommendation notes that this is outside the acceptable range of voice quality, many conversations occur every day over satellite links. As such, voice quality is often defined as what users will accept and use.

In an unmanaged, congested network, queuing delay can add up to two seconds of delay (or result in the packet being dropped). This lengthy period of delay is unacceptable in almost any voice network. Queuing delay is only one component of end-to-end delay. Another way end-to-end delay is affected is through jitter.

Jitter

Simply stated, *jitter* is the variation of packet interarrival time. Jitter is one issue that exists only in packet-based networks. While in a packet voice environment, the sender is expected to reliably transmit voice packets at a regular interval (for example, send one frame every 20 ms). These voice packets can be delayed throughout the packet network and not arrive at that same regular interval at the receiving station (for example, they might not be received every 20 ms; see Figure 7-2). The difference between when the packet is expected and when it is actually received is *jitter*.

Figure 7-2 *Variation of Packet Arrival Time (Jitter)*

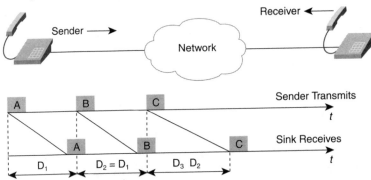

In Figure 7-2, you can see that the amount of time it takes for packets A and B to send and receive is equal (D1=D2). Packet C encounters delay in the network, however, and is received *after* it is expected. This is why a *jitter buffer*, which conceals interarrival packet delay variation, is necessary. Voice packets in IP networks have highly variable packet-interarrival intervals. Recommended practice is to count the number of packets that arrive late and create a ratio of these packets to the number of packets that are successfully processed. You can then use this ratio to adjust the jitter buffer to target a predetermined, allowable late-packet ratio. This adaptation of jitter buffer sizing is effective in compensating for delays.

Note that jitter and total delay are *not* the same thing, although having plenty of jitter in a packet network can increase the amount of total delay in the network. This is because the more jitter you have, the larger your jitter buffer needs to be to compensate for the unpredictable nature of the packet network.

Most DSPs do not have infinite jitter buffers to handle excessive network delays. Sometimes it is better to just drop packets or have fixed-length buffers instead of creating unwanted delays in the jitter buffers. If your data network is engineered well and you take the proper precautions, jitter is usually not a major problem and the jitter buffer does not significantly contribute to the total end-to-end delay.

RTP timestamps are used within Cisco IOS Software to determine what level of jitter, if any, exists within the network.

The jitter buffer found within Cisco IOS Software is considered a dynamic queue. This queue can grow or shrink exponentially depending on the interarrival time of the RTP packets.

Although many vendors choose to use static jitter buffers, Cisco found that a well-engineered dynamic jitter buffer is the best mechanism to use for packet-based voice networks. Static jitter buffers force the jitter buffer to be either too large or too small, thereby causing the audio quality to suffer, due to either lost packets or excessive delay.
The Cisco jitter buffer dynamically increases or decreases based upon the interarrival delay variation of the last few packets.

Pulse Code Modulation

Although analog communication is ideal for human communication, analog transmission is neither robust nor efficient at recovering from line noise. In the early telephony network, when analog transmission was passed through amplifiers to boost the signal, not only was the voice boosted but the line noise was amplified, as well. This line noise resulted in an often-unusable connection.

It is much easier for digital samples, which are comprised of 1 and 0 bits, to be separated from line noise. Therefore, when analog signals are regenerated as digital samples, a clean sound is maintained. When the benefits of this digital representation became evident, the telephony network migrated to pulse code modulation (PCM).

What Is PCM?

As covered in Chapter 1, PCM converts analog sound into digital form by sampling the analog sound 8000 times per second and converting each sample into a numeric code. The Nyquist theorem states that if you sample an analog signal at twice the rate of the highest frequency of interest, you can accurately reconstruct that signal back into its analog form. Because most speech content is below 4000 Hz (4 kHz), a sampling rate of 8000 times per second (125 microseconds between samples) is required.

A Sampling Example for Satellite Networks

Satellite networks have an inherent delay of around 500 ms. This includes 250 ms for the trip up to the satellite, and another 250 ms for the trip back to Earth. In this type of network, packet loss is highly controlled due to the expense of bandwidth. Also, if some type of voice application is already running through the satellite, the users of this service are accustomed to a quality of voice that has excessive delays.

Cisco IOS, by default, sends two 10-ms G.729 speech frames in every packet. Although this is acceptable for most applications, this might not be the best method for utilizing the expensive bandwidth on a satellite link. The simple explanation for wasting bandwidth is that a header exists for every packet. The more speech frames you put into a packet, the fewer headers you require.

If you take the satellite example and use four 10-ms G.729 speech frames per packet, you can cut by half the number of headers you use. Table 7-1 clearly shows the difference between the various frames per packet. With only a 20-byte increase in packet size (20 extra bytes equals two 10 ms G.729 samples), you carry twice as much speech with the packet.

Table 7-1   *Frames per Packet (G.729)*

G.729 Samples per Frame	IP/RTP/UDP Header	Bandwidth Consumed	Latency[*]
Default (two samples per frame)	40 bytes	24,000 bps	25 ms
Satellite (four samples per frame)	40 bytes	16,000 bps	45 ms
Low Latency (one sample per frame)	40 bytes	40,000 bps	15 ms

* Compression and packetization delay only

To reduce the overall IP/RTP/UDP overhead introduced by the 54-byte header, multiple voice samples can be packed into a single Ethernet frame to transmit. Although this can increase the voice delay, increasing this count can improve the overall voice quality, especially when the bandwidth is constrained.

How many voice samples to be sent per frame depends on what codec you choose and the balance between bandwidth utilization and impact of packet loss. The bigger this value, the higher the bandwidth utilization because more voice samples are packed into the payload field of a UDP/RTP packet and thus the network header overhead would be lower. The impact of a packet loss on perceived voice quality will be bigger, however. Table 7-2 lists the values for some of the commonly used codec types.

Table 7-2   *Voice Samples per Frame for VoIP Codecs*

Codec Type	Voice Samples per Frame (Default)	Voice Samples per Frame (Maximum)
PCMU/PCMA	2	10
G.723	1	32
G.726-32	2	20
G.729	2	64
G.728	4	64

Voice Compression

Two basic variations of 64 Kbps PCM are commonly used: µ-law and a-law. The methods are similar in that they both use logarithmic compression to achieve 12 to 13 bits of linear PCM quality in 8 bits, but they are different in relatively minor compression details (µ-law has a slight advantage in low-level, signal-to-noise ratio performance). Usage is historically along country and regional boundaries, with North America using µ-law and Europe and other countries using a-law modulation. It is important to note that when making a long-distance call, any required µ-law to a-law conversion is the responsibility of the µ-law country.

Another compression method used often is *adaptive differential pulse code modulation (ADPCM)*. A commonly used instance of ADPCM is ITU-T G.726, which encodes using 4-bit samples, giving a transmission rate of 32 Kbps. Unlike PCM, the 4 bits do not directly encode the amplitude of speech, but they do encode the differences in amplitude, as well as the rate of change of that amplitude, employing some rudimentary linear prediction.

PCM and ADPCM are examples of *waveform* codecs—compression techniques that exploit redundant characteristics of the waveform itself. New compression techniques were developed over the past 10 to 15 years that further exploit knowledge of the source characteristics of speech generation. These techniques employ signal processing procedures that compress speech by sending only simplified parametric information about the original speech excitation and vocal tract shaping, requiring less bandwidth to transmit that information.

These techniques can be grouped together generally as *source* codecs and include variations such as *linear predictive coding (LPC), code excited linear prediction compression (CELP),* and *multipulse, multilevel quantization (MP-MLQ).*

Voice Coding Standards

The ITU-T standardizes CELP, MP-MLQ PCM, and ADPCM coding schemes in its G-series recommendations. The most popular voice coding standards for telephony and packet voice include:

- G.711—Describes the 64 Kbps PCM voice coding technique outlined earlier; G.711-encoded voice is already in the correct format for digital voice delivery in the public phone network or through Private Branch eXchanges (PBXs).

- G.726—Describes ADPCM coding at 40, 32, 24, and 16 Kbps; you also can interchange ADPCM voice between packet voice and public phone or PBX networks, provided that the latter has ADPCM capability.

- G.728—Describes a 16 Kbps low-delay variation of CELP voice compression.

- G.729—Describes CELP compression that enables voice to be coded into 8 Kbps streams; two variations of this standard (G.729 and G.729 Annex A) differ largely in computational complexity, and both generally provide speech quality as good as that of 32 Kbps ADPCM.

- G.723.1—Describes a compression technique that you can use to compress speech or other audio signal components of multimedia service at a low bit rate, as part of the overall H.324 family of standards. Two bit rates are associated with this coder: 5.3 and 6.3 Kbps. The higher bit rate is based on MP-MLQ technology and provides greater quality. The lower bit rate is based on CELP, provides good quality, and affords system designers with additional flexibility.

- iLBC (Internet Low Bitrate Codec)—A free speech codec suitable for robust voice communication over IP. The codec is designed for narrow band speech and results in a payload bit rate of 13.33 kbps with an encoding frame length of 30 ms and 15.20 kbps with an encoding length of 20 ms. The iLBC codec enables graceful speech quality degradation in the case of lost frames, which occurs in connection with lost or delayed IP packets. The basic quality is higher than G.729A, with high robustness to packet loss. The PacketCable consortium and many vendors have adopted iLBC as a preferred codec. It is also being used by many PC-to-Phone applications, such as Skype, Google Talk, Yahoo! Messenger with Voice, and MSN Messenger.

Mean Opinion Score

You can test voice quality in two ways: subjectively and objectively. Humans perform subjective voice testing, whereas computers—which are less likely to be "fooled" by compression schemes that can "trick" the human ear—perform objective voice testing.

Codecs are developed and tuned based on subjective measurements of voice quality. Standard objective quality measurements, such as total harmonic distortion and signal-to-noise ratios, do not correlate well to a human's perception of voice quality, which in the end is usually the goal of most voice compression techniques.

A common subjective benchmark for quantifying the performance of the speech codec is the *mean opinion score (MOS)*. MOS tests are given to a group of listeners. Because voice quality and sound in general are subjective to listeners, it is important to get a wide range of listeners and sample material when conducting a MOS test. The listeners give each sample of speech material a rating of 1 (bad) to 5 (excellent). The scores are then averaged to get the mean opinion score.

MOS testing also is used to compare how well a particular codec works under varying circumstances, including differing background noise levels, multiple encodes and decodes, and so on. You can then use this data to compare against other codecs.

MOS scoring for several ITU-T codecs is listed in Table 7-3. This table shows the relationship between several low-bit rate coders and standard PCM.

Table 7-3   *ITU-T Codec MOS Scoring*

Compression Method	Bit Rate (Kbps)	Sample Size (ms)	MOS Score
G.711 PCM	64	0.125	4.1
G.726 ADPCM	32	0.125	3.85
G.728 Low Delay Code Excited Linear Predictive (LD-CELP)	15	0.625	3.61
G.729 Conjugate Structure Algebraic Code Excited Linear Predictive (CS-ACELP)	8	10	3.92
G.729a CS-ACELP	8	10	3.7
G.723.1 MP-MLQ	6.3	30	3.9
G.723.1 ACELP	5.3	30	3.65
iLBC Freeware	15.2	20	3.9
	13.3	30	

Source: Cisco Labs

For iLBC codec - COMPARISONS OF FEC AND CODEC ROBUSTNESS ON VOIP QUALITY AND BANDWIDTH EFFICIENCY - WENYU JIANG AND HENNING SCHULZRINNE. Columbia University, Department of Computer Science

Perceptual Speech Quality Measurement

Although MOS scoring is a subjective method of determining voice quality, it is not the only method for doing so. The ITU-T put forth recommendation P.861, which covers ways you can objectively determine voice quality using Perceptual Speech Quality Measurement (PSQM).

PSQM has many drawbacks when used with voice codecs (vocoders). One drawback is that what the "machine" or PSQM hears is not what the human ear perceives. In layman's terms, a person can trick the human ear into perceiving a higher-quality voice, but a computer cannot be tricked. Also, PSQM was developed to "hear" impairments caused by compression and decompression and not packet loss or jitter.

Echo

Echo is an amusing phenomenon to experience while visiting the Grand Canyon, but echo on a phone conversation can range from slightly annoying to unbearable, making conversation unintelligible.

Hearing your own voice in the receiver while you are talking is common and reassuring to the speaker. Hearing your own voice in the receiver after a delay of more than about 25 ms, however, can cause interruptions and can break the cadence in a conversation.

In a traditional toll network, echo is normally caused by a mismatch in impedance from the four-wire network switch conversion to the two-wire local loop (as shown in Figure 7-3). Echo, in the standard Public Switched Telephone Network (PSTN), is regulated with echo cancellers and a tight control on impedance mismatches at the common reflection points, as depicted in Figure 7-3.

Echo has two drawbacks: It can be loud, and it can be long. The louder and longer the echo, of course, the more annoying the echo becomes.

Figure 7-3   *Echo Caused by Impedance Mismatch*

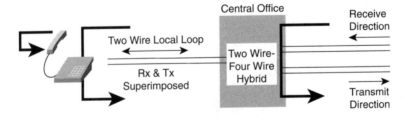

Telephony networks in those parts of the world where analog voice is primarily used employ echo suppressors, which remove echo by capping the impedance on a circuit. This is not the best mechanism to use to remove echo and, in fact, causes other problems. You cannot use Integrated Services Digital Network (ISDN) on a line that has an echo suppressor, for instance, because the echo suppressor cuts off the frequency range that ISDN uses.

In today's packet-based networks, you can build echo cancellers into low-bit-rate codecs and operate them on each DSP. In some manufacturers' implementations, echo cancellation is done in software; this practice drastically reduces the benefits of echo cancellation. Cisco VoIP, however, does all its echo cancellation on its DSP.

To understand how echo cancellers work, it is best to first understand where the echo comes from.

In this example, assume that user A is talking to user B. The speech of user A to user B is called G. When G hits an impedance mismatch or other echo-causing environments, it bounces back to user A. User A can then hear the delay several milliseconds after user A actually speaks.

To remove the echo from the line, the device user A is talking through (router A) keeps an inverse image of user A's speech for a certain amount of time. This is called *inverse speech (–G)*. This echo canceller listens for the sound coming from user B and subtracts the –G to remove any echo.

Echo cancellers are limited by the total amount of time they wait for the reflected speech to be received, a phenomenon known as *echo tail*. Cisco has configurable echo tails of 16, 24, 32, 64, and 128 ms.

It is important to configure the appropriate amount of echo cancellation when initially installing VoIP equipment. If you don't configure enough echo cancellation, callers will hear echo during the phone call. If you configure too much echo cancellation, it will take longer for the echo canceller to converge and eliminate the echo.

Packet Loss

Packet loss in data networks is both common and expected. Many data protocols, in fact, use packet loss so that they know the condition of the network and can reduce the number of packets they are sending.

When putting critical traffic on data networks, it is important to control the amount of packet loss in that network.

Cisco Systems has been putting business-critical, time-sensitive traffic on data networks for many years, starting with Systems Network Architecture (SNA) traffic in the early 1990s. With protocols such as SNA that do *not* tolerate packet loss well, you need to build a well-engineered network that can prioritize the time-sensitive data ahead of data that can handle delay and packet loss.

When putting voice on data networks, it is important to build a network that can successfully transport voice in a reliable and timely manner. Also, it is helpful when you can use a mechanism to make the voice somewhat resistant to periodic packet loss.

Cisco Systems developed many quality of service (QoS) tools that enable administrators to classify and manage traffic through a data network. If a data network is well engineered, you can keep packet loss to a minimum.

Cisco Systems' VoIP implementation enables the voice router to respond to periodic packet loss. If a voice packet is not received when expected (the expected time is variable), it is assumed to be lost and the last packet received is replayed, as shown in Figure 7-4.
Because the packet lost is only 20 ms of speech, the average listener does not notice the difference in voice quality.

Figure 7-4 *Packet Loss with G.729*

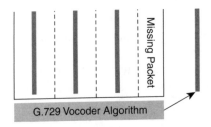

Using Cisco's G.729 implementation for VoIP, let's say that each of the lines in Figure 7-4 represents a packet. Packets 1, 2, and 3 reach the destination, but packet 4 is lost somewhere in transmission. The receiving station waits for a period of time (per its jitter buffer) and then runs a *concealment strategy*.

This concealment strategy replays the last packet received (in this case, packet 3), so the listener does not hear gaps of silence. Because the lost speech is only 20 ms, the listener most likely does not hear the difference. You can accomplish this concealment strategy only if one packet is lost. If multiple consecutive packets are lost, the concealment strategy is run only once until another packet is received.

Because of the concealment strategy of G.729, as a rule of thumb G.729 is tolerant to about five percent packet loss averaged across an entire call.

Voice Activity Detection

In normal voice conversations, someone speaks and someone else listens. Today's toll networks contain a bi-directional, 64,000 bit per second (bps) channel, regardless of whether anyone is speaking. This means that in a normal conversation, at least 50 percent of the total bandwidth is wasted. The amount of wasted bandwidth can actually be much higher if you take a statistical sampling of the breaks and pauses in a person's normal speech patterns.

When using VoIP, you can utilize this "wasted" bandwidth for other purposes when voice activity detection (VAD) is enabled. As shown in Figure 7-5, VAD works by detecting the magnitude of speech in decibels (dB) and deciding when to cut off the voice from being framed.

Figure 7-5 *Voice Activity Detection*

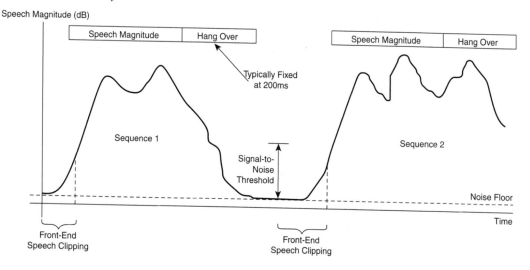

Typically, when the VAD detects a drop-off of speech amplitude, it waits a fixed amount of time before it stops putting speech frames in packets. This fixed amount of time is known as *hangover* and is typically 200 ms.

With any technology, tradeoffs are made. VAD experiences certain inherent problems in determining when speech ends and begins, and in distinguishing speech from background noise. This means that if you are in a noisy room, VAD is unable to distinguish between speech and background noise. This also is known as the *signal-to-noise threshold* (refer to Figure 7-5). In these scenarios, VAD disables itself at the beginning of the call.

Another inherent problem with VAD is detecting when speech begins. Typically the beginning of a sentence is cut off or clipped (refer to Figure 7-5). This phenomenon is known as *front-end speech clipping*. Usually, the person listening to the speech does not notice front-end speech clipping.

Digital-to-Analog Conversion

Digital to analog (D/A) conversion issues also currently plague toll networks. Although almost all the telephony backbone networks in first-world countries today are digital, sometimes multiple D/A conversions occur.

Each time a conversion occurs from digital to analog and back, the speech or waveform becomes less "true." Although today's toll networks can handle at least seven D/A conversions before voice quality is affected, compressed speech is less robust in the face of these conversions.

It is important to note that D/A conversion must be tightly managed in a compressed speech environment. When using G.729, just two conversions from D/A cause the MOS score to decrease rapidly. The only way to manage D/A conversion is to have the network designer design VoIP environments with as few D/A conversions as possible.

Although D/A conversions affect all voice networks, VoIP networks using a PCM codec (G.711) are just as resilient to problems caused by D/A conversions as today's telephony networks are.

Tandem Encoding

As covered in Chapter 1, all circuit-switched networks today work on the premise of switching calls at the data link layer. The circuit switches are organized in a hierarchical model in which switches higher in the hierarchy are called *tandem switches*.

Tandem switches do not actually terminate any local loops; rather, they act as a *higher-layer* circuit switch. In the hierarchical model, several layers of tandem circuit switches can exist, as shown in Figure 7-6. This enables end-to-end connectivity for anyone with a phone, without the need for a direct connection between every home on the planet.

Figure 7-6 *Tandem Switching Hierarchy*

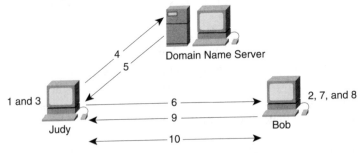

Typically, a voice call that passes through the two TDM switches and one tandem switch does not incur degradation in voice quality because these circuit switches use 64 Kbps channels.

If the TDM switches compress voice and the tandem switch must decompress and recompress the voice, the voice quality can be drastically affected. Although compression and recompression are not common in the PSTN today, you must plan for it and design around it in packet networks.

Voice degradation occurs when you have more than one compression/decompression cycle for each phone call. Figure 7-7 provides an example of when this scenario might occur.

Figure 7-7   *VoIP Tandem Encoding*

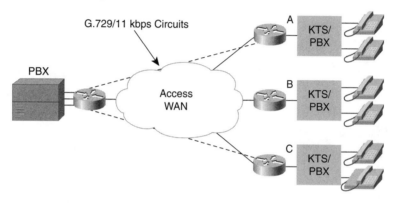

Figure 7-7 depicts three VoIP routers connected and acting as tie-lines between one central-site PBX and three remote-branch PBXs. The network is designed to put all the dial-plan information in the central-site PBX. This is common in many enterprise networks to keep the administration of the dial plan centralized.

A drawback to tandem encoding when used with VoIP is that, if a telephony user at branch B wants to call a user at branch C, two VoIP ports at central site A must be utilized. Also, two compression/decompression cycles exist, which means that voice quality will degrade.

Different codecs react differently to tandem encoding. G.729 can handle two compression/decompression cycles, while G.723.1 is less resilient to multiple compression cycles.

Assume, for example, that a user at remote site B wants to call a user at remote site C. The call goes through PBX B, is compressed and packetized at VoIP router B, and is sent to the central site VoIP router A, which decompresses the call and sends it to PBX A. PBX A circuit-switches the call back to its VoIP router (router A), which compresses and packetizes the call, and sends it to the remote site C, where it is then decompressed and sent to PBX C. This process is known as *tandem-compression*; you should avoid it in all networks where compression exists.

It is easy to avoid tandem compression. This customer simplified the router configuration at the expense of voice quality. Cisco IOS has other mechanisms that can simplify management of dial plans and still keep the highest voice quality possible.

One possible method is to use a Cisco IOS Multimedia Conference Manager (for instance, H.323 Gatekeeper). Another mechanism is to use one of Cisco's management applications, such as Cisco Voice Manager, to assist in configuring and maintaining dial plans on all your routers.

Taking the same example of three PBXs connected through three VoIP routers, but configuring the VoIP routers differently, simplifies the call-flow and avoids tandem encoding, as shown in Figure 7-8.

Figure 7-8   *VoIP Without Tandem Encoding*

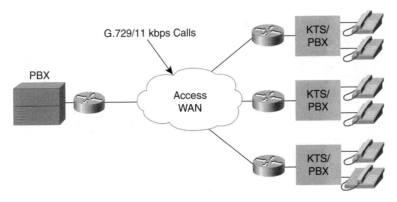

You can see one of IP's strengths in Figure 7-8: a tie-line does not have to be leased from the telephone company to complete calls between two PBXs. If a data network connects the sites, VoIP can ride across that network.

The dial plan is moved from the central-site PBX to each of the VoIP routers. This enables each VoIP device to make a call-routing decision and removes the need for tie-lines. The major benefit of this change is the removal of needless compression/decompression cycles.

Transport Protocols

As explained in Chapter 6, "IP Tutorial," two main types of traffic ride upon Internet Protocol (IP): User Datagram Protocol (UDP) and Transmission Control Protocol (TCP). In general, you use TCP when you need a reliable connection and UDP when you need simplicity and reliability is not your chief concern.

Due to the time-sensitive nature of voice traffic, UDP/IP was the logical choice to carry voice. More information was needed on a packet-by-packet basis than UDP offered, however. So, for real-time or delay-sensitive traffic, the Internet Engineering Task Force (IETF) adopted RTP. VoIP rides on top of RTP, which rides on top of UDP. Therefore, VoIP is carried with an RTP/UDP/IP packet header.

RTP

RTP is the standard for transmitting delay-sensitive traffic across packet-based networks. RTP rides on top of UDP and IP. RTP gives receiving stations information that is not in the connectionless UDP/IP streams. As shown in Figure 7-9, two important bits of information are sequence number and timestamp. RTP uses the sequence information to determine whether the packets are arriving in order, and it uses the time-stamping information to determine the interarrival packet time (jitter).

Figure 7-9 *Real-Time Transport Header*

Version	IHL	Type of Service	Total Length		
Identification			Flags	Fragment Offset	
Time To Live		Protocol	Header Checksum		
Source Address					
Destination Address					
Options				Padding	
Source Port			Destination Port		
Length			Checksum		
V=2	P	X	CC	M	PT	Sequence Number
Timestamp					
Synchronization Source (SSRC) Identifier					

You can use RTP for media on demand, as well as for interactive services such as Internet telephony. RTP (refer to Figure 7-9) consists of a data part and a control part, the latter called RTP Control Protocol (RTCP).

The data part of RTP is a thin protocol that provides support for applications with real-time properties, such as continuous media (for example, audio and video), including timing reconstruction, loss detection, and content identification.

RTCP provides support for real-time conferencing of groups of any size within an Internet. This support includes source identification and support for gateways, such as audio and video bridges as well as multicast-to-unicast translators. It also offers QoS feedback from receivers to the multicast group, as well as support for the synchronization of different media streams.

Another new proposal defined in RFC3 611, RTP Control Protocol Extended Reports (RTCP XR), provides a rich set of data for VoIP management. The data for these extended reports can be provided by technology such as VQmon embedded into VoIP phones or gateways and sent periodically during the call to provide real-time feedback on voice quality. The reports generated present a very useful set of VoIP metrics data on network packet loss, RTP round trip delay, and so on.

Using RTP is important for real-time traffic, but a few drawbacks exist. The IP/RTP/UDP headers are 20, 8, and 12 bytes, respectively. This adds up to a 40-byte header, which is twice as big as the payload when using G.729 with two speech samples (20 ms).
You can compress this large header to 2 or 4 bytes by using RTP Header Compression (CRTP). CRTP is covered in depth in Chapter 8.

Reliable User Data Protocol

Reliable User Data Protocol (RUDP) builds in some reliability to the connectionless UDP protocol. RUDP enables reliability without the need for a connection-based protocol such as TCP. The basic method of RUDP is to send multiples of the same packet and enable the receiving station to discard the unnecessary or redundant packets. This mechanism makes it more probable that one of the packets will make the journey from sender to receiver.

This also is known as *forward error correction* (FEC). Few implementations of FEC exist due to bandwidth considerations (a doubling or tripling of the amount of bandwidth used). Customers that have almost unlimited bandwidth, however, consider FEC a worthwhile mechanism to enhance reliability and voice quality.

Cisco currently utilizes RUDP in its SC2200 product, which enables Signaling System 7 (SS7) to Q.931 over IP conversion. The Q.931 over IP is transmitted over RUDP.

Dial-Plan Design

One of the areas that causes the largest amount of headaches when designing an Enterprise Telephony (ET) network is the *dial plan*. The causes of these head pains might be due to the complex issues of integrating disparate networks. Many of these disparate networks were not designed for integration.

A good data example of joining disparate networks is when two companies merge. In such a scenario, the companies' data networks (IP addressing, ordering applications, and inventory database) must be joined. It is highly improbable that both companies used the same methodologies when implementing their data networks, so problems can arise.

The same problems can occur in telephony networks. If two companies merge, their phone systems (voice mail, billing, supplementary features, and dial-plan addressing) might be incompatible with each other.

These dial-plan issues also can occur when a company decides to institute a corporate dial plan. Consider Company X, for example. Company X grew drastically in the last three years and now operates 30 sites throughout the world, with its headquarters in Dallas. Company X currently dials through the PSTN to all its 29 remote sites. Company X wants to simplify the dialing plan to all its remote sites to enable better employee communication and ease of use.

Company X currently has a large PBX at its headquarters and smaller PBX systems at its remote sites. Several alternatives are available to this company:

■ Purchase leased lines between headquarters and all remote sites.

■ Purchase a telephony Virtual Private Network (VPN) from the telephone company and dial an access code from anywhere to access the VPN.

■ Take advantage of the existing data infrastructure and put voice on the data network.

Regardless of which option Company X chooses, it must face dial-plan design, network management, and cost issues.

Without getting into great detail, most companies must decide on their dial-plan design based on the following issues:

■ Plans for growth

■ Cost of leased circuits or VPNs

■ Cost of additional equipment for packet voice

■ Number overlap (when more than one site has the same phone number)

■ Call-flows (the call patterns from each site)

■ Busy hour (the time of day when the highest number of calls are offered on a circuit)

Depending on the size of the company, the dial plan can stretch from two digits to seven or eight digits. It is important that you not force yourself down a particular path until you address the previous issues.

Company X plans on sustaining 20–30 percent growth and decides on a seven-digit dial plan based on its growth patterns. This choice also cuts down on the number overlap that might be present.

Company X will have a three-digit site code, and four digits for the actual subscriber line. It made this decision because it does not believe it will have more than 999 branch offices.

> **NOTE**   For companies that have hundreds of branch offices, it is common to have more site codes and fewer subscriber lines. If a company has several hundred branch offices and needs thousands of subscriber lines, it must use more digits (that is, it must use an eight- or nine-digit dial plan).

End Office Switch Call-Flow Versus IP Phone Call

To simplify a TDM or end office switch call-flow and an IP call-flow, this section looks at ways you can call your next-door neighbor using both the PSTN and the Internet. Figure 7-10 shows a basic call-flow in the PSTN today. Compare this to an IP phone call-flow and notice the similarities of necessary call setup.

Figure 7-10   *Calling My Neighbor with Today's PSTN*

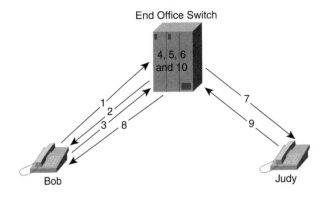

In this example, Bob calls his neighbor Judy. They are both subscribers on the local end office switch, and therefore, no SS7 is needed. The following steps occur:

1. Bob picks up his handset (off hook).

2. The local end office switch gives Bob a dial tone.

3. Bob dials Judy's seven-digit phone number.

4. The end office switch collects and analyzes the seven-digit number to determine the destination of the phone call. The end office switch knows that someone from Bob's house is placing the call because of the specific port that it dedicated to Bob.

5. The switch analyzes the seven-digit called number to determine whether the number is a local number that the switch can serve.

NOTE   If the same end office switch does not service Judy, Bob's end office switch looks in its routing tables to determine how to connect this call. It can add prefix digits to make the number appear as a fully qualified E.164 number when contacting Judy.

6. The switch determines Judy's specific subscriber line.

7. The end office switch then signals Judy's circuit by ringing Judy's phone.

8. A voice path back to Bob is cut through so that Bob can hear the ring-back tone the end office switch is sending. The ring-back tone is sent to Bob so that he knows Judy's phone is ringing. (The ringing of Judy's phone and the ring-back tone that Bob hears need not be synchronized.)

9. Judy picks up her phone (off hook).

10. The end office switch cuts through the voice path from Bob to Judy. This is a 64 Kbps, full-duplex DS-0 (Digital Service, Level 0) in the end office switching fabric to enable voice transmission.

Figure 7-11 demonstrates the call-flow necessary to complete an Internet phone call using a PC application.

Figure 7-11 *Calling with an Internet-Phone Application*

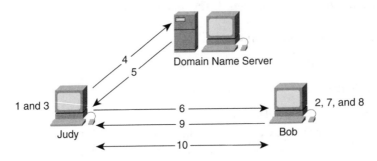

Both Bob and Judy need to be on the Internet or have some other IP network between their homes to talk to each other. Assuming this IP network exists or that both neighbors have a connection to the Internet, you can then follow this possible call-flow:

1. Judy launches her Internet phone (I-phone) application, which is H.323-compatible.

2. Bob already has his I-phone application launched.

3. Judy knows that Bob's Internet "name," or Domain Name System (DNS) entry, is bob@nextdoorneighbor.com, so she puts that into the "who to call" section in her I-phone application and presses Return.

4. The I-phone application converts Bob.nextdoorneighbor.com to a DNS host name and goes to a DNS server that is statically configured in Judy's machine to resolve the DNS name and get an actual IP address.

5. The DNS machine passes back Bob's IP address.

6. Judy's I-phone application takes Bob's IP address and sends an H.225 message to Bob.

7. The H.225 message signals Bob's PC to begin ringing.

8. Bob clicks on the Accept button, which tells his I-phone application to send back an H.225 connect message.

9. Judy's I-phone application then begins H.245 negotiation with Bob's PC.

10. H.245 negotiation finishes and logical channels are opened. Bob and Judy can now speak to one another through a packet-based network.

The example does not show all the steps and omits some details that a service provider needs to deploy a VoIP network. Because IP is a ubiquitous protocol, as mentioned in Chapter 6, when a call is packetized, it could be destined to your next-door neighbor or to a relative in Norway.

Summary

This chapter brought up many of the issues surrounding VoIP. Many of these issues, such as compression/decompression of the speech frame and propagation delay, are inherent to VoIP, and you can't do much to minimize these effects on VoIP networks.

With careful planning and solid network design, however, you can control and possibly avoid many problematic issues. Some of these issues are jitter, overall latency, handling delay, sampling rates, tandem encodings, and dial-plan design.

References

The following Requests For Comments (RFCs) will help you to continue researching VoIP:

RFC 1889—RTP: A Transport Protocol for Real-Time Applications
RFC 2327—SDP: Session Description Protocol
RFC 2326—RTSP: Real-Time Streaming Protocol
ITU-T Recommendation H.323
ITU-T G. specifications for codecs
ITU-T G.113 Voice Quality Specification
ITU-T P.861 Perceptual Speech Quality Measure(ment), PSQM
iLBC Codec—http://www.ilbcfreeware.org/

Part II: Networking Technology Guide Series

Knowledge to Master the Challenge of the Network

Networking Technology Guide Series titles offer valuable information for **constructing efficient networks**, **understanding new technologies**, and building successful networking careers. Titles in the Networking Technology Guide Series cover topics of importance to **experienced networking professionals**, such as IP communications, security, routing, switching, network design, and wireless networks.

Book features such as **case studies** and **example configurations** provide you with **real-world applications and solutions** you can apply in your network.

ISBN: 1-58705-253-9

SECURITY

Self-Defending Networks:
The Next Generation of Network Security

ciscopress.com

Duane De Capite

This chapter covers the following topics:

- Network admission control overview
- NAC Framework benefits
- NAC Framework components
- Operational overview
- Deployment models

CHAPTER 6

Implementing Network Admission Control

Network Admission Control (NAC) is a technology initiative led by Cisco Systems working in collaboration with many leading security vendors, including antivirus and desktop management. Their focus is the creation of solutions that limit security threats, such as worms and viruses.

This technology provides a framework using existing Cisco infrastructure to enforce network admission policies on NAC-enabled endpoint devices, guaranteeing software compliance before network access is granted. If an endpoint device is determined noncompliant, a variety of admission actions are available to administrators, and how the actions are implemented is at the discretion of the network administrator. For example, a noncompliant endpoint may be placed in a quarantine area of the network and redirected to a remediation server to load the necessary software or patches. A notification is displayed to the user warning that their device is not compliant or, in the worse case, that they are denied network access entirely.

This chapter describes the Cisco NAC Framework, identifies benefits, describes the solution components and how they interoperate, and describes common deployment models.

Network Admission Control Overview

Worms and viruses continue to be disruptive, even though many businesses have significantly invested in antivirus and traditional security solutions. Not all users stay up to date with the many needed software security patches of antivirus files. Noncompliant endpoints are frequent and the reasons vary; for example:

- A user might choose to wait and install a new update later because they don't have the time

- A contractor, partner, or guest needs network access; however, the business may not control the endpoint

- The endpoints are not managed

- The business lacks the capability to monitor the endpoints and determine whether they are updated to conform to the business's security policy

When infected endpoints connect to the network, they unsuspectingly spread their infections to other improperly protected devices. This has caused businesses to examine how they should implement endpoint compliance enforcement besides user authentication before granting access to their networks.

Cisco Systems provides two network admission control solution choices:

- NAC Appliance
- NAC Framework

Chapter 7, "Cisco Clean Access," describes NAC Appliance, which was originally marketed as Cisco Clean Access (CCA). NAC Appliance is a turnkey self-sufficient package that does not rely on third-party products for determining and enforcing software compliance. This chapter focuses on NAC Framework.

NAC Framework is an integrated solution that enables businesses to leverage many of their existing Cisco network products, along with many third-party vendor products such as antivirus, security, and identity-based software. Vendor products must be NAC-enabled in order to communicate with the NAC-enabled network access devices. NAC Framework is more robust than NAC Appliance because it can enforce more features available from other vendors' products. A comparison of customer preferences for choosing the NAC Appliance and NAC Framework is shown in Table 6-1.

Table 6-1   *NAC Customer Profile*

NAC Framework	NAC Appliance
Uses an integrated framework approach, leveraging existing security solutions from other vendors	Prefers bundled, out-of-the-box functionality with preinstalled support for antivirus and Microsoft updates
Complex network environment, leveraging many types of Cisco network access products	Heterogeneous network infrastructure
Longer, phased-in deployment model	Rapid deployment model
Can integrate with 802.1x	Independent of 802.1x

Source: Cisco Systems, Inc.[1]

NAC Framework Benefits

Following are some benefits that can be recognized by businesses that have implemented NAC Framework:

- **Protects corporate assets**—Enforces the corporate security software compliance policy for endpoints.

- **Provides comprehensive span of control**—All the access methods that endpoints use to connect to the network are covered, including campus switching, wireless, router WAN links, IP Security (IPSec), and remote access.

- **Controls endpoint admission**—Validates all endpoints regardless of their operating system, and it doesn't matter which agents are running. Also provides the ability to exempt certain endpoints from having to be authenticated or checked.

- **Offers a multivendor solution**—NAC is the result of a multivendor collaboration between leading security vendors, including antivirus, desktop management, and other market leaders. NAC supports multiple security and patch software vendors through APIs.

- **Leverages existing technologies and standards**—NAC extends the use of existing communications protocols and security technologies, such as Extensible Authentication Protocol (EAP), 802.1x, and RADIUS services.

- **Leverages existing network and antivirus investments**—NAC combines existing investments in network infrastructure and security technology to provide a secure admission control solution.

NAC Framework Components

The initial release of the Cisco NAC Framework became available in June 2004 and continues to evolve in phases. The functions of the solution architecture remain consistent; however, as each phase is introduced, more capabilities and deeper integration are added to the NAC framework architecture. To stay up to date with NAC and partner products, refer to the URL www.cisco.com/go/nac.

NAC Framework includes the following main components, as shown in Figure 6-1:

- Endpoint security application
- Posture agent
- Network access devices
- Cisco Policy server
- Optional servers that operate as policy server decision points and audit servers
- Optional management and reporting tools are highly recommended (not shown)

Figure 6-1 *NAC Framework Components*

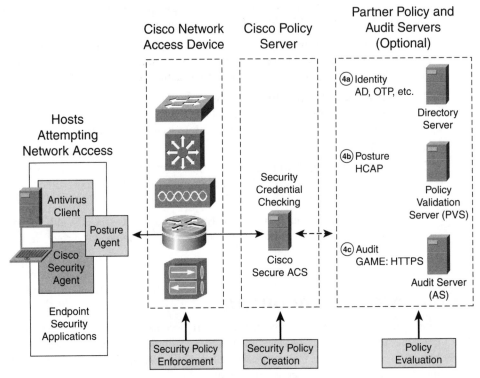

The next sections describe the main components in more detail.

Endpoint Security Application

An endpoint security application is security software that resides on a host computer. Depending on the application, it can provide host-based intrusion prevention system (HIPS), antivirus scanning, personal firewall, and other host security functions. Cisco Security Agent is a HIPS example.

NAC partners provide NAC-enabled security applications that use a posture plug-in that communicates their credentials and state with a posture agent, both residing on the same endpoint. Many endpoint security applications provide antivirus capabilities, and some provide additional identity-based services. For a list of NAC partners, refer to www.cisco.com and search for "Network Admission Control Current Participants."

Posture Agent

A posture agent is middleware or broker software that collects security state information from multiple NAC-enabled endpoint security applications, such as antivirus clients. It communicates the endpoint device's compliance condition. This condition is referred to as the *posture* of an endpoint. The posture information is sent to Cisco Secure Access Control Server (ACS) by way of the Cisco network access device.

The *Cisco Trust Agent* is Cisco's implementation of the posture agent. Cisco has licensed the trust-agent technology to its NAC partners so that it can be integrated with their security software client products. The trust agent is free and is also integrated with the Cisco Security Agent. Cisco Trust Agent can work with Layer 3 Extensible Authentication Protocol over User Datagram Protocol (EAPoUDP), and Cisco Trust Agent (CTA) version 2 can also work with Layer 2 with Extensible Authentication Protocol over 802.1x (EAPo802.1x) or Extensible Authentication Protocol over LAN (EAPoLAN).

Network Access Devices

Network access devices that enforce admission control policy include Cisco routers, switches, wireless access points, and security appliances. These devices demand endpoint security credentials and relay this information to policy servers, where network admission control decisions are made. Based on customer-defined policy, the network will enforce the appropriate admission control decision—permit, deny, quarantine, or restrict. Another term for this device is security policy enforcement point (PEP).

Policy Server

A policy server evaluates the endpoint security information relayed from network access devices (NADs) and determines the appropriate admission policy for enforcement. The Cisco Secure ACS, an authentication, authorization, and accounting (AAA) RADIUS server, is the foundation of the policy server system and is a requirement for NAC. Cisco Secure ACS is where the admission security policy is created and evaluated to determine the endpoint device's compliance condition or posture.

Optionally, Cisco Secure ACS may work in concert with other policy and audit servers to provide the following additional admission validations:

- **Identity**—User authentication can be validated with an external directory server and the result is communicated to Cisco Secure ACS. Examples include Microsoft Active Directory and one-time password (OTP) servers.

- **Posture**—Third-party, vendor-specific credentials such as antivirus and spyware can be forwarded using the Host Credential Authentication Protocol (HCAP) to NAC-enabled Policy Validation Servers (PVS) for further evaluation. This enables businesses to leverage existing policies maintained in their PVS to validate and forward the software compliance result to Cisco Secure ACS, ensuring that a consistent policy is applied across the entire organization.

- **Audit**—Determines the posture for a NAC Agentless Host (NAH), which is a host without the presence of a posture agent such as Cisco Trust Agent. The Audit server works out of band and performs several functions:

  — Collects posture information from an endpoint.

  — Acts as a posture validation server to determine compliance of an endpoint and determine the appropriate compliance result in the form of a posture.

  — Communicates the result to Cisco Secure ACS using Generic Authorization Message Exchange (GAME) over an HTTPS session. GAME uses an extension of Security Assertion Markup Language (SAML), a vendor-neutral language enabling Web services to exchange authentication and authorization information.

The optional validation policy servers communicate the user authentication status or compliance status or both to Cisco Secure ACS, which makes the final determination as to the admission policy for the endpoint. *Policy decision point* is a term used to describe the function Cisco Secure ACS performs.

Management and Reporting Tools

In addition to the required NAC components, a management system is recommended to manage and monitor the various devices. Reporting tools are available to operation personnel to identify which endpoints are compliant and, most importantly, which endpoints are not compliant. Examples include Cisco Security Monitoring Analysis and Response System (CS-MARS) and CiscoWorks Security Information Manager Solution (SIMS).

Operational Overview

This section describes how NAC determines admission compliance and how it then uses the network to enforce the policy to endpoints.

Network Admission for NAC-enabled Endpoints

This section describes the process in which a noncompliant endpoint device is discovered and is denied full access until it is compliant with the admission policy. This scenario is shown in Figure 6-2.

Figure 6-2   *Admission Process for Noncompliant Endpoint*

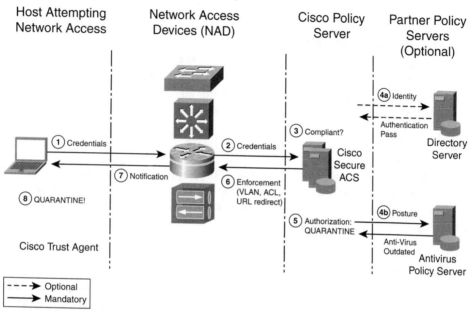

The following list is a summary of the admission process for a noncompliant endpoint shown in Figure 6-2:

1 An endpoint attempts to access the network.

2 The NAD notifies the policy server (Cisco Secure ACS) that an endpoint is requesting network access.

3 Cisco Secure ACS checks the NAC policy to determine whether the endpoint is compliant.

4 Cisco Secure ACS forwards specific information to other partner policy servers.

   a Identity information is sent to a directory server for authentication validation.

   b Host credentials are sent to an antivirus policy server for posture determination.

5 Cisco Secure Access uses information from the all-policy servers and decides the endpoints authorization. In this example, the endpoint is not compliant and is assigned a quarantine posture.

6 Quarantine enforcement actions are sent from Cisco Secure ACS to the NAD servicing the endpoint.

7 NAD enforces admission actions and communicates posture to Posture Agent.

8 Posture Agent notifies the user that the endpoint is quarantined.

The following sections explain each step in more detail.

Endpoint Attempts to Access the Network

In step 1, the admissions process begins when an endpoint attempts to access the network. What triggers the process is dependent upon the NAD's capabilities and configuration. The NAD initiates posture validation with Cisco Trust Agent using one of the following protocols:

- EAPoUDP
- EAPo802.1x

The protocol used is dependent upon the NAD to which the endpoint connects. Both of these protocols serve as a communication method between the endpoints using Cisco Trust Agent and the NAD. Cisco Trust Agent gathers credentials from NAC-enabled security applications such as antivirus.

NAD Notifies Policy Server

In step 2, the NAD notifies the policy server (Cisco Secure ACS) that an endpoint is requesting network access. A protected tunnel is set up between the policy server and the endpoints posture agent. Once communication is established, the credentials from each of the posture plug-ins are sent to Cisco Secure ACS.

Cisco Secure ACS Compares Endpoint to NAC Policy

In step 3, Cisco Secure ACS looks at the admission control policy and compares the endpoint credentials to the policy to determine whether it is compliant. It determines which of the following posture states to assign to the endpoint:

- **Healthy**—Endpoint is compliant; no network access restrictions.
- **Checkup**—Endpoint is within policy, but an update is available. This state is typically used to proactively remediate a host to the Healthy state or to notify a user that a more recent update is available and recommend remediation.
- **Transition**—This state became available in NAC phase 2. The endpoint posturing is in process; provide an interim access, pending full posture validation. This state is applicable during an endpoint boot in which all services may not be running or audit results are not yet available.
- **Quarantine**—Endpoint is out of compliance; restrict network access to a quarantine network for remediation. The endpoint is not an active threat but is vulnerable to a known attack or infection.

- **Infected**—Endpoint is an active threat to other endpoint devices; network access should be severely restricted or totally denied all network access.

- **Unknown**—Endpoint posture cannot be determined. Quarantine the host and audit or remediate until a definitive posture can be determined.

Cisco Secure ACS Forwards Information to Partner Policy Servers

In step 4, Cisco Secure ACS can optionally send user login (4a) and credentials (4b) to other policy decision servers. When this is done, Cisco Secure ACS expects to receive authentication status and a posture state from each of the policy decision servers.

In step 4a when NAC L2-802.1x is used, Cisco Secure ACS can send identity information to an authentication server. It confirms that the username and password are valid and returns a passed authentication message to Cisco Secure ACS. If identity authentication fails, no posture is checked and the endpoint fails authentication, resulting in no network access.

In step 4b in this example, an antivirus policy server determines that the device is out of compliance and returns a quarantine posture token to Cisco Secure ACS.

Keep in mind that NAC partner policy servers vary and offer a variety of compliance checks besides antivirus. For example, some vendors offer checking for spyware and patch management.

Cisco Secure ACS Makes a Decision

In step 5, Cisco Secure ACS compares all the posture states and determines which posture is the worst; infected is the worst and healthy is the best. It always assigns the worst state and takes the action for that posture. In this example, the user has passed authentication but the endpoint has been assigned a quarantine posture.

Cisco Secure ACS Sends Enforcement Actions

Cisco Secure ACS takes the actions assigned to a quarantine state. In this quarantine example, they can include the following:

- Enforce quarantine access; this varies based on the NAD.

- For NADs using NAC-L3-IP, the enforcement actions include a quarantine Access Control List (ACL) being applied to the endpoint.

- For NADs using NAC-L2-IP, the enforcement actions include a quarantine ACL being applied to the endpoint.

- For NADs using NAC-L2-802.1x, the enforcement action includes a quarantine virtual LAN (VLAN) being applied to the endpoint device.

- Optionally, the endpoint device may be assigned a URL redirect to the remediation server.

- Optionally, a notification message can be sent to the user, indicating that their device is not compliant and is being redirected for remediation.

NAD Enforces Actions

In step 7, the NAD receives the quarantine policy enforcement from Cisco Secure ACS and responds accordingly. In this example, such a response would be to quarantine the endpoint, enforce an endpoint URL redirect to the remediation server, and send a quarantine message to the posture agent.

Posture Agent Actions

In step 8, the posture agent displays the quarantine message, and the user is redirected to the remediation server.

Actions available vary by NAC partner products. Cisco Secure ACS is capable of sending different application actions from HCAP-compliant policy servers to their specific application plug-ins. This can trigger actions such as the following:

- Force an auto-remediation to a designated remediation server

- Force an auto-patch by instructing the host to download and apply a patch automatically

- Restart a stopped application service

In this example, the endpoint is now quarantined, and the user has been notified by a message. The user can elect to do nothing and remain quarantined, or comply and allow their computer to be updated.

The admission control process can take very little time, as little as milliseconds. The time varies and is based on many factors, including:

- Where the endpoint is located in relation to the policy server and optional partner policy servers

- Where the remediation server is located

- NADs performance capability

- Network bandwidth

- How busy the policy servers are

As shown in Figure 6-3, an endpoint is changing from quarantine to healthy posture state.

Figure 6-3   *Admission Process for Endpoint Changing from Quarantine to Healthy State*

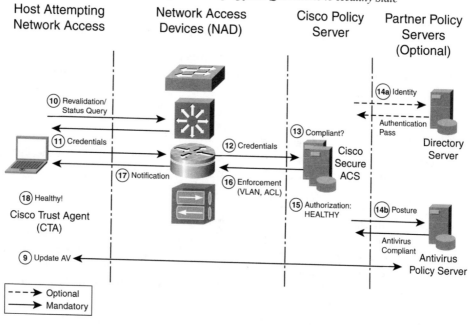

The following list explains the process shown in Figure 6-3:

9 Endpoint remediated.

10 Endpoint polled for change of compliance.

11 Host credentials gathered from endpoint.

12 Host credentials passed to Cisco Secure ACS.

13 Cisco Secure ACS rechecks the NAC policy to determine whether the endpoint is compliant.

14 Cisco Secure ACS forwards specific information to other partner policy servers.

  a Identity information is sent to a directory server for authentication validation.

  b Host credentials are sent to an antivirus policy server for posture determination.

15 Cisco Secure Access uses information from all policy servers and decides the endpoints authorization. In this example, the endpoint is compliant and is assigned a healthy posture.

16 Healthy enforcement actions are sent from Cisco Secure ACS to the NAD servicing the endpoint.

17 NAD enforces admission actions and communicates healthy posture to Posture Agent.

18 Posture Agent can notify the user that the endpoint is healthy. Many businesses prefer that a healthy posture be transparent to the user with no message notification displayed.

Endpoint Polled for Change of Compliance

Once an endpoint has been assigned a posture, it stays in effect and is not checked again until a NAC timer has expired or a posture agent trigger occurs.

The following are configurable timers for NAC:

- **Status Query**—Ensures that an endpoint remains compliant with the admission policy. The timer begins at policy enforcement for the endpoint; compliance is rechecked after the timer expires. Different Status Query timers can exist for different posture states. A shorter amount of time is beneficial for noncompliant states such as quarantine; the device can be rechecked sooner than a healthy device, in order to regain full network access.

- **Revalidation**—A time in which the posture remains valid. It can be set lower when an outbreak occurs, to force all endpoints to go through the admission policy process again. This enables endpoints to timeout at different intervals depending on where their timers are, versus forcing all endpoints to go through the validation process at the same time.

In phase 2 with NAC-L2-802.1x, there is no capability to send a status query from the NAD by way of 802.1x. To overcome this, beginning with version 2 of Cisco Trust Agent, an asynchronous status query capability exists. Cisco Trust Agent can send an Extensible Authentication Protocol Over Lan (EAPOL)-Start to the NAD, or CTA can frequently poll all registered NAC application posture plug-ins looking for a change in credentials. If a change exists, it will trigger an EAPOL-Start signaling for a new posture validation.

In step 10 of Figure 6-3, the quarantine status query timer has expired.

The NAD is aware that the timer has expired for the endpoint, so it begins rechecking for compliance. The posture agent gathers credentials from the posture plug-ins of NAC-enabled security applications such as antivirus.

Revalidation Process

From step 11 through step 18, the process is the same as the example described in Figure 6-2. The NAD notifies the policy server (Cisco Secure ACS) that an endpoint requests network access. This time, the Cisco Secure ACS determines that the posture is healthy for all admission checks and that the user login is valid. Authentication is successful, and Cisco Secure ACS assigns the healthy policy.

The NAD receives the healthy policy enforcement from Cisco Secure ACS and responds accordingly by allowing full network access. The timers begin for the healthy state.

The NAD informs the posture agent of the healthy status, but no message is sent to the user this time. The user can now resume normal network activity.

Network Admission for NAC Agentless Hosts

The previous example described the admission process for a NAC-enabled endpoint running a posture agent, such as Cisco Trust Agent. This section describes the process for endpoints that do not have a posture agent.

NAC agentless hosts (NAH) can be accommodated by several methods, as shown in Table 6-2. A NAH exception list and whitelist can be created to identify known endpoints that do not have a posture agent installed and running. The option chosen is dependent upon the NAC Framework component and the NAD enforcement method used.

Table 6-2   *NAC Agentless Host Exceptions and Whitelisting*

Component	Administration Model	NAC-L2 IP	NAC-L3 IP	NAC-L2 802.1x
NAD	• Distributed, managed at the device level • Does not scale	Device Type, IP, or MAC Enforcement by intercept ACL (IP/MAC)	Device Type, IP, or MAC Enforcement by intercept ACL (IP)	MAC-Auth-Bypass (identity + posture)
Cisco Secure ACS whitelist	• Centralized • Scales	MAC (posture only)	MAC (posture only)	MAC-Auth-Bypass (identity + posture)
Audit	• Centralized • Scales	Active network scan, remote login, browser object, hardware/software inventory	Active network scan, remote login, browser object, hardware/software inventory	Not supported at the time of this writing

Source: Cisco Systems, Inc.[2]

The audit server can be used for NAH in all enforcement methods and is a single centrally managed server. As shown in Figure 6-4, an audit server can be included as a decision policy server for NAH. The audit server can determine the posture credentials of an endpoint without relying on the presence of a posture agent.

Figure 6-4 *Admission Control for NAC Agentless Host*

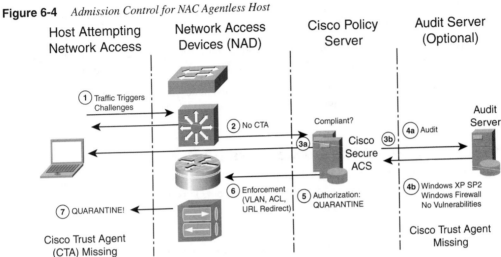

The following list explains the process shown in Figure 6-4:

1 An endpoint attempts to access the network. The trigger mechanism is dependent upon the NAD's capabilities and configuration. The NAD attempts to initiate posture validation with the posture agent, but no posture agent (Cisco Trust Agent) exists.

2 The NAD notifies the policy server (Cisco Secure ACS) that an endpoint is requesting network access with no Cisco Trust Agent (CTA) present.

3 Cisco Secure ACS cannot determine whether the NAH is compliant because no posture agent exists. Cisco Secure ACS performs the following:

   a Assign a transition posture to grant a temporary, limited network access to the agentless host while the audit server is determining the full posture validation. The NAD enforces the transition admission policy.

   b Notify the external audit server that the NAH is requesting admission.

4 Cisco Secure ACS cannot determine whether the NAH is compliant, so it notifies the audit server using GAME to conduct a scan on the endpoint.

   a The audit server scans the endpoint. It evaluates the endpoint's software information against the audit server's compliance policy. It determines that the operating system patch level is compliant or healthy, but the posture agent is missing, so it is considered noncompliant.

   b Quarantine is the application posture token (APT) assigned by the audit server for this NAH and is communicated to Cisco Secure ACS.

5   Cisco Secure ACS uses quarantine as the final posture, which is referred to as the system posture token (SPT), and takes the actions assigned to a quarantine state. The actions can include the following:

   — **Enforce quarantine access**—This varies based on the NAD.

      For NAC-L3-IP, the enforcement actions include a quarantine ACL being applied to the endpoint.

      For NADs using NAC-L2-IP, the enforcement actions include a quarantine ACL being applied to the endpoint.

      For NADs using NAC-L2-802.1x, the enforcement action includes a quarantine VLAN.

   — **Enforce Redirection (optional)**—In this example, the endpoint device is assigned a URL redirect to the remediation server.

6   The NAD receives the quarantine policy enforcement from Cisco Secure ACS. It quarantines the endpoint and sends the endpoint a redirect URL to go to the remediation server.

7   The endpoint is now quarantined and redirected to a remediation server. With NAH, the URL redirect is the only way to provide feedback to the user because there is no posture agent present. At this point, the user can elect to do nothing and remain quarantined, or comply and allow their host to remediate by installing Cisco Trust Agent.

From this point, the NAC Framework process is the same as the example in which the endpoint state changed from quarantine to healthy as shown in Figure 6-3.

Deployment Models

Cisco NAC Framework is a flexible solution providing protection to connected endpoints regardless of network connectivity. As shown in Figure 6-5, it operates across all access methods including campus switching, wired and wireless, WAN and LAN links, IP Security (IPSec) connections, and remote access links.

Figure 6-5 *NAC Deployment Scenarios*

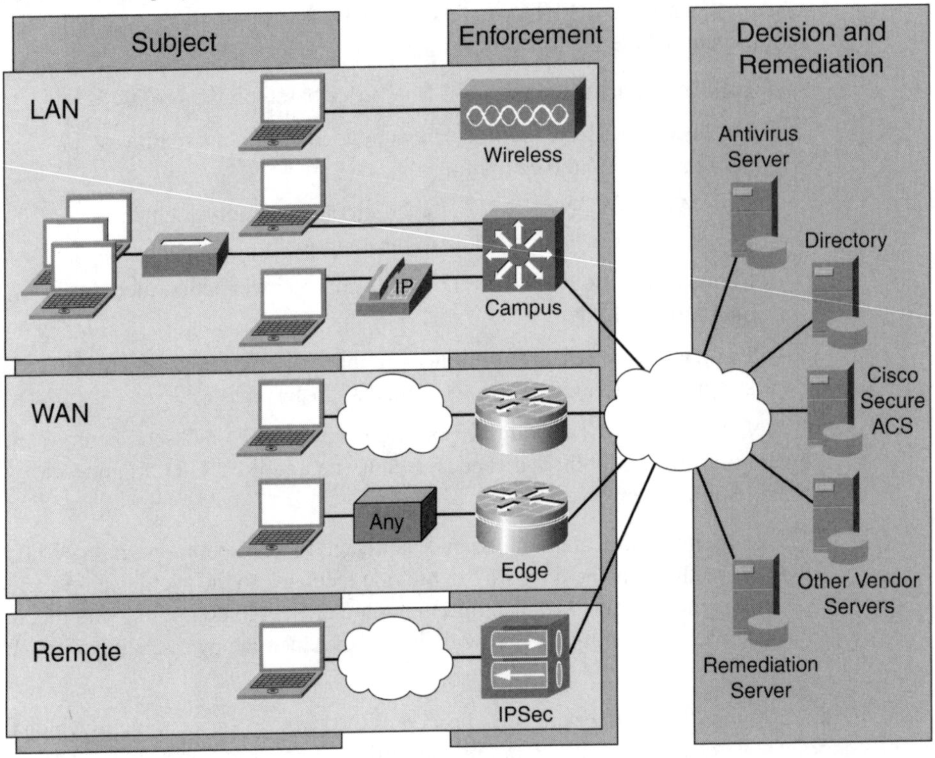

Source: Cisco Systems, Inc.[3]

The first NAC Framework deployment rule of thumb is to use the NAC-enabled NAD closest to the endpoints for checking compliance, helping enforce a least-privilege principle. The second rule is that compliance checking for an endpoint should occur at one NAD (closest to the endpoint), not throughout the network. The NAD might not be capable of performing compliance checks or enforcing the admission policy. Examples include non-Cisco devices or an older NAD that does not support NAC. As a result, NAC deployments will vary.

The following sections describe common NAC deployment scenarios.

LAN Access Compliance

NAC monitors desktops and servers within the office, helping to ensure that these endpoints comply with corporate antivirus and operating system patch policies before granting them LAN access. This reduces the risk of worm and virus infections spreading within an organization by expanding admission control to Layer 2 switches.

NAC Framework can also check wireless hosts connecting to the network to ensure that they are properly patched. The 802.1x protocol can be used in combination with device and user authentication to perform this validation using the NAC-L2-802.1x method. Some businesses might not want to use the 802.1x supplicant, so instead they may choose to use the NAC-L2-IP method using either IP or MAC.

NAC can be used to check the compliance of every endpoint trying to obtain network access, not just those managed by IT. Managed and unmanaged endpoints, including contractor and partner systems, may be checked for compliance with antivirus and operating system policy. If the posture agent is not present on the interrogated endpoint, a default access policy can be enforced limiting the endpoint to a specific subnet, thus limiting its ability to infect other devices on the entire network.

WAN Access Compliance

NAC Framework can be deployed at branch or home offices to ensure that endpoints comply with the latest antivirus and operating system patches before allowing them access to WAN or Internet connections to the corporate network. Alternatively, compliance checks can be performed at the main office before access is granted to the main corporate network.

Remote Access Compliance

NAC Framework helps to ensure that remote and mobile worker endpoints have the latest antivirus and operating system patches before allowing them to access company resources through IP Security (IPsec) and other virtual private network (VPN) connections.

Summary

The Cisco Network Admission Control is a framework comprising Cisco networking infrastructure along with a variety of partner products to enforce network admission policies on NAC-enabled endpoint devices, guaranteeing software compliance before granting network access.

The Cisco NAC Framework consists of the following components:

- NAC-enabled security applications such as antivirus and host intrusion protection systems such as Cisco Security Agent
- Posture agents such as Cisco Trust Agent
- Network access devices such as routers, switches, and wireless access points
- Cisco Secure ACS, which is the Cisco Policy Server
- Optional third-party validation policy servers
- Optional management and reporting tools

NAC allows the appropriate level of network access only to compliant and trusted endpoint devices such as PCs, servers, and PDAs. NAC can also identify noncompliant endpoints, deny them access, and place them in a quarantined area or give them restricted access to computing resources.

NAC agentless hosts can be identified by exception lists, whitelisting, or audit servers and can be evaluated before granting network access.

NAC Framework operates across all network access methods including campus switching, wired and wireless, router WAN and LAN links, IPSec connections, remote access, and dial-up links.

References

[1] Cisco Systems, Inc. NAC Customer Profile Reference by Russell Rice. Network Admission Control (NAC) Cisco Security SEVT Update. April 6, 2005.

[2] Cisco Systems, Inc. NAC Agentless Host Exceptions and Whitelisting. 2005.

[3] Cisco Systems, Inc. Network Admission Control (NAC). 2005.

CISCO SYSTEMS

ISBN: 1-58705-220-2

Building Multiservice
Transport Networks

Jim Durkin
John A. Goodman
Michael Rezek
Michael E. Wallace
Frank Fernandez-Posse

ciscopress.com

This chapter covers the following topics:

- MSPP Network Design Methodology
- Protection Design
- Network Timing Design
- Network Management Considerations
- MSPP Network Technologies
- Linear Networks
- UPSR Networks
- BLSR Networks
- Subtending Rings
- Subtending Shelves
- Ring-to-Ring Interconnect Diversity
- Mesh Networks

Multiservice Provisioning Platform Network Design

You must consider many factors when you plan to design Multiservice Provisioning Platform (MSPP) networks. Some are obvious and are a function of the traffic requirements and growth forecast for the network: fiber cable sizing, span bandwidth(s), circuit allocation, and so on. However, you must consider other factors that are foundational to the design and that help determine the extent of the network's flexibility and resiliency, as well as its operational characteristics. This chapter examines many of these design components, including protection options, synchronization (timing) design, and network management. In addition, this chapter presents a survey of the various MSPP network topologies, such as linear, ring, and mesh configurations.

MSPP Network Design Methodology

Network designers must address three important questions during the transport network planning process:

- What level of reliability must the transport system provide to meet end-user availability requirements?

- How will the network be synchronized to ensure that all transmissions from each of its elements are precisely timed?

- How will the network be managed to facilitate fault management, provisioning, and performance evaluation of the system?

This section covers these design parameters and the factors to consider when making decisions related to these.

Protection Design

A key feature of MSPPs is the capability to provide a very high level of system reliability because of the multiple forms of redundancy or protection provisionable in the platform. These protection mechanisms are available to the MSPP network designer:

- Redundant power feeds
- "Common control" redundancy

- "Tributary" interface protection
- Synchronization source redundancy
- Cable route diversity
- Multiple shelves, or chassis
- Protected network topologies (rings)

Redundant Power Feeds

MSPPs require a power source with a -48 V potential (within a certain tolerance) to operate. Two separate connections for power supply cabling are generally provided on the rear of an MSPP chassis. These are typically referred to as Battery A and Battery B. The internal power distribution is designed so that the system can continue to function normally if one of the supply connections is removed or fails. If only one of these supply connections is cabled to the power source, which is typically an alternating current (AC)–to direct current (DC) rectifier plant, an alarm is raised in the system's software (such as "Battery Failure B").

For maximum protection from service interruption from power issues, the MSPP design should include connections for both the A and B terminals. Power feed cable sizing and the associated fusing should follow the local electrical codes. If possible, separate power supplies should provide these redundant feeds, to avoid losing both feeds in a single-supply failure. Finally, it is strongly recommended that you use power supplies that include battery back-up systems, to maintain service if a commercial power outage occurs.

Common Control Redundancy

Most fully featured MSPP systems employ a modular architecture. This means that various cards (also called blades or plug-ins) can be inserted into the chassis to provide various functionality or service interfaces. Typically, a subset of the cards installed in the chassis is known as common control cards. These cards provide functions that all the installed interface cards need, and also control and monitor the operation of the system. Consider some examples of the functions that the common control cards in an MSPP provide:

- System initialization
- Configuration control
- Alarm reporting and maintenance
- System and network communications
- Synchronization
- Diagnostic testing
- Power monitoring
- Circuit cross-connect setup and maintenance

Because many of these functions are critical to the proper operation of the system, the cards that perform these functions typically must be installed in pairs. For example, the Cisco ONS 15454 MSPP reserves five chassis slots for common control cards; four of these are used to house two redundant pairs. The Timing, Communications, and Control (TCC) card and the Cross-connect (XC) card are essential to the system and are always placed in an active/standby pair. If the active card fails, the standby card takes over. Failure to install the secondary common control card(s) normally results in an alarm condition in the MSPP, such as a "Protection Unit Not Available" alarm.

Tributary Interface Protection

Interface cards that connect an MSPP to external equipment, such as routers, Ethernet switches, and private branch exchange (PBX) switches, are sometimes referred to as tributary interfaces. MSPP cards can be protected to ensure service continuity in case of card failure. MSPPs provide protection in many ways, which include one or more of the following:

- **1:1 protection**—A single protect, or standby, interface card protects a single working, or active, service interface card. This type of protection can be provided for electrical time-division multiplexing (TDM) interfaces, such as DS1, DS3, or EC-1. If the working card fails or is removed, traffic switches from the working card to the protection card. The standby card slot is linked through the MSPP chassis backplane to the working card slot so that it can reuse the cabling (such as coax cables for a DS3 interface) from the working slot if a protection switch occurs.

- **1:N protection**—In this protection scheme, a single standby card is used to protect multiple working cards (such as a single DS3 interface card used to protect up to five working DS3 cards). This is an advantage economically because fewer total cards are required to protect the working service interfaces. In addition, non-revenue-generating protection cards consume less valuable chassis real estate. As in 1:1 protection, some MSPP systems provide this type of redundancy for electrical TDM interfaces.

- **1+1 protection**—Optical (OC-N) interfaces can use this protection type in a failover scenario. 1+1 protection implies that a standby card or port protects a single working optical card (or port on a multiport card). Each of the optical cards must be cabled to the external equipment to provide this functionality.

- **Higher-layer protection**—Data interfaces, such as native Ethernet cards, are typically unprotected. However, if required, you can protect these interfaces by installing separate cards, with each having a 100-Mbps or Gigabit Ethernet (GigE) connection to a switch or router. This external networking equipment can then be configured to provide protection at Layer 2 or Layer 3. As an example, separate GigE links with load balancing can be configured between the MSPP Ethernet interface and the external switch or router.

- **0:1 protection**—This is also known as unprotected operation. This can be an option with certain designs, as in the case of Ethernet or Storage-Area Network (SAN) extension services, and when Layer 3 is used to protect data traffic.

Figure 5-1 gives an example of an MSPP (a Cisco ONS 15454) with multiple service interfaces configured with the various tributary protection methods. For critical service requirements that cannot be subjected to outage caused by the failure of a single interface card, it is strongly recommended that you provide tributary interface protection. In addition to avoiding traffic loss, these protection mechanisms can be used to defer time-consuming repair visits (truck rolls) for card replacements until regularly scheduled maintenance visits.

Figure 7-1   *MSPP with Multiple Tributary Protection Methods*

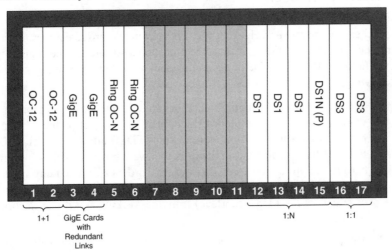

Synchronization Source Redundancy

Timing is an essential element of Synchronous Optical Network (SONET)/Synchronous Digital Hierarchy (SDH) networks. MSPP systems enable network operators to provision multiple synchronization sources to provide redundancy. Primary timing can be provided for a node either externally, through wired connections to a digital clocking source, or from a connected OC-N interface. In either case, MSPP systems also must be equipped with internal clocking sources (usually contained within the common control cards) for failover in case the primary sources fail.

For MSPP locations that have a clock source installed, such as a Cesium clock or Global Positioning System (GPS) clock receiver, the MSPP typically provides redundant clock source connection terminals. These are normally referred to as Building Integrated Timing Supply (BITS) connections. These should be wired to diverse timing interfaces on the BITS clock system for maximum redundancy. In this type of arrangement, the network operator can configure three timing sources for the MSPP node and rank them in order of preference to use. For example, the first-choice timing reference source would be the BITS-1 connection. The second choice would be the BITS-2 connection (in case the BITS-1 connection fails), followed by the internal system clock as a last resort.

Similarly, MSPP locations that do not have an external clocking source can be configured with three timing source options. The first two options would be the East and West OC-N ring interfaces, which can be traced back to another node's clocking source. The third option is the internal clock.

Cable Route Diversity

Physical cable route diversity should be considered to ensure service continuity in case of a cable break or inadvertent disconnection. Cable route diversity can be provided on both a system-level and a network-level basis.

At the system or node level, diverse pathing and ducting for direct system connections can be provided during shelf installation, with one cable lead routed away from the shelf on the left side of the network bay frame or cabinet, and the other cable lead on the right. Connections that can provide diversity in this manner include power feeders, timing leads, optical fibers, and Category 5 Ethernet cables.

At the network level, optical cable diversity can be provided for MSPP nodes configured in ring topologies. This protection can be provided both inside the building in which the MSPP is located and in the exterior (or outside-plant) cabling that is used to connect to other node locations. For example, a carrier operating an MSPP network might choose to use diverse routing for each pair of fibers connecting MSPP nodes in a two-fiber ring, such as a unidirectional path switched ring (UPSR). This could include separate underground conduit runs leaving a building and diverse geographical cable routes. If only one route exists between two locations, such as to a "spur" site on a ring, diversity can be provided by using two fibers in a buried fiber cable and two fibers in a cable lashed to a utility pole line. This would be the case when a particular site is limited to a single physical-access route (such as one roadway) from the remaining sites on the network.

Multiple Shelves

In an MSPP network that is used to transport critical services, such as medical or E911 applications, consideration should be given to providing chassis-level protection for service-termination nodes. For example, a hospital using a resilient SONET ring to carry real-time video for remote robotic-assisted surgery might elect to install MSPP nodes for interface diversity in separate data rooms or closets in a building or campus, to protect against a power outage, fire, or flooding hazard.

Protected Network Topologies (Rings)

Protected network topologies, or rings, can be used to protect a network if a single node or fiber span fails. Rings allow protected traffic to be rerouted automatically over an alternate path if the active path becomes unavailable. Ring topologies are covered in detail in the sections "UPSR Networks" and "BLSR Networks."

Network Timing Design

SONET MSPPs rely on highly accurate clocking sources to maintain proper network synchronization. Each element in the network should be timed from a Stratum Level 3 (or better) source traceable to a primary reference source (PRS). The PRS is typically a Stratum Level 1 clock.

Timing Sources

For timing design, the first consideration should be the type of timing source available at each location. As discussed previously, the possible timing sources for MSPPs include the following:

- External sources, such as a Cesium or GPS clocks
- Line sources, which include the SONET optical ports
- Internal clock, which is normally a Stratum 3 clock built into a system common control card

Based on these different timing source types, a network designer has several options to choose from when deciding how the network will be synchronized. The following are the most common recommended designs:

- **External/line-timed configuration**—In this configuration, one MSPP in the network is timed from an external clocking source, such as a BITS clock; the other MSPP nodes are line-timed from their optical interfaces. The clocking source for the externally timed node is traceable to the PRS. This is a typical timing design for a carrier access ring, in which one (or more than one) node is located in a telco central office and the other nodes are located at remote locations. Figure 5-2 shows this configuration.

- **Externally timed configuration**—If external clocking sources are available at all MSPP locations, each node can be cabled and configured as externally timed. Figure 5-3 shows an example of this type of design. Because this requires clocks at each site, this type of configuration is normally seen in interoffice transport applications, in which each MSPP is located in a telco central office. If all clock sources are traceable to a single primary reference source, the network is said to be synchronous. However, if the various local clocks are traceable to two or more primary reference sources with nearly the same timing (such as an MSPP network that spans more than one carrier), the network is referred to as plesiochronous.

Figure 7-2   *External/Line-Timed Network Synchronization Configuration*

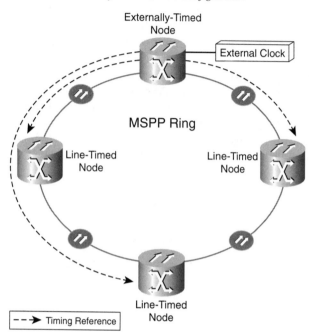

Figure 7-3   *Externally Timed Network Synchronization Configuration*

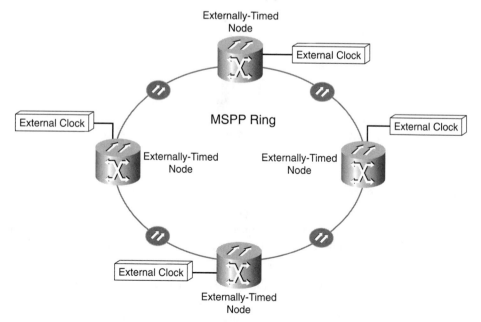

- **Internal/line-timed configuration**—For networks in which no external clocking source is available, such as a private corporate network, a single MSPP node can be configured for internal timing from its embedded Stratum 3 clock, with the remaining nodes deriving their timing from their connected optical interfaces. Some MSPP vendors refer to configured Internal clocking as "free-running" mode. This type of design is unacceptable for rings in which SONET connections (such as OC-3 or STS-1) are required to other networks. Also, additional jitter is introduced on low-speed add/drop interfaces, such as DS1s. This can cause problems if these interfaces are connected to external equipment that is sensitive to such jitter. One example is a voice switch that contains a Stratum 3 clock of its own. Figure 5-4 depicts a ring configured for the internal/line-timed configuration.

Figure 7-4   *Internal/Line-Timed Network Synchronization Configuration*

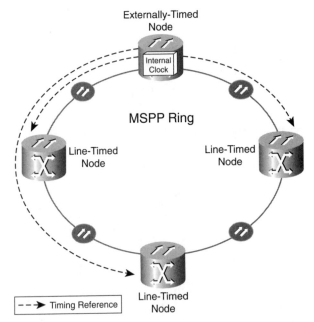

Timing Reference Selection

After selecting the timing configuration, the network designer must assign the prioritized list of timing references to be provisioned for each MSPP node. The MSPP system software uses this prioritized list to determine its primary reference source for timing and the order of failover switching in case the primary source becomes unusable or unavailable.

Typically, this list can be set up in the MSPP node to be revertive or nonrevertive. Revertive means that, if the primary reference fails and a switch to the secondary reference occurs, the node switches back to the primary source after the problem that forced the switch is corrected. A countdown timer is implemented for this reversion switch so that the network operator can set an amount of time (such as 5 minutes) to allow the primary reference to stabilize before the node switches back. This prevents multiple clock source switches from a "flapping" primary timing source.

The order of prioritization for timing sources varies based on whether the node is externally timed, line-timed, or internally (free-running) timed. For externally timed nodes, in which the MSPP is synchronized to DS1 timing leads cabled to the chassis from an external clocking source, the primary and secondary options for timing should be the redundant pair of connections, usually referred to as BITS-1 and BITS-2. Generally, it is recommended that you use the internal Stratum 3 clock as the third option so that if both BITS inputs fail, the MSPP fails over to internal timing. However, some MSPP systems allow for another option, which is to provision an optical port for the third selection. Cisco calls this mixed timing mode. This is an option for a network that is configured in the external/line-timed configuration, in which more than one node uses external timing. Using mixed timing can be tricky, however, as you will see in the examples later in this chapter. Although the Cisco ONS 15454 allows for mixed timing configuration, Cisco does not recommend its use and urges caution if you are implementing it.

For line-timed nodes, a typical recommended prioritization list includes the "main ring" optical ports, East and West, for the first and second options, with the internal clock as the third option. Internally timed nodes should be provisioned to use the internal clock for all three references.

Synchronization Status Messaging

To maintain adequate timing in an MSPP network, SONET provides a protocol known as Synchronization Status Messaging (SSM) to allow for communication related to the quality of timing between nodes. This information is carried over 4 bits in the S1 byte of the line overhead, with each node transmitting its current status to the adjacent line-terminating equipment (LTE). Recall that an LTE is a piece of SONET equipment that can read and modify the line overhead bytes. These messages enable each MSPP in the network to select alternate timing sources, as defined in the prioritized reference list, when events in the network make a change necessary. Two sets of SSM codes are in use today: The older and more widely used version is Generation 1; Generation 2 is a newer version that defines additional quality levels. Table 5-1 defines the message set for Generation 2.

Table 7-1   *Synchronization Status Messaging Generation 2 Message Set*

Message Description	Message Acronym	S1 Bits 5–8	Quality Level
Stratum 1 Traceable	PRS	0001	1
Synchronized–Traceability unknown	STU	0000	2
Stratum 2 Traceable	ST2	0111	3

continues

Table 7-1   *Synchronization Status Messaging Generation 2 Message Set (Continued)*

Message Description	Message Acronym	S1 Bits 5–8	Quality Level
Transit Node Clock	TNC	0100	4
Stratum 3E Traceable	ST3E	1101	5
Stratum 3 Traceable	ST3	1010	6
SONET Minimum Clock Traceable	SMC	1100	7
Stratum 4 Traceable	ST4	—	8
Do Not Use for Synchronization	DUS	1111	9
Provisionable by Network Operator	PNO	1110	User assignable

To understand how these SSM messages are used in a SONET MSPP network, consider the example network shown in Figure 5-5. This network is configured in the externally timed/line-timed arrangement, with Node 1 being externally timed from a collocated BITS clock and Nodes 2–6 being line-timed traceable back to the timing source at Node 1. Because Node 1 is being timed by a Stratum 1 clock, the last 4 bits of the S1 byte transmitted in both the East and West directions are set to the value 0001, indicating the primary reference source.

NOTE   Node 1 has the two BITS inputs as its primary and secondary timing sources, with the internal clock as the last resort.

Proceeding clockwise in the network, nodes 2, 3, 4, 5, and 6 have been provisioned to select the timing from the OC-N card installed in their West slot (in Figure 5-5, this is Slot 6) as their first choice for timing.

Note that each of these nodes receives the SSM value of PRS on their Slot 6, indicating that the timing being received is of Stratum 1 quality. Each node passes that along in the daisy chain to the next node in the ring.

In the reverse direction (counterclockwise), each MSPP node transmits the SSM value of DUS (Don't Use for Synchronization) back in the direction from which primary timing is received. This is required to prevent a timing loop from occurring somewhere in the network if the primary timing source fails. Note that at the Node 6–to–Node 1 connection, the PRS value is being both transmitted and received by each of the two network elements. This is a normal scenario. Node 1 always ignores the PRS being received on its Slot 6 OC-N card because that optical line is not among its possible timing references. Meanwhile, Node 6 makes use of the SSM information received on its Slot 12 only if its primary reference source fails.

Figure 7-5   *SSM Operation*

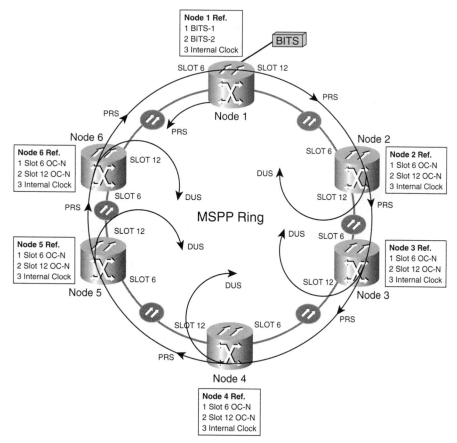

The example shown in Figure 5-5, in which each of the line-timed nodes has the same Reference 1, is one typical method of timing configuration in externally timed/line-timed designs. Another method for this type of network is to provision the ring OC-N interface that is closest to the primary reference source as Reference 1. For example, in Figure 5-5, Nodes 2 and 3 would have the OC-N interface in Slot 6 as their Reference 1, whereas Nodes 5 and 6 would have Slot 12 for their first selection. Node 4 could be provisioned either way, since it is the same number of "hops" in either direction back to the BITS-connected Node 1. Cisco recommends the latter selection criteria for their MSPP, the ONS 15454.

Network Management Considerations

Network management is an important consideration in MSPP network design. The designer has various options, depending upon the type of network environment in which the equipment is deployed. Fault detection, configuration and provisioning, performance monitoring, and security management are all functions of the network-management system.

In an enterprise campus or privately owned metro MSPP network, each MSPP node can have the capability to connect to the local LAN for remote management. Figure 5-6 shows this type of scenario. From the standpoint of fault recovery, this is an advantageous arrangement because no single network connection failure will isolate the network from the network-management system. Each MSPP node has its own connectivity for management purposes.

Figure 7-6 *An MSPP Network with LAN Connections to Each Node for Network Management*

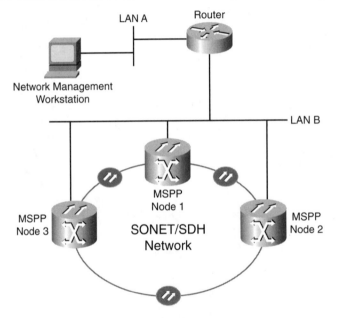

Figure 5-7 shows a more typical service provider scenario. Service provider MSPP networks typically have one or more network elements located in secure, company-owned locations, such as a telco central office. The other nodes are normally located on the premises of the service provider's customers or in common locations serving multiple customers. The node(s) located in the service provider's central office (sometimes referred to as a point of presence, or POP) can be linked back to the network operations center (NOC). This node is known as the gateway network element (GNE). The other nodes, called external network elements (ENEs), use the SONET in-band management channel, known as the data communications channel (DCC), to communicate to the NOC via the GNE. In this example, a single MSPP node (Node 1, the GNE) is attached to the management network; the other nodes, ENEs, use the DCC for management connectivity. If additional MSPP nodes in the network are located in facilities that the service provider owns and can also be used as GNEs, the single point of failure for network-management connectivity shown in this example could be eliminated.

Figure 7-7   *An MSPP Network with a LAN Connection to a Single GNE Node for Network Management*

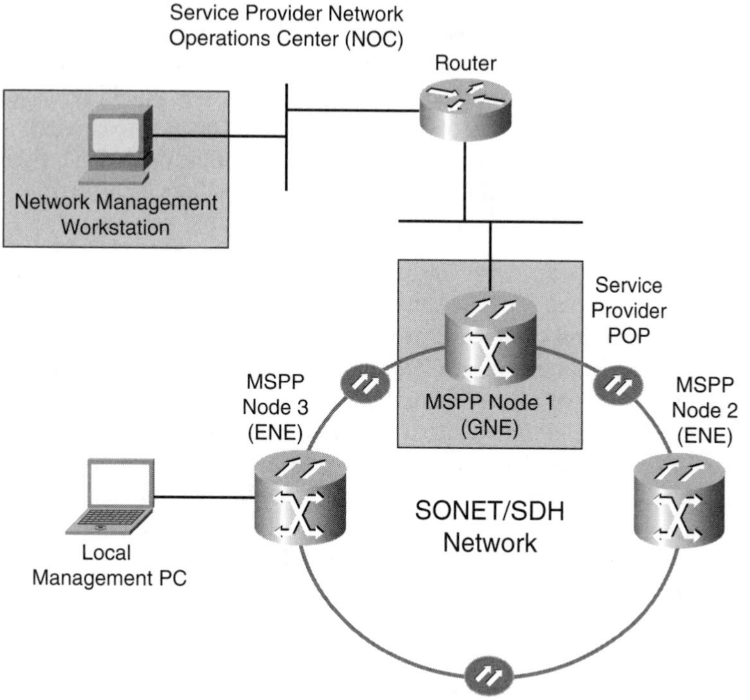

MSPP Network Topologies

Network-protection characteristics and total system payload capacity are determined largely by the type of network topology deployed. SONET MSPPs provide support for multiple available topologies, with varying levels of resiliency and traffic-carrying capabilities. These topologies include linear, ring, and mesh networks. This section covers these topologies and describes their operation and applications.

Linear Networks

One topology option for MSPP network design is the linear network. Linear networks are typically used when all the traffic to be serviced by the network is routed in a point-to-point manner, or point-to-point with intermediate add/drop locations. Linear networks that transport all traffic between two nodes are commonly referred to as point-to-point or terminal mode networks. If some traffic needs to be inserted into the network at intermediate sites, a linear add/drop network, sometimes called a linear add/drop chain, can be used.

Figure 5-8 shows an example of a terminal mode MSPP network. All traffic is routed from Node A to Node B. The connection between the nodes can be protected against facility failures, or it can be designed as unprotected if protection is not a requirement or is provided through some other network connection. If the terminal mode network will be unprotected, a single optical interface card, such as an OC-12 or OC-48, should be installed at each node (or terminal) and a single pair of optical fibers should be used to connect between them. In this case, a failure on the fiber cable span or of one of the optical interface cards causes traffic to be interrupted, and information will be lost unless it can be routed between the sites through some alternate connection.

In the protected scenario, two optical interfaces are needed in each terminal. These can be provided either on separate cards or on different ports of the same multiport card. A type of protection known as 1+1 is provided for this type of network. This means that one of the optical ports on each end (and the associated fiber connection) is set up as "working" or "active"; the secondary ports are the "protect" or "standby" ports. If a port failure or fiber facility failure occurs on the working link, the network switches the traffic to the protection link. To decrease the chances of a failure-related service interruption, terminal mode networks can be designed so that the working and protect ports are on different interface cards in each terminal, and the working and protect fiber pairs are physically routed in separate cable sheaths following diverse paths between the two endpoints.

Figure 7-8   *A Terminal Mode MSPP Network*

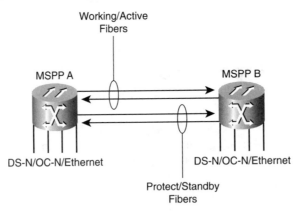

In a linear add/drop chain MSPP network, the intermediate nodes each have a connection to their neighboring MSPP nodes, one facing East and the other facing West. Again, these connections can be either 1+1 protected or unprotected. In the protected scenario, the intermediate add/drop nodes require two pairs of optical interfaces, with a pair facing East and a pair facing West. Figure 5-9 shows an example of a linear add/drop chain network.

Figure 7-9   *A Linear Add-Drop Chain MSPP Network*

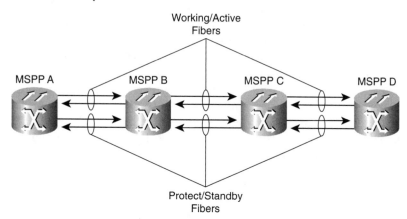

In modern MSPP networks, linear systems are rarely deployed. This is because of the availability of ring-based networks, which are more fault tolerant and often more economical to deploy. In a ring network, a single-node failure causes a service disruption only for traffic that terminates in that particular node. However, in a linear network, a single node failure can disrupt traffic servicing additional network locations. For example, in Figure 5-9, if MSPP C experienced a failure affecting the entire node (such as a power supply failure), traffic routed from MSPP A to MSPP D would be lost because this traffic transited MSPP C. In a ring network, this transit traffic would be rerouted via an alternate path. This network also can be provided with facility protection much more economically in a ring-based architecture. MSPP C would require a total of four costly optical interfaces if it were installed in a protected linear add/drop configuration, with two interfaces for East and two for West. However, a ring network would require only a single interface in each direction. Ring networks are covered in detail in the following sections.

UPSR Networks

A UPSR is a SONET protection topology used to maintain service across the optical network in case of a failure condition, such as a fiber span break or optical interface card failure. In a UPSR, traffic between MSPP nodes is safeguarded by carrying duplicate copies of the signals around diverse East and West paths from origin node to destination node, ensuring a swift failover to the opposite path. Because of this method of operation, a UPSR is sometimes referred to as a dual counter-rotating, self-healing ring.

UPSR Operation

To understand the operation of a UPSR, consider Figure 5-10, which shows a typical four-node OC-12 UPSR network. In this example, a client signal is being transported across the network from MSPP A to MSPP C. In the case of a bidirectional signal, such as a time-division multiplexing (TDM) circuit (such as a DS3), the signal consists of a transmit side and a receive side at each termination point; however, for clarity, Figure 5-10 shows only one direction. In the transmit direction from A to C, the signal enters MSPP A through a traffic interface card and is internally routed to the node's cross-connect matrix. Within the cross-connect matrix, the signal is bridged, or duplicated, and connected to both the East-facing and West-facing UPSR optical interface cards for transmission across the optical network. The circuit is assigned to travel on the UPSR on STS-1 path number 1, on both the East and West interfaces. At the intermediate MSPP nodes B and D, the signals are passed through. At MSPP C, a selector switch locks to the highest-quality signal from the two available STS-1 paths.

Figure 7-10 *UPSR Operation*

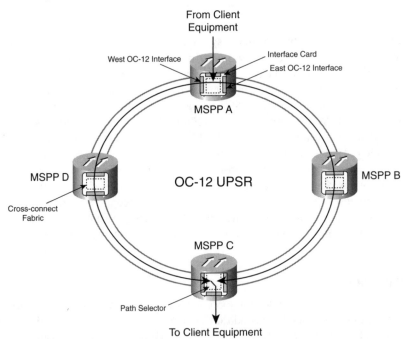

If a problem occurs with the selected signal, such as a high bit-error rate, the selector mechanism switches to the back-up path. Figure 5-11 shows the resulting path switch from a facility failure.

Because each signal transported on the UPSR consumes the same amount of bandwidth on both sides of the ring between the source and destination, the total amount of traffic carried (in Synchronous Transport Signal [STS] equivalents) is limited to the ring's transmission bandwidth, regardless of the origin and destination of the circuits. Therefore, an OC-12 UPSR is limited to transporting 12 total STS-1s, whereas an OC-48 UPSR can handle a total of 48 STS-1s.

Figure 7-11 *UPSR Path Switch Example*

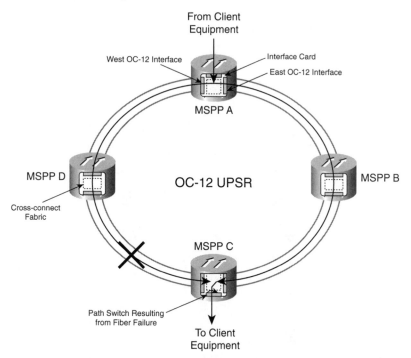

For example, in the OC-12 network in Figure 5-10, if an STS-3c signal was being carried between MSPP A and MSPP C, and was assigned to use the first three STS-1s (STS-1-1, STS-1-2, and STS-1-3), it would traverse the East path through MSPP B, as well as the West path through MSPP D on these same three STS-1s. This is a major difference between UPSR and bidirectional line switch ring (BLSR) topologies. Depending on the number of nodes in the network and the traffic pattern, a BLSR can accommodate more traffic than the transmission bandwidth.

Within the cross-connect matrix of the MSPP, a UPSR-protected circuit consumes three ports on the source and destination nodes, and two ports on the intermediate, "pass-through" nodes. Figure 5-10 shows this. At MSPP A, which is a source/destination node, the DS3 signal is mapped into an STS-1 and enters the cross-connect matrix on a single input/output (I/O) port. Because copies of this signal are to be transported around both the East and West sides of the ring, the signal is sent to two different I/O ports leaving the matrix. One of these will connect to the East optical line interface, the other to the West.

Meanwhile, at MSPP B, which is a pass-through node for this circuit, the signal enters one optical interface, gets passed through the matrix by entering one I/O port and exiting another, and then exits through the opposite optical interface. Figure 5-12 shows the details of how this works at each of the circuit-termination nodes. At each of these sites, three STS-1 I/O ports on the cross-connect matrix are consumed for this drop/add circuit.

For example, if this were a 60-Gbps cross-connect fabric, with a total of 1,152 STS-1 ports (1,152 × 51.84 Mbps = 59.71968 Gbps), this connection would use 3 of the 1152 ports, or approximately 0.26 percent of its STS-1 capacity.

Figure 7-12 *MSPP Cross-Connect Matrix Use at a UPSR-Protected Circuit Source or Destination Node*

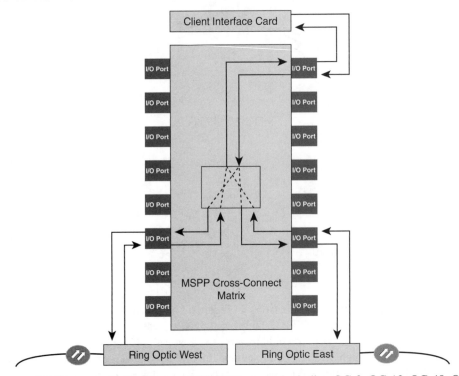

UPSRs can be built using any SONET line rate, including OC-3, OC-12, OC-48, OC-192, and OC-768. In an MSPP configured for UPSR operation, you need two optical interface cards, one designated East and the other designated West. A node design using a multiport optical interface card with separate ports used for East and West would be ill advised because a card-level failure (such as a card power supply failure) would result in losing both ring interfaces. That would cause service disruption on any traffic terminating at that node.

SONET MSPPs are typically configured so that an East-designated interface on one node is connected via the fiber-optic network links to the West-designated interface on the next adjacent node, and vice versa. For example, in an ONS 15454 MSPP OC-48 UPSR, a network designer might choose to designate an OC-48 interface card in chassis Slot 5 as the West interface, and an OC-48 interface card in chassis Slot 6 as the East interface. The card in Slot 5 would connect to a similar card in Slot 6 of the adjacent node to the west of this node, and the card in Slot 6 would connect to a similar card in Slot 5 of the adjacent node to the east. Figure 5-13 shows such a design. For simplicity, it is usually recommended that you keep this scheme consistent throughout the network.

Figure 7-13 *Typical UPSR Fiber Cable Interconnection*

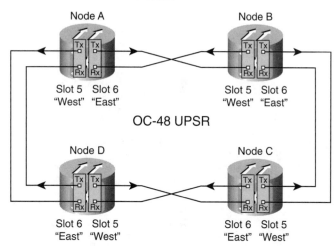

UPSR Applications

UPSRs are best suited for networks in which the traffic requirements call for most circuits to have a single common endpoint, or hub location. Some examples of this type of network requirement include the following:

- A local exchange carrier access ring in which voice and data traffic from residential or commercial areas is required to be carried to the local carrier central office for connection to the public switched telephone network (PSTN) or interoffice facilities

- A private corporate network in which Ethernet connectivity is needed from various branch offices to a main location or server farm

- A storage-area network extended via a SONET backbone for linking physically diverse locations to a common data/storage center

Figure 5-14 shows one such example. A carrier has deployed an OC-12 ring to service a neighborhood called East Meadow. This MSPP ring needs to service three locations: a residential area, a wireless provider cellular tower, and a business park.

The residential area, served by the Fairview Avenue Remote Terminal Cabinet, needs DS1 circuits for connecting a digital loop carrier (DLC) system and a DS3 for the trunk feeder for a remote digital subscriber line access multiplexer (DSLAM). The DLC is used to provide plain old telephone service (POTS) for the neighborhood. The remote DSLAM provides broadband DSL service for high-speed Internet connections. The POTS DS1s is transported back to the Oak Street central office for connection to the PSTN via a Class 5 switch. The DSLAM DS3 must connect to the Asynchronous Transfer Mode (ATM) network equipment at Oak Street.

Figure 7-14 *East Meadow OC-12 UPSR Network*

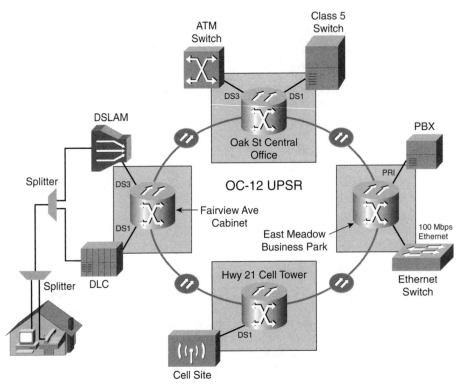

The Highway 21 cellular tower site has a requirement for multiple DS1 circuits. The wireless provider, which purchases this service from the carrier, needs to connect its cell site equipment to its mobile telephone switching office (MTSO). The carrier will connect the DS1s at the Oak Street office to interoffice facilities that route to the MTSO. Customers served by the East Meadow Business Park Site require a variety of services, including primary rate ISDN (PRI) circuits for PBX trunks and 100-Mbps Ethernet links for Internet service provider (ISP) connectivity. These circuits will also need to be routed back to the Oak Street central office to interface with the PSTN or the Internet.

Because all traffic for this network needs to be tied back into the Oak Street central office, a UPSR is an excellent choice for the MSPP network topology.

BLSR Networks

As in a UPSR, a BLSR network is designed to allow traffic continuity in case of a fiber span or MSPP node failure. The key differentiator versus UPSR, however, is that the BLSR is not capacity-limited to the transmission bandwidth of the ring. For example, depending on the number of nodes in the network and the traffic distribution, a two-fiber OC-192 BLSR can be used to transport more than 1000 STS-1 equivalents. BLSRs accomplish this via a method called spatial reuse. The same bandwidth, or traffic channels, can be used to transport different signals on different parts of the network. This is shown for both 2-Fiber and 4-Fiber BLSRs in the next sections.

2-Fiber BLSR Operation

In a 2-Fiber BLSR, a pair of optical fibers is used to connect the MSPP nodes on the ring, just as is the case with a UPSR. However, unlike in a UPSR, active traffic is connected through the ring in only one direction from source to destination: either the East route or the West route. In the opposite direction, spare capacity is held in reserve as "protection" bandwidth, in case a failure occurs in the assigned route. This is the case on every fiber link in a 2-Fiber BLSR: Exactly half the SONET bandwidth is used for assigned, working traffic; the other half is held in reserve for protection.

Consider the example four-node 2-Fiber OC-192 BLSR shown in Figure 5-15. Each fiber link in the ring, such as the one between Node 1 and Node 2, consists of two fibers transmitting in opposite directions. The bandwidth carried on each fiber is divided equally, with the first sequential half transporting production traffic and the second half reserved for protection. For example, in the link from Node 1 to Node 2 OC-192, the clockwise fiber path can use the first 96 STS-1s to map SONET circuits; STS-1s 97-192 are designated as the protection path for use during a fault-initiated switch. The counterclockwise fiber works in the same manner while transmitting the OC-192 signal in the reverse direction.

Figure 7-15 *A 2-Fiber BLSR Example*

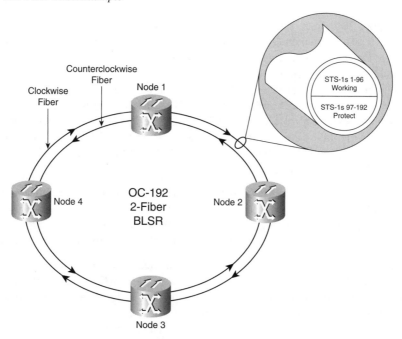

To illustrate the fault-recovery process for a BLSR, reference the scenario shown in Figure 5-16; this is the same network from Figure 5-15, with an STS-3c circuit mapped from Node 1 to Node 3 through the route passing through Node 2 using STS-1s 1 to 3.

Figure 7-16 *A 2-Fiber BLSR with an STS-3c Circuit-Routed from Node 1 to Node 3*

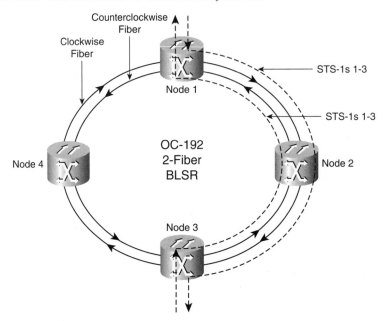

Suppose that a fiber failure occurs on the span between Node 1 and Node 2, with both clockwise and counterclockwise fibers affected as shown. In this case, the traffic would switch as shown in Figure 5-17. The original route for the transmit side (from Node 1 to Node 3) for the signal was rerouted from the clockwise fiber (STS-1s 1 to 3) to the counterclockwise fiber (STS-1s 97 to 99), reaching Node 3 through Node 4. The opposite side of the signal, which is the Node 3–to–Node 1 transmit direction, traverses the counterclockwise fiber (STS-1s 1 to 3) from Node 3 to Node 2. However, because of the fiber facility failure that has occurred between Node 1 and Node 2, this side of the signal is switched to STS-1s 97 to 99 on the clockwise fiber at Node 2, and reaches Node 1 through Node 3 and Node 4, as shown in the figure.

To facilitate the protection switching in a BLSR, the network elements in the ring use the K1 and K2 bytes in the line overhead to communicate protection-switch requests and status. These bytes are known collectively as the Automatic Protection Switch (APS) bytes. The switching is accomplished by the nodes that are adjacent to the failure (optical line or network node).

BLSR operation and protection-switch performance requirements are defined in a Telcordia (formerly BELLCORE) document called GR-1230-CORE. In this document, the total completion time for protection switching and traffic restoration is defined to be less than or equal to 50 ms, not including detection time. This requirement is for networks consisting of a maximum of 16 nodes with up to 1200 km of fiber.

Figure 7-17 *A 2-Fiber BLSR Line-Switch Example*

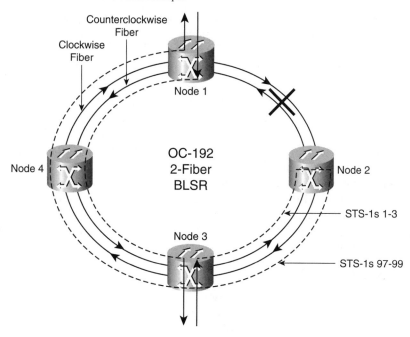

2-Fiber BLSR System Capacity

Because of the protection scheme employed in the 2-Fiber BLSR architecture, the total capacity of a fiber span between two network nodes in this configuration is equal to half the transmission bandwidth, or $n/2$, where n is the ring's STS-1 capacity (for example: $n = 48$ in an OC-48 ring, so the capacity of a single OC-48 span is equal to 48/2, or 24). In addition, the protection channel(s) held in reserve on the side of the ring opposite to the assigned working link is defined as $c + (n/2)$, where c is the assigned working STS-1 channel (or first STS-1 in a concatenated signal, such as a STS-12c) and n is the ring STS-1 capacity. For example, in an OC-48 ($n = 48$) 2-Fiber BLSR, the protection channel for a signal using STS-1 5 ($c = 5$) would be 5 + (48/2), or 29.

Because the total number of STS-1 equivalents that a 2-Fiber BLSR can carry depends on the number of spans, or nodes, in the ring, you need to define an equation for calculating this capacity. The variables in the equation are the number of nodes in the network, the bandwidth, and the traffic pattern for the ring, which is defined in the equation as the number of nonterminated, "pass-through" STS-1s transiting any node in the network. If you use X as the number of nodes, N as the network bandwidth, and A as the number of pass-through STS-1s in the ring, the capacity (or number of circuits that can be carried) for the ring is defined as $(N/2) \times X - A$. For each possible 2-Fiber BLSR configuration, Table 5-2 shows the capacity equations.

Table 7-2 *2-Fiber BLSR STS-1 Capacity Equations*

2F Ring Bandwidth	N	Working STS-1 Channels	Protect STS-1 Channels	Ring Capacity
OC-12	12	1–6	7–12	$(12/2) \times X - A$
OC-48	48	1–24	25–48	$(48/2) \times X - A$
OC-192	192	1–96	97–192	$(192/2) \times X - A$
OC-768	768	1–384	385–768	$(768/2) \times X - A$

To illustrate the application of these equations, consider the example in Figure 5-18. This is a representation of a four-node, 2-Fiber, OC-48 BLSR, with the traffic pattern as shown in the accompanying chart. The double-ended arrowed lines in the chart indicate the termination points for the various circuits shown. For example, the first line in the chart indicates that there are 10 STS-1 circuits routed on the ring from Node 1 to Node 2 (directly, with no pass-through nodes); the fifth line in the chart indicates that eight STS-1 circuits are riding the ring from Node 1 to Node 3, passing through Node 2.

Figure 7-18 *Traffic Routing in a 2-Fiber BLSR Example*

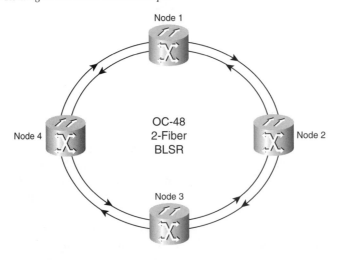

Circuits	Node 1	Node 2	Node 3	Node 4
10 STS-1	←———→			
12 STS-1		←———→		
6 STS-1			←———→	
18 STS-1	——→			←—
8 STS-1	←———— PT ————→			
4 STS-1		←——— PT ———→		

PT = Pass Through

To calculate the circuit capacity of this ring, you can apply the formula $(N/2) \times X - A$, where $N = 48$ (because the ring is an OC-48), $X = 4$ (number of nodes), and $A = 12$. You arrive at the value of A by adding the number of pass-through circuits for each pair of source-destination defined circuit sets. Proceeding through the traffic chart from top to bottom, then, yields $0 + 0 + 0 + 0 + 8 + 4 = 12$ total STS-1 pass-through circuits. Substituting these values into the equation, you get a total possible ring capacity, given the current traffic mapping, of $(48/2) \times 4 - 12 = 96 - 12 = 84$ STS-1 circuits. Because the ring is currently carrying 58 STS-1s (the summation of all the current services), a network planner can determine that there is space for up to 26 additional STS-1 circuits on this network, depending on their future routing.

Protection Channel Access

In their normal mode of operation, BLSRs inherently have some unused capacity in the form of the traffic channels held in reserve for protection switching. For instance, in an OC-48 2-Fiber BLSR, channels 25 to 48 on all ring spans are normally unused. Most protection-switch events (such as fiber cable cut and human provisioning error) are unplanned and unpredictable; however, it is theoretically possible that a network will operate in a normal, switch-free state for many months, or even years. Because of this, many network operators choose to use the BLSR protection channels to carry live production traffic. In the case of telecom carrier networks, this capability, referred to as protection channel access (PCA), represents an opportunity to generate additional revenue.

The caveat to using PCA circuits is that they are typically unprotected, or preemptible. This is because, if a line switch occurs, these PCA circuits will be dropped in favor of the working (protected) traffic. Carriers (which use this arrangement to provide service) typically sell the bandwidth to their customers at a lower rate and offer a more lenient service-level agreement (SLA) to accommodate the possible service interruptions from line switches. This might be a perfectly acceptable arrangement to an end user, who is willing to forgo the reliability of SONET-protected traffic in favor of the economic benefits, or who may not require 99.999 percent network availability.

For example, a company that requires a 1-Gbps connection for 4 hours per day for regularly scheduled data backup might be a good candidate for a PCA-based service. The carrier could use a STS-24c or STS-1-21v PCA circuit on an OC-192 BLSR with Fibre Channel interfaces to provide this service to a customer, and still be capable of carrying a normal "full load" of protected traffic. Figure 5-19 shows this application. The STS-24c connection for a Fibre Channel application between Nodes 3 and 4 uses a PCA circuit on STS-1 paths 97 to 120, which is the protection bandwidth for the GigE link between Nodes 1 and 2. Those nodes use STS-1 paths 1 through 24. Of course, STS-1s 1 through 24 can also be used on the other links for carrying traffic because this is a BLSR network. If a line switch occurs on the GigE link, the Fibre Channel circuit is preempted to allow protection for the GigE.

Figure 7-19 *PCA Use in an OC-192 2-Fiber BLSR for a SAN Extension Application Example*

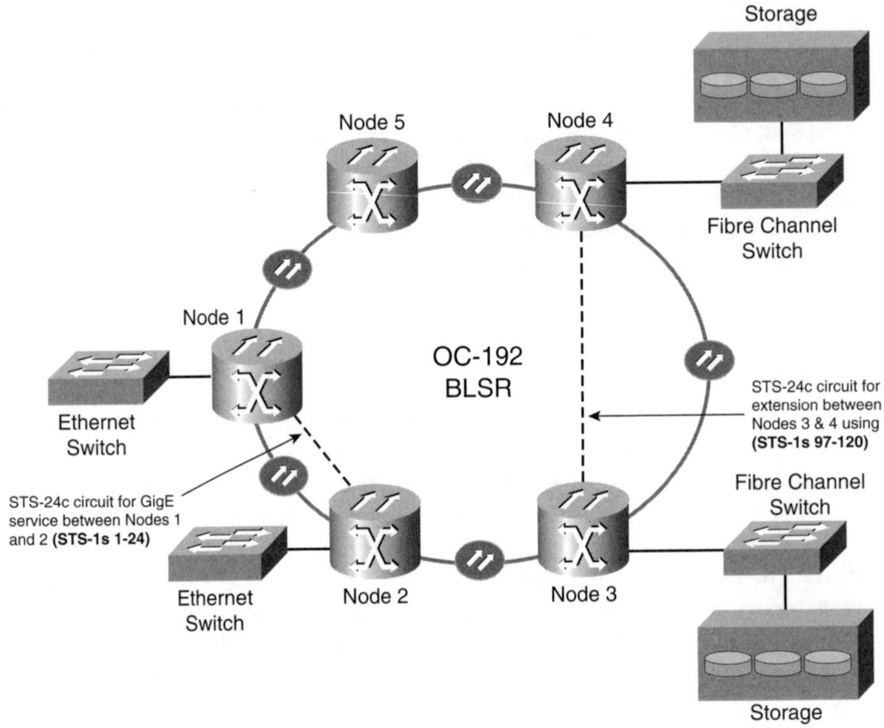

4-Fiber BLSR Operation

4-Fiber BLSRs provide twice the available bandwidth of a bandwidth-equivalent 2-Fiber BLSR, but they require additional costs and fiber facility resources to implement. As the name implies, four fiber strands (or two fiber pairs) are required between adjacent network elements in a 4-Fiber BLSR; two fibers are designated as working and two fibers are designated as protect. The entire bandwidth of the working pair can be assigned, whereas all the channels of the protection pair are held in reserve. This is shown in the 4-Fiber OC-192 BLSR in Figure 5-20, in which 192 STS-1 protected channels are available for assignment on the working fiber pair.

Figure 7-20 *A 4-Fiber BLSR Network Example*

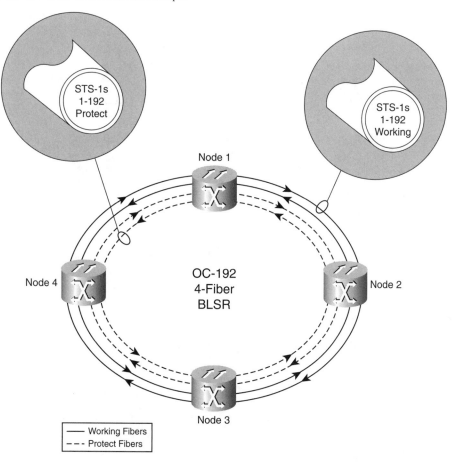

The 4-Fiber BLSR adds a layer of protection over the 2-Fiber version. In a 4-Fiber BLSR, a facility failure, which affects the working fibers, can be restored using a span switch. Figure 5-21 shows this. If the failure affects the working and protect fibers in the same segment, such as with a fiber cable cut, which severs all four strands, a ring switch occurs, as shown in Figure 5-22.

Figure 7-21 *A 4-Fiber BLSR Span Switch Example*

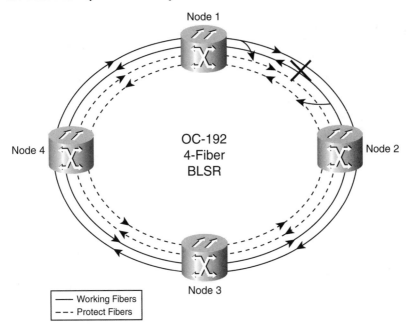

Figure 7-22 *A 4-Fiber BLSR Ring Switch Example*

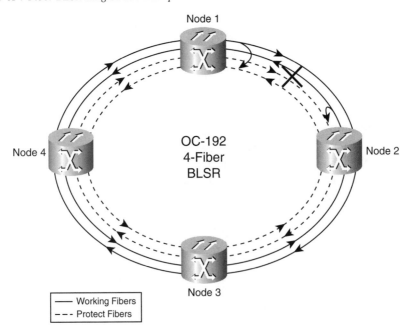

Although a 4-Fiber BLSR yields twice the bandwidth and offers enhanced protection from facility failures, it requires twice the number of optical fibers and also increases the number of optical interfaces required by a factor of 2. This topology is generally used in high-capacity long-distance carrier networks, such as those owned by U.S. interexchange carriers (IXCs). Typical MSPP implementations of 4-Fiber BLSRs are at the OC-48 and OC-192 levels.

4-Fiber BLSR System Capacities

The equation for determining the maximum channel-carrying capability of a 4-Fiber BLSR is similar to the 2-Fiber version, except that the ring bandwidth (N) is not halved in the formula. Table 5-3 shows the equations for performing these calculations, where X is the number of nodes in the 4-Fiber BLSR ring and A is the number of pass-through STS-1 circuits:

Table 7-3   *4-Fiber BLSR STS-1 Capacity Equations*

4F Ring Bandwidth	N	Working STS-1 Channels (Fiber Pair 1)	Protect STS-1 Channels (Fiber Pair 2)	Ring Capacity
OC-48	48	1–48	1–48	$(48 \times X) - A$
OC-192	192	1–192	1–192	$(192 \times X) - A$
OC-768	768	1–768	1–768	$(768 \times X) - A$

BLSR Applications

BLSR networks are well suited for distributed, nonhubbed traffic patterns because they can handle traffic requirements that exceed their transmission bandwidth. This characteristic of BLSRs makes it the topology of choice for metro or regional carrier networks in which TDM circuits for PSTN switch trunk links and data circuits for Ethernet or ATM networks are needed among multiple central offices.

Subtending Rings

In legacy SONET environments, traffic routing between two or more rings is typically accomplished using low-speed drop connections at digital cross-connect (DSX) panels, or through a separate device called a Digital Crossconnect System (DCS). This is because the older equipment was very limited in terms of ring terminations and cross-connect fabric sizes. With the current MSPP systems in the marketplace, these restrictions no longer apply. In many cases, a single MSPP add-drop multiplexer (ADM) can replace racks of cumbersome DSX panels or expensive DCS gear. This is done by terminating (or "closing") multiple SONET rings on a single MSPP chassis, also known as creating subtending rings.

In a large MSPP network, a carrier can use a single MSPP node to aggregate multiple access rings into a single backbone interoffice ring, as shown in Figure 5-23. In this figure, Node A is used to terminate and interconnect several subtended OC-12/48 UPSR access rings into a core OC-192 BLSR for metro or regional transport. These access rings can consist of the same type of MSPP chassis as the core ring, or they can include compatible miniature MSPP systems, which many manufacturers include in their portfolio for the access and customer premise market. For example, the Cisco ONS 153xx series includes several models for both the SONET and SDH markets, which are geared toward OC-3 or OC-12 (and even OC-48) access rings for aggregation of TDM and Ethernet connections. The 153xx series, which includes the 15302, 15305, 15327, and 15310, is compatible with the ONS 15454, which is the Cisco flagship SONET/SDH MSPP.

Figure 7-23 *An OC-192 Metro Core Ring with Multiple Subtended Rings*

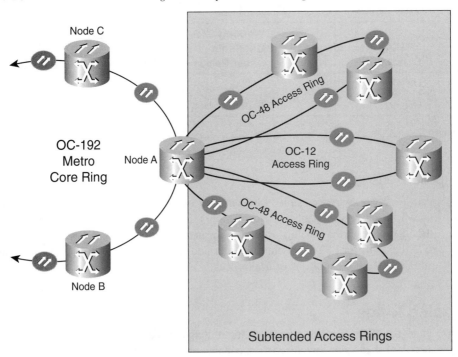

This MSPP capability can also be leveraged (in some systems) to bridge large backbone rings without costly interconnection solutions, as in the case of two OC-192 BLSRs terminated in a single MSPP chassis (see Figure 5-24).

Figure 7-24 *Two OC-192 Metro Core Rings Interconnected at a Single MSPP Node*

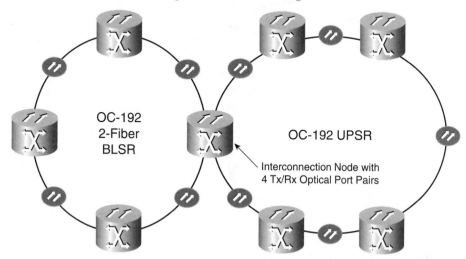

Subtending Shelves

Because of the relatively high cost of high-bandwidth and long-reach optical interfaces (for example, OC-192 long-reach 1550-nm cards are typically some of the most expensive MSPP blades), it is sometimes advantageous to stack or subtend additional shelves from a primary shelf at an MSPP site. For example, if a particular site has a heavy concentration of DS1 interfaces, along with other traffic requirements, it might be more economical to place the DS1 cards in a second shelf and use lower-rate optics, such as OC-3 or OC-12, to interconnect to the primary shelf for routing the DS1s onto the network. Figure 5-25 shows such an arrangement, with a primary node participating in an OC-192 ring with a subtended shelf, interconnected to the primary OC-192 node through OC-12 optical interfaces, used for a high concentration of DS1 drops. This allows the interface slots in the primary shelf to be used for other services, such as DS3, OC-3/12/48, and GigE.

Figure 7-25 *An OC-192 MSPP Ring Node with a Subtended OC-12 Chassis for DS1 Handoffs*

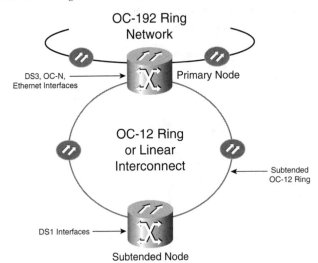

Ring-to-Ring Interconnect Diversity

One potential issue with connecting two or more rings at a single site (refer to Figure 5-24) is the creation of a nonredundant point of failure—the interconnection node. If a serious problem, such as a loss of power or natural disaster, occurs at this location, traffic passing between the ring networks through this node will be lost. A method of connecting rings to avoid this issue is known as Dual Ring Interconnect (DRI). In a DRI configuration, rings can be connected at two nodes to eliminate the single point of failure. If these two interconnection points are geographically diverse, such as in different carrier central offices, an even greater level of fault protection is provided. DRI can be achieved with UPSRs, BLSRs, or a combination of the two. DRI can be accomplished in two methods (see Figure 5-26):

- **Traditional DRI**—Uses four nodes to perform the interconnection, with two nodes on each of the separate rings optically linked to form the protection paths.

- **Integrated DRI**—Uses only two nodes, with the two nodes at the junction points participating simultaneously in each of the two rings. This requires a pair of optical links between the two interconnect nodes.

Figure 5-27 shows an example of how this is installed with optical interfaces and fibers. Because the integrated DRI solution uses fewer nodes and optical interfaces, it can be installed with less capital outlay and with fewer network elements to manage.

Figure 7-26 *Traditional and Integrated DRI Examples*

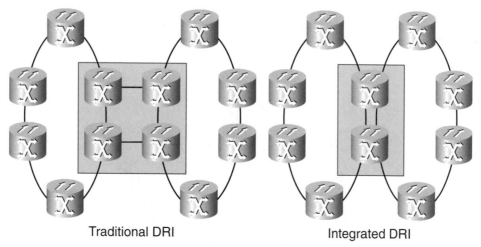

Traditional DRI   Integrated DRI

Figure 7-27 *Shelf Fiber Interconnections for Integrated DRI Example*

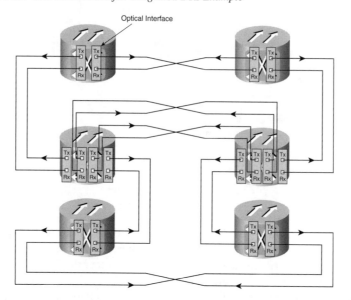

Figure 5-28 shows the operation of DRI in a UPSR, in the integrated DRI configuration. Nodes 4 and 5 are the interconnection nodes for the two rings. As shown in the figure, a signal entering Node 1 and bound for Node 8 is bridged in the cross-connect fabric at Node 1. At Node 5, the path selector chooses the primary signal. Using a circuit-creation method known as drop and continue, this signal is also bridged to Node 4 for protection. Similarly, the second copy of the signal bridged at Node 1 is used as the secondary or backup and is dropped to the path selectors at Nodes 4 and 5. This ultimately allows for two copies, a working signal and a protect signal, to be present at the path-selector switch on the receive side at Node 8. This duplication of signals at the interconnect nodes avoids service interruption from the failure of either of these network elements.

Figure 7-28 *Integrated DRI Configuration*

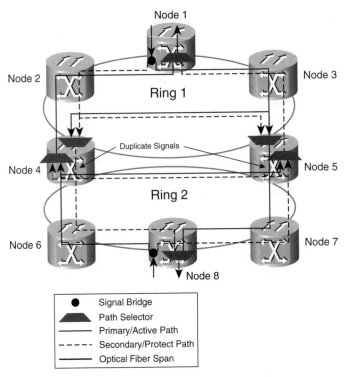

Mesh Networks

A mesh network is any set of interconnected locations (for example, MSPP nodes) with at least one loop pathway. Each site in the mesh can be reached from any other site by at least two completely separate routes. Any network other than a point-to-point or purely linear network can be considered a mesh, even a UPSR or BLSR network. However, some of the distinctive features and advantages of a mesh network include these:

- Mesh networks can contain spans with varying SONET optical rates, or even dense wavelength-division multiplexing (DWDM) spans for high-capacity routes.

- Reduced dedicated protection bandwidth requirements because of distributed backup capacity.

- Automated, algorithmic route optimization, requiring the network operator to specify only the ingress and egress points of traffic connections to establish service.

Figure 5-29 shows an example of a mesh network. The interconnecting fiber spans can contain a variety of SONET (OC-N) line rates and DWDM links.

Figure 7-29   *A Mesh Network*

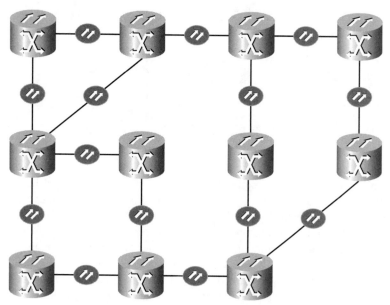

Cisco provides a supported mesh networking topology on the ONS 15454 MSPP known as a path-protected mesh network (PPMN). Coupled with the automatic circuit-routing feature of the 15454, PPMN provides an effective and efficient means of rapidly provisioning protected traffic across complex meshed networks. Each working and protection path pair effectively forms a virtual UPSR for the circuit. Figure 5-30 shows an example of this.

Figure 7-30   *Protected Circuit Routing in a Mesh Network Example*

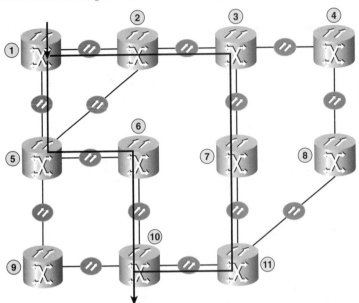

In this case, a protected circuit is specified to connect Nodes 1 and 10. The network software determines the shortest path between those nodes and routes the circuit accordingly, automatically creating the pass-through cross-connections at Nodes 5 and 6. Traffic between the terminating nodes initially traverses this link. The optimal protection path is calculated to be through Nodes 2, 3, 7, and 11, and pass-through cross-connections are created at those locations as well. If the primary link into Node 10 fails, the MSPP performs a protection switch and selects traffic on the protection link from Node 11 instead of the primary link from Node 6. Note that the loop formed by Nodes 1, 2, 3, 7, 11, 10, 6, and 5 is a UPSR for this particular circuit.

Summary

In this chapter, you learned some considerations in the design of MSPP networks, and you explored the operation and application of various MSPP network topologies.

With regard to network resiliency and protection, multiple mechanisms and design features are available with MSPPs to ensure high availability for critical services. These include the use of redundant power feeds, common control cards, tributary interfaces, synchronization sources, and MSPP chasses. In addition, system reliability can be substantially improved through diverse cable routing and ring network topologies.

MSPP network topologies include linear networks, UPSRs, BLSRs (both 2-Fiber and 4-Fiber), mesh networks, subtended rings and nodes, and diverse ring interconnections. Whereas linear networks are not commonly used in current MSPP networks, UPSR and BLSR networks are standard configurations in service-provider and enterprise networks. UPSRs are advantageous because of their design simplicity and fast protection switch times, but they are inefficient in terms of bandwidth use for meshed traffic patterns between MSPP network sites. UPSRs are typically used in access networks, where all traffic hubs to a central site (such as a telco central office). BLSRs, which have slower protection-switching times because of the required internode switching protocol, can accommodate a much higher amount of traffic in a meshed traffic pattern, such as a service provider core network.

ISBN: 1-58705-248-2

Network Virtualization

Kumar Reddy
Victor Moreno

ciscopress.com

CHAPTER 8

Business Drivers Behind Enterprise Network Virtualization

Today's enterprises service diverse groups of users, each with specific needs. The different business needs of these groups translate into varying network requirements. In some enterprises, these requirements can be so dissimilar that the different groups must be treated as totally separate customers by the enterprise's IT department.

Network virtualization is an architectural approach to providing a separate logical networking environment for each group within the enterprise. These logical environments are created over a single shared network infrastructure. Each logical network provides the corresponding user group with full network services similar to those provided by a traditional nonvirtualized network. The experience from the end-user perspective is that of having access to a dedicated network with dedicated resources and independent security policies. Thus, the virtualization of the network involves the logical segmentation of the network transport, the network devices, and all the network services.

Because the diverse logical networks share a common network infrastructure and a common, often centralized, set of service appliances and servers, user groups can collaborate with enhanced flexibility and manageability. This enhanced collaboration enables new business processes that would not be possible (or even imaginable) over a traditional network. Throughout this chapter, you will see examples of enterprises that rely on the virtualization of their network to modify their processes and operations. You will see how some enterprises can transform their network into a revenue-generating asset or increment the volume of operations possible at a specific facility or even open new streams of revenue by exploiting otherwise idle resources in creative ways.

Why Virtualize?

Consider the diverse networking needs of different enterprises. At one end of the spectrum is the enterprise that might require the separation of a single user group from the rest of the network for security purposes. For this enterprise, segmenting traffic seems easy to address by means of proper cabling and firewall positioning. For example, guests at a company site would be expected to access the network only from certain areas, such as lobbies or guest meeting rooms, where they can be easily isolated from the rest of the network through the use of firewalls. This setup works relatively well for separating guests from employees, provided that guest physical access to the enterprise network is strictly restricted. However, the separation becomes more complex when it is not possible to confine specific users to specific areas in the network, or when the number of user groups increases beyond just guests and employees. When this occurs, the physical positioning of firewalls can no longer address the problem in a scalable manner (not to mention the huge management challenge that this scenario represents).

At the other end of the spectrum are enterprises in which a common campus is home to many different and often competing customers. Multitenant campuses such as technology incubators, universities, airports, and even cooperatives fall under this category. Such enterprises leverage their high-capacity intelligent networking infrastructure to provide connectivity and network services for many groups and in many cases transform the IT department into a profit center providing billable services. For instance, different airlines could share the airport network and use it as a billable service. This arrangement accelerates the return on network infrastructure investment, optimizes network operations and operational expenses through economies of scale, and can ultimately help transform the business model of the different groups on the network by providing an enhanced collaboration environment that enables new business processes and efficiencies. For an airline, being able to easily create virtual communication environments for each flight removes a lot of the overhead and delay present in the current flight-launch process, allowing more flights per day, but also allowing the airline to seamlessly change gates or even terminals. We take a detailed look at the alteration of business processes in a later section.

Many business drivers are behind the virtualization of enterprise networks, including the following:

- Productivity gains derived from providing visitors with access to the Internet so that they can connect to their own private networks.

- Increasing network availability by quarantining hosts that are infected by viruses or not compliant with the enterprise security policies.

- A business model that involves the services of in-house consultants, partners, or even contractors requires the enterprise to provide this personnel connectivity to the Internet and select internal resources.

- Legal/regulatory compliance. Acts such as HIPAA and Sarbanes-Oxley define privacy and integrity standards for health and financial data.

- Creation of secure network areas that are partially or totally isolated.

- Consolidation of multiple networks onto a single infrastructure.

- Collocation of diverse competing customers on a shared infrastructure.

- Integration of subsidiaries and acquisitions.

- Next-generation business models aimed at improving efficiencies, reducing costs, and generating new streams of revenue. For instance, the IT department could become a revenue-generating service provider, or the airlines could optimize their use of shared services such as baggage handling.

Visitors, Partners, Contractors, and Quarantine Areas

It is important for today's enterprise to provide network access for groups of users who are not members of the enterprise. Visitors bring much more business benefit if they have access to the Internet and can get their information dynamically while they visit. Having this connectivity could make the difference between concluding business in one visit or having to schedule a follow-up meeting because some information was not readily available at the time of the meeting. Because these users are not part of the enterprise, they should be able to access only specific resources, and their connectivity should resemble that of a network that is separate from the main enterprise network.

Guest access should be limited to the Internet, and enterprises should ensure that guests cannot connect to any internal network resources. Enterprises could easily provide such limited access by deploying a totally separate network just for guests to access the Internet. However, owning a separate network solely for the purposes of providing guests with Internet access is not a viable alternative. The goal is to leverage the existing network infrastructure and the existing Internet access services to provide guest access as if guests have a dedicated network that connects them solely to the Internet.

One coarse way to achieve this is to define physical locations in the campus as guest-access locations (conference rooms, lobbies, cafeterias, and so on) and isolate them using firewalls. The guest locations become small dedicated networks for visitors. Even employees would be restricted to accessing the Internet only when connected at these locations. The success of this scheme relies heavily on the effectiveness of the physical-access restriction mechanisms in place at the enterprise facilities. If a visitor enters an employee-only area, there is the potential for guests accessing the internal network unless the appropriate security mechanisms are in place. A pervasive mechanism is required to create a guest virtual network segment that can be accessed by guests from anywhere in the enterprise.

A dynamic mechanism for authenticating guests and employees and authorizing and restricting them to the appropriate *virtual network* (VN) segment is also required. A network-based authentication and authorization mechanism removes the dependency on physical-access restriction for securing the network. Dynamic authentication also allows users from different groups to work in the same room while still connected to their appropriate VN. Thus, visitors and employees can attend the same meeting and enjoy network connectivity levels in accordance with their roles.

Network admission control mechanisms call for the creation of a quarantine network segment to isolate devices that are found to be either infected with a virus or simply do not comply with the enterprise security policies. In either case, these devices must be isolated and fixed. The isolation of the devices calls for the creation of a quarantine VN segment. Because infected or noncompliant hosts can connect anywhere in the network, the quarantine VN must be accessible from any port in the enterprise. Hence, rudimentary solutions based on physical network segmentation, such as that proposed for guest access, are not viable.

Providing access for in-house partners or consultants is also an interesting scenario that calls for the virtualization of the infrastructure. In-house consultants generally require access to the Internet plus a few select internal resources. These internal resources can be distributed across the enterprise, making the connectivity requirements for partners slightly more sophisticated than those imposed by guests.

Both guest access and quarantine VN segments provide access to a single resource for many users. In the case of guest access, the single resource is the Internet, whereas the quarantine segment provides access to a remediation server only. This defines a many-to-one connectivity requirement easily serviced by a simple hub-and-spoke topology. Meanwhile, partners require connectivity to several resources, which are not necessarily located at a single site. Therefore, partners present a many-to-few requirement that is better served by an overlay of several hub-and-spoke topologies, in which case it might be easier to deploy an any-to-any topology. It is important to highlight this distinction because the business requirements will clearly determine the viability of different virtualization technologies and the complexity of the solution that is required.

When we separate guests from employees and these from contractors, we are basically creating user groups based on their role. A dramatic example of the value of creating groups based on roles and actually providing virtual environments for each group is seen in the separation of contractors and employees. Contractors and employees have different types of benefits, different levels of compensation, and overall their relation with their employer is governed by different laws. In a recent lawsuit, a large group of contractors claimed full employee rights based on the fact that their work environment was no different from that of an employee. This work environment largely involved the network. With this precedent in place, enterprises are making sure that a clear differentiation exists in the connectivity provided to a contractor from that provided to a full-time employee.

Regulatory Compliance

Data security and integrity is the subject of tight controls. Some of these controls are imposed by internal policies, whereas others are required by law and specified in a detailed regulatory framework. This regulatory framework is captured in acts such as the *Health Insurance Portability and Accountability Act* (HIPAA) and the Sarbanes-Oxley Act. Although these acts do not explicitly call for specific security features or functionality, they do require that appropriate controls contain and detect fraud. Furthermore, these controls must be part of the periodic reporting process and must be endorsed by the CFO and CEO of the company, who are directly responsible for the integrity of the data in question.

Network virtualization is instrumental in achieving compliance with many of these regulations in a cost-effective manner. Because one VN cannot communicate with another unless the security policies are explicitly opened, the virtualization of the network adds an extra layer of security that restricts the number of users who have access to critical resources and thus simplifies the necessary controls and makes them more effective.

Often, enterprise user groups are defined by departments or roles. In this scenario, users are grouped according to their role in the enterprise. For example, an engineering firm may be interested in keeping the finance personnel and resources on a VN separate from that devoted to engineering contractors. This separation keeps the financial information out of the reach of curious computer-savvy engineers, while all engineering traffic is also kept away from the administrative personnel. The Sarbanes-Oxley Act regulates the protection of financial data in the enterprise. Many technical measures must be taken to comply with these regulations, and the virtualization of the network is one tool to be considered.

Secure Service Areas

Many enterprises converge services onto their IP network. Some examples of services that are typically converged onto an IP network include telephony, surveillance systems, badge readers, and energy-efficiency systems for intelligent buildings. Enterprises that own a production line also converge their production robots and controllers (such as *Programmable Logic Controller* [PLC]) onto the IP network.

This convergence brings a special type of endpoint onto the network. These endpoints do not require connectivity to the Internet and are not subject to the broad variety of network traffic a user PC would be subject to. These endpoints are part of closed systems with a task that is static in terms of the type of traffic they handle. Therefore, each one of these systems can be isolated in its own VN segment. This isolation provides the systems and services with protection from the Internet or even viruses that spread from hosts in the internal network.

Many of the systems already mentioned (PLCs, PCs, and so on) are business critical; therefore, it is important to provide the maximum amount of protection possible to them. Furthermore, many of the systems leverage mainstream operating systems such as Windows or Linux and are therefore susceptible to common network attacks. However, most of these systems cannot be fixed rapidly, and an infected station could be rendered unusable and beyond repair by such an attack.

A sample scenario is that of a car manufacturer in which the assembly line consists of robots and PLCs that are all interconnected by an IP network. Because the assembly line is located in a specific physical plant and does not really require external connectivity, it is tempting to physically isolate the network in the plant from the rest of the enterprise. This approach is not cost-effective because two separate infrastructures would need to be maintained, increasing both the operational and capital costs. Furthermore, most plants are collocated with administrative offices, and the demarcation is blurry to say the least. Many employees actually require network access from within the plant. This brings to the table the requirement to dynamically and pervasively virtualize the network to provide the appropriate access to users, while maintaining the isolation of the production line. In this specific scenario, the robots on the assembly line had a long *mean time to repair* (MTTR) in the case of a virus attack. Hence, the preferred policy was to avoid attacks at all costs. Given that the assembly line did not require any type of Internet, intranet, data-center connectivity, or even human intervention, the assembly line was kept isolated. The necessary isolation can be achieved by creating a VN segment for the assembly line robots and PLCs, instead of deploying a separate physical network for the assembly line.

Network Consolidation

Because of their operations and the way in which they have grown, many enterprises maintain multiple physical networks. The operational cost associated with the ownership of this multitude of networks is extremely high. Therefore, it is desirable for the enterprise to consolidate the multiple networks onto a single infrastructure. The value of an infrastructure capable of supporting VNs is evident because consolidating the networks does not necessarily mean that the security boundaries between the networks are to disappear with the consolidation. Thus, each physical network will usually be migrated onto a VN in the consolidated infrastructure.

We use the example of airports to discuss the subject of network consolidation.

Airports run separate physical networks for each airline serviced. Imagine a fully meshed network of fiber deployed for each airline. Not only is this expensive, it is also hard to maintain and provides little to no flexibility when it comes to moving airlines around the airport. The reason for these separate physical networks is to preserve the privacy and security of the individual airlines. In these networks, the fiber runs only to specific places, so certain sectors of the airport are dedicated to certain airlines. Airports also run all their internal operations over their LAN. Baggage services, air traffic control, maintenance, and governmental agencies controlling immigration and security—all require LAN services and privacy. The ability to virtualize the network infrastructure allows enterprises to converge these separate physical networks onto a shared infrastructure and still preserve the privacy of the different groups.

The degree of sophistication in the virtualization technology to be used is determined by the enterprise business processes. For some enterprises, the business processes are such that failure of a single network would halt the entire operation. In this case, maintaining separate networks does not increase the availability of the business, and the benefit to consolidating the networks is clear. For other enterprises, the use of multiple networks is aimed at increasing the resiliency of the business that could continue to partially function in case of a failed network. In the latter case, sophisticated virtualization technologies involving the use of separate memory spaces and even separate processors are required so that the different networks can be consolidated while still maintaining the availability benefits of physically separate networks.

The financial results of multinetwork consolidation are capital investment savings and reduced operational expenses. The maintenance of a single network is much cheaper than maintaining separate networks. Note that policies that previously had to be applied in a distributed and complex manner can now be centralized and simplified.

Acquisitions and Mergers

IT departments often have to integrate the network infrastructure and resources of an acquired company into the existing network. A similar scenario is presented when two companies merge.

After an agreement has been reached to acquire or merge with another company, IT must start the process of integrating the network resources. However, a time lag occurs between the time when the acquisition is agreed upon and when all regulatory clearances have been granted by governing bodies (for example, the *Federal Communications Commission* [FCC] in the United States). IT departments require a way of laying out the foundations for the integration to enable connectivity in a phased manner as the regulatory clearances are granted. By laying out the foundation for the integration ahead of time, the integration of acquired companies is expected to be as nondisruptive as possible.

One significant way to avoid operational disruption is to preserve the network structure of the acquired company. The creation of VNs accommodates the integration of acquisitions by creating a separate environment to interface with the acquired infrastructure. In this way, the acquired network does not have to change basic things, such as its IP addressing scheme or its routing protocols, which can be independently supported within its assigned VN. Communication between the VN for the acquired network and the VNs containing the traffic for the parent (acquiring) network can be gradually opened as the regulatory clearances are obtained.

Multitenant Enterprises

Business centers provide office space to many different companies within a physical space that is equivalent to a campus. The companies lease the physical space and the network infrastructure along with voice, video, surveillance, and paging services. In some cases, even server farms are available for lease. Deploying a dedicated data center for each customer can be extremely expensive because of the intelligence necessary at the data center front end. Many customers require only a small server farm, which makes the expense of deploying a dedicated data center per customer even more difficult to justify. Therefore, a high-performance network that can be virtualized to provide private services to the different customers is desirable.

Similarly, universities host many faculties that need to be kept separate. Universities are also home to numerous research groups (often privately funded). It is usually a requirement of the funding institution that the project's network be isolated, while still being able to access all the university's network resources. Furthermore, the funding institution often requires that the network section on campus be directly connected to their corporate network, thus extending their enterprise into the university campus and raising the bar in terms of security and routing requirements. This arrangement becomes expensive when the university has to deploy separate physical networks with dedicated firewall and routing appliances. Therefore, a virtualized shared infrastructure is desired.

Virtual Project Environment: Next-Generation Business Processes

The speed and dynamic nature of today's business environment calls for the frequent creation of virtual teams. These teams include individuals from many groups inside and outside of a company. The virtual teams are usually formed to complete a specific project. For some enterprises, these projects are long term; other enterprises start and finish projects in a single day. Whichever the case, the interactions within each of these virtual teams can be enhanced by the creation of a virtual environment that provides an optimal set of resources, communication, and security policies for each virtual team to complete its project. A virtual project environment allows the virtual team to work in an environment customized for their mission, making communications much more efficient.

A significant challenge in the creation of a virtual project environment is that of managing the policies and connectivity between members of the virtual team. The creation of a VN for each project greatly simplifies this task, with users being assigned to project networks as required. The policies associated with the VN are inherited by any user who is allowed access to the VN. This scenario reduces the problem to the creation of a policy for each project (instead of having to maintain a set of policies for each user and resource).

Let's take a closer look at how the creation of virtual project environments can impact the business process.

Most personnel in the enterprise have a relatively well-defined role. As part of their role, they must carry out certain tasks. Tasks and roles are defined to support different processes. Therefore, by enhancing communications, through the creation of virtual work environments, it is possible to modify the tasks that are carried out by certain personnel (making these tasks easier, faster, or sometimes even automating them and eliminating the need for human intervention). Taken to the extreme, the modification of tasks will alter the roles of the personnel. More important, the added flexibility in the definition of tasks impacts the business process directly. This flexibility allows for the implementation of new models and processes that were impractical over a nonvirtualized infrastructure.

So far, we have defined a *process* as a group of tasks that are carried out by different personnel in their corresponding roles. When these roles meet to get the process rolling, they are part of a *project*. Projects are governed by the existing business processes, which, as discussed, depend directly on the different type of tasks possible within the organization.

An intelligent network can dynamically create groups of users and resources on a per-project basis. In the airport example, a typical example of a project is a specific flight. To launch a flight, many instances (roles) within the airline and the airport operations need to come together in a common project and use certain resources in a dedicated manner during a well-defined time window. By creating virtual groups (or what some call an "extended enterprise"), the users involved in the project of launching a flight have secure access to their private resources and those shared resources that are common to the project.

A sample project group for a flight launch would include runway personnel, traffic control, baggage handling personnel, ground crew, maintenance technicians from vendor A (vendor B, C, and so on), load calculation resources, maintenance manuals, procedure manuals, overhead paging systems, announcement boards, and so forth. These resources need to work closely together while the specific flight is being launched. After the flight has launched, these resources must be able to dynamically be liberated and assigned to another flight (project). Having the resources "on the same page" eliminates communication delays that were implicit with the use of technologies such as fax, telex, and even phone conversations.

This type of connectivity allows for communication efficiencies that translate into faster operations and opens the potential for new forms of revenue. A salient consequence for the air transportation industry is that such increased efficiencies allow for faster loading and reloading of cargo on a passenger plane. In the past, the speed of the processes related to load-distribution recalculations drastically limited the amount of cargo that could be transported on passenger planes. By creating virtual project environments, it is possible to redesign the business operations and ultimately allow the airlines to tap into new sources of revenue, such as an increased cargo allowance, a higher number of flights per day, and perhaps a lower cost per flight in terms of man-hours. From the airport's perspective, the dynamic creation of these virtual environments allows resources (gates, for instance) that used to be dedicated to a certain airline to be shared by different airlines, thus maximizing the utilization of the resource and servicing more customers with fewer resources, which clearly leads to considerable operational expense reduction.

The creation of virtual project groups is also necessary in university environments, where expensive resources could be shared by many groups. Some examples include electronic microscopes, particle accelerators, and clean rooms. Although we use universities as an example, these requirements are typical of any campus hosting research groups, including technology incubators and shared business parks. In an industry setting, it is not uncommon to find different companies developing competing products in parallel with a common technology provider while being collocated in the same campus. The security requirements of such interactions are demanding, and even though they could become complex, the virtualization of the network allows for their simplification.

Business Requirements Drive Technical Requirements

Enterprises face many technical challenges when attempting to fulfill the requirements described so far, including the following:

- Guarantee total privacy between groups
- Assign users to their appropriate group based on some sort of authentication
- Enforce independent security policies for each group
- Enable secure collaboration mechanisms between groups
- Provide basic networking services for the different groups
- Provide independent routing domains and address spaces to each group
- Provide group extensibility over the WAN
- Implement billing and accounting mechanisms for each group
- Enforce the previous policies regardless of the physical location of the user in the network

Many technologies could be used to solve the problems listed; some are perceived as simple, whereas others are perceived as complex. Different business requirements will call for different degrees of connectivity and a different subset of the functionality described previously. Fulfilling the subsets of functionality will in turn demand varying degrees of technology sophistication. In general, an overlap of diverse business drivers will result in increased technological sophistication. For simple business requirements, simple technologies suffice. As the requirements become more complex or numerous, however, simple technologies cease to scale or even provide adequate connectivity.

A simple example of how business requirements drive the use of different technologies can be seen when we compare the connectivity requirements for simple guest access against the connectivity needed when supporting a secure service area. Guest access requires many-to-one connectivity (many guests to one Internet access point), whereas a secure service area will most likely require any-to-any connectivity. When providing many-to-one connectivity, the technology used could be as simple as *access control lists* (ACLs) or a mesh of tunnels that connect to a head end. However, providing any-to-any connectivity with either ACLs or a static mesh of tunnels is highly impractical. Therefore, more sophisticated *virtual private networking* (VPN) technologies, such as those discussed throughout this book, are necessary.

Summary

Modern enterprises can benefit in many ways from the creation of VNs and the virtualization of network services. Network virtualization capabilities must considered as a key network service when defining the network strategy for an enterprise.

Existing business pressures and the potential to enable change in business processes make network virtualization relevant in the agenda of any IT discussion. This chapter has explored some of the business requirements that are driving the virtualization of the network, including the following:

- Support for visitors (guests, partners, and contractors)
- Quarantining of infected servers
- Isolation of critical resources such as assembly line robots
- Consolidation of separate networks
- Regulatory compliance
- Infrastructure integration for mergers and acquisitions
- Dynamic creation of virtual project groups

VNs can be created in a number of ways. The sophistication of the technique used directly correlates with the complexity of the business requirements.

Cisco Marketplace Bookstore

Shop the Cisco Bookstore for the latest
Cisco Press books, including networking,
business, and certification
titles to help you learn and
understand Cisco technology.

Just use your Cisco.com
user name and password
to log into the site and
automatically **receive a
discount on books**.

Visit **www.cisco.com/go/marketplace/networkers2006** today.

Learning is serious business.   **Invest wisely.**

Cisco Press

SEARCH THOUSANDS OF BOOKS FROM LEADING PUBLISHERS

With Safari® Bookshelf you can

- **Search** the full text of thousands of technical books

- **Read** the books from cover to cover online, or just flip to the information you need

- **Browse** books by category to research any technical topic

- **Download** chapters for printing and viewing offline

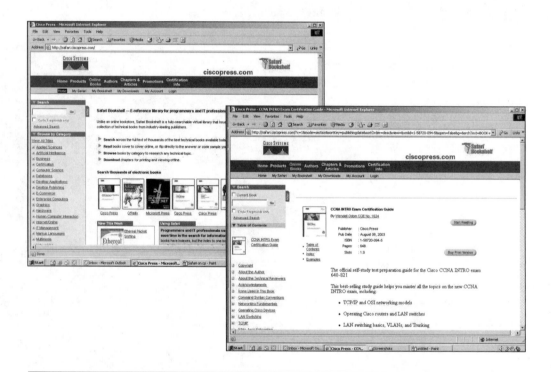

http://safari.ciscopress.com